THE FIRST BATTLE
OF MANASSAS

AN END TO INNOCENCE, JULY 18–21, 1861

JOHN J. HENNESSY

STACKPOLE
BOOKS

Published in paperback by
STACKPOLE BOOKS
5067 Ritter Road
Mechanicsburg, PA 17055
www.stackpolebooks.com

Printed in the United States of America

Distributed by NATIONAL BOOK NETWORK

Cover design by Wendy A. Reynolds

Library of Congress Cataloging-in-Publication Data

Hennessy, John J., 1958– author.
    The First Battle of Manassas : an end to innocence, July 18–21, 1861 /
John J. Hennessy. — Revised edition.
        pages cm
    Includes bibliographical references and index.
    ISBN 978-0-8117-1591-1
1. Bull Run, 1st Battle of, Va., 1861.   I. Title.
    E472.18.H55 2015
    973.7'31—dc23

                                                                2015028962

Contents

Introduction to the Original Edition

It was the climax of a half century of burgeoning turmoil. For fifty years, men had feared its occurrence. Now, ironically, on its eve, they heralded its arrival. In the predawn light of a warm Sunday morning, they gathered their wives, their picnic baskets, and their carriages, and sallied forth over dusty roads deep into the countryside. Some carried with them only a morbid fascination, but most were spurred forth by a sense that they were going to witness something spectacular, something momentous. Indeed they would. They were going to watch a nation do battle with itself.

These people in their fine suits and pretty skirts symbolized a nation's attitude toward war. And it was these attitudes, faithfully shared by the men who would do the fighting that Sunday afternoon, that made the First Battle of Manassas an event like none other in American history. Never did an American army take to the field so convinced of its righteousness, so confident of success, yet so deluded as to the price that success would exact, as did the armies of 1861.

"It would be as easy for Abe Lincoln to reduce the White Mountains to the level of the oceans as to conquer these states," one Southerner boasted. One Confederate, reasoning went, could "whup" three, four, or six Yankees, depending on the need at the moment. Conversely, most Northerners speculated that a few shells tossed over enemy lines would be sufficient to set the ragamuffin rebels to irretrievable flight. "It is generally believed that the contest will be a short and decisive one," forecasted one New Hampshireman. "It is [also] thought it will be a comparatively bloodless one."

These naive illusions served only to speed a nation toward something for which it was as yet unprepared. The men who would do the killing were half-trained at best, still awkward at drill and loath to obey orders. Their officers were often of little help, sometimes ill-chosen and always unprepared. Few had commanded so much as a company in the field, much less a brigade. (Even Union army commander McDowell had never commanded more than eight men at one time.) Equipment was varied, shoddy, and usually burdensome. Men on both sides carried weapons of all calibers and ferocious-looking cutlery galore. Accoutrements and accessories rarely matched, and there were invariably too many of them. One soldier brought an iron breastplate to the field, while a Union colonel brought his wife and his beehive (presumably for culinary rather than defensive purposes).

Short on time, neither side had been able to clothe its army. The resultant multitude of state- and local-issued uniforms created a kaleidoscope of color. Indeed, they were bedizened as no armies had been, as though their clothing would somehow conceal their soldierly nascence. Zouave units wore blood-red pants, bright white spats, and tasseled fezzes. Some militia battalions marched in threads that were indeed little more than that—better suited for the gazes of giggly girls around the parade ground than for the battlefield. Some New York and Wisconsin troops dressed in gray, while two North Carolina and Louisiana regiments dressed in blue (and one in stripes). Into battle soldiers wore firemen's shirts and belts, and stovepipe hats, derbies, kepis, and forage caps. Some soldiers wore simple outfits that betrayed their true station: citizens' clothes.

And so, filled with expectation and excitement, they came, citizens and soldiers, Northerners and Southerners. What they saw and experienced stunned them. In eight hours of the heaviest, bloodiest fighting this country had ever seen, their naive misconceptions and grand illusions were obliterated, consumed in the dirt, death, and devastation of battle: 900 dead, 3,000 wounded. Never again would we so excitedly chafe for blood. Never again would we send such ill-prepared armies into the field. Never again would the citizenry flock to the countryside to watch the men in those armies die. So costly, so destructive, so sad, the First Battle of Manassas changed the way a nation viewed war.

Chapter One

THE CERTAINTY
OF TRIUMPH

The prospects at Marble Hill Plantation and the neighborhood of Sudley seemed good the spring of 1861. The farm's owner, Massachusetts-born Christopher Cushing, wrote his son in late May, "The people here have nearly done planting corn, the wheat looks better than usual." Neighbor Tom Crawford seemed especially well fixed, with promising crops, 130 sheep, and more than 100 lambs. "Crawford has engaged his wool at Buckland at 25 cts per pound," wrote Cushing—a good price.

But the hint of coming war hovered over the promise of a happy planting season. Alex Compton, the son of the pastor at Sudley Methodist Church, had enlisted in the 8th Virginia Infantry. His mother and sister sent him off to war in a sharp gray uniform with green trim. Wheelwright John Thornberry, whose house and shop stood across the road from Sudley Church, also became an infantryman, he in the 49th Virginia. When Thornberry enlisted, he left behind his wife, Martha, and four children, including feisty six-year-old Laura, who would remember far more of her seventh year of life than most children might (and years later would write about it).

A bit more than a mile down the road from the Thornberrys, the venerable and bedridden Mrs. Judith Carter Henry clung to a life most had long ago expected her to yield. Her daughter Ellen lived with her in a one-story frame house atop a prominent hill; she and a slave named Lucy attended to Mrs. Henry's many needs. Son Hugh Henry lived in Alexandria, but getting out to see his mother had suddenly become an uncertain thing. The Union army occupied Alexandria, and the regular trains along the Orange and Alexandria Railroad to Manassas Junction had ceased. Still, Hugh harbored few worries for his sister

1

and mother should troops pass through the neighborhood: "[You] need not fear them, as your entire helplessness, I should think would make you safe."[1]

Two miles still farther south of the Henrys stood a cluster of buildings and farms called Tudor Hall—better known to the world in the spring of 1861 as Manassas Junction. Smattered across its landscape were farms so typical of Northern Virginia: 100- or 200-acre operations run by modest men who generally worked side by side in the fields with a handful of slaves. The farmers adorned their homes with names that suggested elegance and prestige—Liberia, Mayfield, Birmingham, Hazel Plain—but more often they were simple two-story frame structures surrounded not by fancy gardens, but cornfields, wheat fields, or grazing cattle, hogs, or fowl. Interspersed among the farms stood the simple homes of slaves, laborers, carpenters, coopers, and merchants.

What distinguished the area from the rest of Virginia were the two railroads that rendered it Manassas Junction. The Orange and Alexandria ran into Tudor Hall from the lush Piedmont region to the southwest, and then on to the markets in Alexandria. The other, the Manassas Gap, joined the O & A after a 60-mile trek from the Shenandoah Valley, across the Blue Ridge, and through the fertile farmlands of Fauquier and Prince William Counties. Like the community it in large part had created, Manassas Junction itself hardly reeked of prosperity. Along more than a mile of siding stood a tallow factory, a hotel, a one-story station, an express office, a telegraph office, and some modest workshops put up by the Orange and Alexandria. The junction's motley appearance belied its importance: In the summer of 1861, few places mattered more to the new Southern Confederacy than Manassas Junction.

At this early stage of the war, the Confederacy, like its soldiers, was bold, ambitious, and territorial. The men in power intended to defend their new nation as close to its northern border as possible. In Virginia, however, that presented a special problem. As the Confederate leaders eyed their maps of the Old Dominion, they could foresee two possible routes of Federal advance. The most obvious of these, and most likely, was an overland route along the rail lines between Washington and Richmond. The roads and railroads along the route—especially the Orange and Alexandria—were ample to move and supply a sizable Union army. The only natural obstacle for the Federals would be the numerous streams and rivers that wound across Northern Virginia and offered the Confederates their best opportunity for defense.

The other potential "invasion" route was less conspicuous and less of a direct threat to Richmond, but nonetheless ominous to the Confederates: the Shenandoah Valley. Lush and fertile, the Valley was vital to the sustenance of Southern civilians and soldiers alike. But more than that, the tree-clad mountains bordering it (the Blue Ridge on the east and the Alleghenies on the west) could, with diligent screening of their many gaps, conceal a Union army's advance until it had reached more than a hundred miles southward, to the very heart of Virginia.

Once there, a Yankee army would have outflanked any Confederate force still in Northern Virginia, and could quickly pass east of the mountains and move on Richmond from the northwest.

If the Confederates were to defend Northern Virginia, they would have to do so on two fronts; defending one without the other would not do. But even this early in the war, the Confederates wrestled with what would become a chronic problem: too few men and too much work to do—two fronts to defend, but not enough men to meet the Yankees on equal terms on both at the same time. They might be able to feign a defense in the Valley and in front of Washington simultaneously, but when it came time to shoulder arms and do some serious fighting, the Confederates would need to combine their limited forces against the enemy on one front, beat him there, and then rush back to the other to thrash him again if necessary. To do this, they needed two allies: time and a means to move their armies fast.

Whisking armies from the Valley to the Washington front, or vice versa, was no small matter and would clearly demand more than the raw foot speed of Southern soldiers. Instead, it would require—for the first time in an American war—the use of technology, namely the Manassas Gap Railroad. Running from Mount Jackson northward to Strasburg, then eastward through the Blue Ridge to Manassas Junction, the Manassas Gap could neatly connect any Confederate force defending the valley with one standing in front of Washington. Though it would be used and abused heavily later in the war, during these first months the line seemed most vulnerable at its eastern terminus at Manassas Junction. Only 30 miles from Washington, the Junction would undoubtedly be an objective of any Federal army moving out from Washington, requiring either a direct assault or a deft maneuver to force the Confederates to give up the place. At the same time, if the Confederates intended to defend Virginia as close to its northern border as possible, they simply had to have Manassas Junction.

And so, as June turned into July that summer of 1861, the eyes of the world turned to Manassas Junction as the likely locale for what many thought would be the Civil War's first and only major battle—"the most important strategical point now in Virginia," as one South Carolinian described it.[2]

To defend this critical spot, the Confederates assembled their then-largest army. Throughout the early summer, Southern soldiers poured into Tudor Hall, transforming a typical, bucolic Virginia neighborhood into an armed camp. Where once grazed cattle and hogs now appeared trenches and forts intended to defend Manassas Junction. Into these works they hauled 3-ton, 32-pounder naval cannon, strange rifled 6-pounder guns, and almost anything else they could find that might throw a cannonball in the direction of the enemy. By July 1, cannon poked out of embrasures, ready to confront an enemy from the direction of Washington. "If they do reach this place (which is scarcely possible) then [they] cant [sic] pass it," boasted a Confederate naval officer.[3]

Nature provided a welcome complement to the earthworks protecting Manassas Junction: Bull Run. The stream meandered lazily north to south about three miles east of the Junction. The stream itself amounted to little—rarely did it exceed three feet in depth—but its steep banks rendered it a formidable obstacle with few crossing points. The Confederates knew that any Union army marching from Washington to Manassas Junction had to cross Bull Run to get there, so the Southerners piled defenses at every possible crossing along an 8-mile stretch from the Warrenton Turnpike on the north (where a stone bridge carried the road across) to Union Mills Ford on the south. East of Bull Run, beyond the crossroads community of Centreville, the Southerners established outposts along all the major roads leading from Washington. Along those roads—today bearing names like Route 50, Route 236, and Braddock Road—jumpy Confederates awaited the first signs of the Federal advance. Ready to pass the word of that approach was a novel system of wigwagging signal stations, commanded by a young captain named Edward Porter Alexander.[4]

In June and July, as trains deposited more and more Confederates at the Junction, it became a social magnet, a fashionable place. "It is the point of attraction for the whole South," the "place . . . for meeting people," wrote one correspondent, "not unlike New York."[5] Many of the soldiers saw drills, occasional alarms, and discipline in any form not as functional necessities, but as social inconveniences. "We cannot go outside the line of sentinels without written permission from our officers," a South Carolinian who saw camp as "nothing more or less than a social jail" complained. Nonetheless, he admitted, "We have quite a jovial time of it and all seem to enjoy themselves finely."[6] The most common lament, especially early on, was the absence of women (though many officers managed to bring their wives for visits). "There are as yet no women, and there will not be, I suppose," moaned one private. "They cannot pack as close as men and would, of course, be miserable with a single carpet bag."[7]

Gen. Pierre Gustave Toutant Beauregard, the most famous military man in the South, presided over this awkward reconciliation of the social and the military. Hero-starved, the new Confederacy had clutched Beauregard to its collective bosom after he supervised the reduction of Fort Sumter in April. While that in itself was a military conquest of small merit, the general brought with him to Manassas an outlook on this new war that faithfully reflected that of most of his countrymen. "We are certain to triumph at last," he wrote, "even if we have for arms only pitchforks and flintlocks." The enemy, he said, was little more than "an armed rabble, gathered hastily on a false pretense, and for an unholy purpose. . . . None but the demented can doubt the issue."[8]

Beauregard also seemed to embody at least the physical qualities requisite for a prospective hero. "He is jaunty in his gait, dashing in manner, and evidently takes delight in the circumstance of war," wrote a foreign officer serving with the army. Even out of uniform, he "could not anywhere be mistaken for a civilian." (Beauregard was at times subject to fits of vanity. Later in the war he would cause a sensation when his brown hair suddenly—in mere weeks—turned snow white because he could no longer get his French-made hair dye through the blockade.) His experience, however, was perhaps not what most Southerners would have conjured for their most prominent leader. Beauregard was an engineer by training (West Point Class of 1838) and had seen combat in the Mexican War, receiving two brevets, but prior to Fort Sumter he had never even led more than a company in the field. He, like the men he commanded, would have to learn as he went along.[9]

If Beauregard failed to bring battle-tried experience to Manassas, he at least could see the military needs of the moment. He knew if he were to win the glorious victory he envisioned, he would need help. The feverish drilling and digging that went on near Manassas Junction during June and early July helped assure Beauregard could get that help when he needed it from the Confederate army guarding the Shenandoah Valley. There Gen. Joseph Eggleston Johnston had amassed a force of four brigades, about 11,000 men.

Joseph E. Johnston, though Beauregard's senior in rank, operated in the obscurity of the Creole's shadow. His prewar experience suggested far more promise than did Beauregard's. Few solders in either army could boast better credentials: service in the Black Hawk expedition, the Seminole War, the Utah Expedition, and the Mexican War, where he received five wounds and three well-earned brevets. But compared to Beauregard, Johnston seemed to possess few of the qualities of the heroic figure the South so desperately wanted. For one, he was relatively old (fifty-four) and phlegmatic. And, though dignified, he shared an old regular's disdain for pretention and shunned contrived drama. His current assignment in the Shenandoah Valley also held less allure than Beauregard's: his force was smaller, his enemy less imposing, and, to the less informed, the consequences of his success or failure seemed far less dramatic. Even the men in his own army sensed that the denouement would come in the distant east, near Manassas Junction. Their letters and diaries reveal a persistent, yet veiled, fear—not that they would be wounded or killed in the coming battle, but rather that they might miss it altogether. It would be Johnston's job to ensure that did not happen.[10]

Thirty miles from Manassas Junction, the Federal army in Washington prepared its onslaught on Beauregard and Johnston. A thundering blow it promised to be, for gathered around the capital was the largest army this country had ever seen: 35,000 men, poised for action and, as many saw it, adventure. Their leader was a man few Americans had even heard of three months before, a man who seemed somewhat bewildered at the position in which he now found himself. He was Irvin McDowell, a forty-three-year-old Ohioan and 1838 graduate of West Point (he ranked well below cadet-mate Beauregard in class standing) who, like

Beauregard, had never before commanded as many as a dozen men in the field. A large man, he possessed none of the dash or verve of his primary adversary, Beauregard. A British correspondent described his "broad jowl and smooth face, keen blue eye, good brow, block head, [and] square stout clumsy figure and limbs." McDowell could be friendly and engaging at one moment, especially when talking about his favorite subject of fishing, and arrogant and aloof the next. Subsequent service would prove him to be self-serving and calculating, though at this early stage he was wont to solicit others' opinions and act upon them. Not long after the battle, he admitted, "I was the last man in the world pledged to my own views." Events would validate that self-assessment.[11]

Few men have ever been hoisted into as difficult a position as was McDowell that summer of 1861. The sting of the Fort Sumter affront was still fresh in the public's mind, and the press agitated for action: "On to Richmond!" So too clamored congressmen, cabinet officers, and even the soldiers. To his credit, McDowell resisted impetuosity. His men were not ready, he argued. Some had been with the army only weeks and had received only the most rudimentary training. Even the Regular army officers under his command had never maneuvered brigades or divisions in the field—a fact even Winfield Scott seemed to overlook. When McDowell held a review of eight regiments (two brigades), Scott chastised him for "trying to make a show." McDowell protested that his officers needed the experience, but to no avail. "I wanted very much a little time," McDowell later said. "We did not have a bit of it."

Nor were his troops in physical condition to march in the summer heat. But the pressure for immediate action only increased, and in the end, McDowell could not resist two immutable forces. First, many of his regiments had enlisted for only ninety days, and late July and August would see those men leaving the army. If McDowell did not wage war soon, he might not have an army to do it with later. Second, the pressure from the president, the public, Congress, and the recruits could not be ignored. "You are green, it is true," Scott told McDowell, "but they are green also." McDowell would march in mid-July.[12]

McDowell's plan called for his army to use the overland route. "The objective point . . . is the Manassas Junction," he informed his superiors in late June. He expected the Confederates to fight for it and planned to turn Beauregard out of his position at Manassas by crossing Bull Run below the Junction. He hoped to cut Beauregard's link to the South by destroying the bridge over Broad Run at Bristoe Station, but most of all he expected the Confederates to accept battle somewhere near Manassas. "The consequences of that battle will be of the greatest importance to the country," he understated, by "establishing the prestige in this contest of one side or the other."

McDowell's initial plan envisioned no attempt to sever the rail line linking Beauregard with Johnston, the Manassas Gap Railroad. Instead, the Union commander would rely on the 18,000-man army under the command of sixty-nine-year-old Robert Patterson to detain Johnston in the Shenandoah Valley. Patterson's simultaneous advance on Winchester should at least immobilize Johnston, thus improving McDowell's numerical advantage in front of Manassas. This was the very two-pronged operation the Confederates feared most. If everything proceeded as planned, McDowell's victory near Manassas might clear the road to Richmond within the month, and the war would end. If, that is, everything went as planned.[13]

While the Federal high command schemed, and as one after another projected date for marching passed without action, McDowell's army chafed, becoming increasingly dismayed by the reality of army life. Unlike their foes at Manassas Junction, life in the Federal army in June and July 1861 had a decidedly urban aspect to it. Sizable numbers of troops slept in the Patent Office, the Treasury Building, and the Capitol, the basement of which was for a time turned into a bakery. In idle hours, knots of soldiers roamed the streets, strolling into and stumbling out of saloons at their leisure (until the authorities ordered the watering holes closed). The 11th New York Infantry "Fire Zouaves," comprised mostly of New York City firemen, became famous not just for prodigious drinking, but also for rushing out of their camp to battle a fire at Willard's Hotel.

In the camps outside the city rumors ruled, and false reports of Confederate advances often played havoc with the daily routine. "There was never a moment's peace, day or night," remembered one artillery officer. The slightest noise would frighten nervous sentinels into firing, which in turn would bring whole regiments out on the run. "Horses were shot, mules killed as they grazed," the artilleryman wrote. "Nine men were shot in one day."

Like the Confederates, the Federals placed unbounded confidence in their cause and in the outcome of the impending battle. Many thought the Confederates would run at the first fire and that tossing a few shells at them would suffice to win the war. Indeed, the Union army put great stock in their artillery, especially the 3-ton, 30-pounder Parrott rifle, the size and sound of which was particularly fearsome. More than 250 men volunteered to serve this magnificent piece, which required a team of ten horses to pull it. "I remember well how the men loved that huge gun," recalled Lt. Peter Hains, the gun's commander. "I have seen them come to it and pat its breech affectionately. 'Good old boy, you'll make 'em sit up—just wait a bit,' they would say."[14]

By July 15, the army and virtually the whole world sensed the moment had come, and the Union camps bustled with preparation and buzzed at the prospect of advance. "We are sure to go this time," wrote an anxious Ai Thompson of the 2nd New Hampshire, "or there will be a mutiny in camp. We have been disappointed so many times that to disappoint us again would be hazardous in the extreme." Rumors abounded as to the immediate objective, but gamblers in the ranks wagered Manassas Junction. "The main body of the rebel forces is said to be in that direction," wrote Thompson, "and the 'plan' of course is to meet and annihilate them. If the two armies do ever meet, there will be some cowardly backing down or terrible fighting."[15]

The sudden realization that they might be fighting and dying within the week changed many a soldier's outlook. "Well Jimmy," one soldier from Wisconsin wrote to a friend, "we have at last got into the land of business, where playing soldier is played out, and acting soldier has become a reality, and Home Guards are not known, and Fourth of July soldiering is among the things that were."[16]

Other soldiers stoutly proclaimed their willingness to die, and a few predicted their own demise. Sullivan Ballou, lawyer, father, and the untrained major of the 2nd Rhode Island, was one such grim-minded man. Before setting out, he wrote his wife "a few lines that may fall under your eyes when I shall be no more," and declared, "If it is necessary that I shall fall on the battlefield for my Country, I am ready."[17]

Col. Israel B. Richardson, a newlywed and old army officer in command of a brigade in Tyler's division, wrote no dramatic missives to his wife, Fannie, because she had joined him in the field. She came with a beautiful horse, a fine sidesaddle, and an active beehive to sustain a constant supply of honey (surely the most unusual component of either army's commissary). The men in Richardson's brigade soon learned that Mrs. Richardson's word ruled in ways her husband's did not. During the march, the quartermaster of the 2nd Michigan dared to touch the honey in her beehive; she promptly intervened and had him sent back to Michigan. The campaign to Bull Run would produce several of the war's novelties, but few match the strong-willed Fannie Richardson in the field with her beehive.[18]

Despite dire premonitions and luxurious baggage, the army marched with high spirit as it swung onto the turnpikes, heading west late on the afternoon of July 16. The first day's march was smooth and uneventful—adrenaline as much as anything pushed the tender-footed soldiers on to their destinations. Brig. Gen. Daniel Tyler's division, the largest in the army, trudged into Vienna that evening. Farther south, Col. David Hunter's two brigades and Col. Dixon Miles's division made it as far as Annandale. On the extreme left, grizzled Samuel Heintzelman's columns marched well into the night along the Old Fairfax Road until they reached Pohick Creek.

The next day's march did not go as well. McDowell believed he would find enemy outposts somewhere around Fairfax Courthouse or Fairfax Station and implored caution on his division commanders, an admonition that was hardly necessary. To his jumpy officers and men, every fallen tree became a Rebel breastwork, every turn in the road concealed a masked battery, and every stray shot brought forth the "long roll." The three major columns lurched along, their progress a succession of forward spasms followed by maddening stops. The frequent halts goaded temptation. July is blackberry season in Virginia, and every stop saw a slew of soldiers take to the roadside fields in search of the juicy fruit. At every stream, hordes more fell out of ranks to replenish canteens, whether or not they needed to do so. "They would not keep in ranks, order as much as you pleased," recalled McDowell. "They were not used to denying themselves much."[19]

Still, an army on active campaign presented a memorable spectacle. Congressman Elihu Washburne of Illinois joined Sen. James Lane of Kansas and future Speaker of the House Schuyler Colfax of Indiana in a ride to catch up with the army that day. They found it near Fairfax Courthouse. "The column extended three or four miles," Washburne reported to his wife, "and it was the most exciting scene I ever witnessed—a great army on its march to the battlefield." Washburne and his cohorts rode for a time with Burnside's brigade. "There were the two Rhode Island Regiments, with their white forelocks and red blankets on their backs—their bright bayonets gleaming in the sun. Then followed the long trains of heavy artillery, some immense guns requiring eight horses to haul one of them." New Hampshiremen followed, then a regiment dressed in Zouave uniforms, "their red breeches making a magnificent appearance."[20]

Shortly before noon on July 17, four hours behind McDowell's prescribed timetable, the Federals approached Fairfax Courthouse. Confederate trenches loomed on the landscape, and many expected a fight. "It became vastly exciting," wrote Washburne, "as nobody knew whether we were to have a fight, or a foot race." But when the skirmishers fanned out and moved forward, they found only the burning campfires of abandoned Confederate camps. Anticlimactic though it was, the Yankees unfurled their flags, rushed bands to the front, and, as if they were the first conquerors of the war, strutted into the town. The Stars and Stripes replaced the Stars and Bars over the courthouse, bells tolled, and the looting began. "It seemed as if the men from every regiment tried to see who could do the most foolish thing," remembered an artilleryman. The soldiers ran rampant. "Our dirty fingers were plunged into their jam pots," wrote a Rhode Islander, "and we drank their whiskey, tea, and coffee, and ate their sardines and pickles with gusto, and hunted indefatigably for relics." The soldiers found a Confederate mailbag and circulated the contents among the men of the 2nd New Hampshire. The letters, said one, "were as good as a circulating library."[21]

In Germantown, a paltry collection of rundown shacks just west of Fairfax, the looting turned ugly. The soldiers of Tyler's division broke into homes and barns, taking what they could carry and burning the rest. By late afternoon, the hamlet was in shambles. But one New Yorker saw it as no great loss: "$200 would probably cover any damage done to it."[22]

Officers sometimes joined the frolic (in this army, they often had little more military qualifications than the most common foot soldier). A captain of the 79th New York "Highlanders," clad in a kilt of his native homeland, spied a hog, and his good sense yielded to his hunger. He broke from ranks, his kilts flying up with each stride, and gave hearty chase. His men, who had long ago given up their kilts in the name of practicality, cheered him lustily. "Go it piggy." "Catch him captain!" "Put on your drawers," they razzed him. "The climax was reached," wrote one of the spectators, "when the porker, hard pressed, ran through a snake fence." As the pig squeezed under, the captain threw himself over the top, "and in the act made such an exhibition of his attenuated anatomy as to call forth a roar of laughter from all who witnessed it." The pig escaped, and the captain, mellowed considerably, appeared the next morning in regulation uniform.[23]

Anxious to move on, McDowell urged his men back on the road. The fitful morning march, however, had worn out the soldiers, and the columns melted under the hot sun. By nightfall on July 17, Tyler's division had managed only a few miles beyond Fairfax, while 5 miles to the south, Heintzelman pulled up at Sangster's Station along the Orange and Alexandria Railroad.[24]

Though all this may not have been quite the day's march he had hoped for, McDowell seemed nonetheless satisfied with the prospects for the morrow. The Confederates, as expected, had likely fallen back to the line of Bull Run, but he had no intention at this point of attacking them frontally. Instead, he hoped to move around their right by sending Heintzelman's division across the Occoquan River at Wolf Run Shoals and then cut the Orange and Alexandria southwest of Manassas.

McDowell's need to reconnoiter opposite the Confederate right, combined with worry over the arrival of much-needed but delayed provisions, led him to issue modest marching orders for July 18. No part of his main body, located along the Warrenton Turnpike between Fairfax and Centreville, was to move more than six miles that day, a meager movement that amounted only to a demonstration. "Keep up the impression that we are moving on Manassas," he told Tyler.[25]

McDowell intended Tyler's movement to be nothing more than a diversion in favor of the move around Beauregard's right via Wolf Run Shoals. Soon after issuing the orders to his column on the Warrenton Turnpike that morning, McDowell rode southward to Sangster's Station to have a look at the ground himself to assess the possibility of Heintzelman's flank movement. Arriving there about noon, McDowell found the roads leading to the Occoquan crossing to be poor and the terrain difficult. After discussing the matter with Heintzelman, the commanding general concluded the movement around Beauregard's right would be unwise. Though this had been his plan for fully a month, a few hours of observation on the ground convinced him to cancel it. He would now have to find another way to get at or around the Confederates.[26]

While McDowell's plan met its demise, Beauregard's unfolded precisely as engineered. Beauregard had fully anticipated the Federal advance—indeed, thanks to spy Rose Greenhow, he knew about it almost as it began—and had previously issued minutely detailed orders for his advance forces, namely Milledge Bonham's brigade at Fairfax and Richard Ewell's brigade at Sangster's, to pull back toward Bull Run at the first sign of Union movement.[27] Thus, Bonham's and Ewell's camps stirred early the morning of July 17. Bonham's South Carolina infantrymen, ignorant of Beauregard's standing orders to retreat, grabbed their guns and excitedly rushed into the earthworks around Fairfax Courthouse to do battle. But as soon as the Yankees came in sight, Bonham's officers ordered the Carolinians to fall in and march west, toward Centreville. "Oh! Let's give them a fire before we go," they protested. "I'd rather fight it out right here!" But before the Federals had closed to within a mile, the Confederates were trudging westward along the Warrenton Turnpike, leaving behind smoldering fires and uneaten breakfasts. Ewell's men fell back along the Orange and Alexandria as well, burning bridges and obstructing roads as they went. That night, as planned, all of Beauregard's men filed into positions behind Bull Run.[28]

If he were to fight along Bull Run, Beauregard knew he would need help. Consequently, he wrote to President Jefferson Davis on the seventeenth: "The enemy has assailed my outposts in heavy force. Send forward any re-enforcements at the earliest possible instant and by every possible means." The president acted quickly. To Col. Eppa Hunton's 8th Virginia at Leesburg went orders to march to Manassas. Similar orders went to Gen. Theophilus Holmes's two regiments at Fredericksburg and to Wade Hampton's Legion and the 6th North Carolina in Richmond. But most importantly, orders went to Johnston: "General Beauregard is attacked. To strike the enemy a decisive blow a junction of your effective force [with his] will be needed." If you can get away from Patterson, Davis told Johnston, do it.[29]

Meanwhile Beauregard prepared his positions along Bull Run for what he had already styled his "desperate stand." He had chosen Bull Run as his defensive bastion for the simple reason that crossing the stream would be no easy matter for the Federals—and to get at Manassas, they had to get across. Between the Warrenton Turnpike's stone bridge on the north and the Orange and Alexandria's bridge at Union Mills on the south, a distance of 8 miles, there were only seven crossings, and of these only one, Mitchell's Ford, could be considered major. The rest amounted to little more than farm roads. At nearly all of them Beauregard's men constructed the war's first field earthworks. Each crossing could therefore be defended by a relatively small number of men, allowing Beauregard to spread his troops over an expansive front.

Despite the extensive preparations, fighting on the defensive did not suit Beauregard. He intended to fight an offensive battle—the South expected as much. Indeed, he had put the plan in place for his counterattack long before the Federals had taken so much as an angry step in the direction of Manassas. Beauregard remained confident McDowell would be unimaginative enough to test only the center of the Confederate line, at Mitchell's Ford, where the main road leading from Centreville to Manassas crossed the run and where his line was strongest. (The four South Carolina regiments of Bonham's brigade, four cavalry detachments, and two batteries of artillery held the gentle heights above the ford.) Beauregard calculated that when the Yankee attack at Mitchell's Ford materialized, Bonham's men could hold on long enough for the rest of his army to deliver a sweeping, dramatic counterblow to the enemy's left flank and rear. James Longstreet's brigade of Virginians would dash across at Blackburn's Ford, a quarter mile south of Mitchell's, and D. R. Jones's Carolinians and Mississippians, covering McLean's Ford, would sweep around and lash at the Federal rear. Richard Ewell's and Jubal Early's brigades would also leave their positions near Union Mills Ford and try to cut off the Yankees. At the northern crossings, Philip St. George Cocke's at Lewis and Balls Fords and Nathan Evans's at the Stone Bridge would rush forward in vigorous, victorious pursuit.

A glorious victory it would be—if only the Federals would follow Beauregard's grand design.[30]

Chapter Two

FIRST BLOOD

McDowell of course had no inkling of Beauregard's designs, but judging from the haste with which the Confederates retreated before him, he presumed that whatever the Creole's plans were, they must be now in disarray. "Their retreat . . . must have had a damaging effect upon them," he observed. But with the abandonment of the proposed move around the Confederate right, it was McDowell's plans, not Beauregard's, that stood in disorder. Still his army, with Tyler's division in the lead, crept closer to its foe.

Tyler's orders that July 18 morning were simple and cautious. Move along the Warrenton Turnpike to Centreville (about six miles from Manassas Junction), McDowell told him. Once at that crossroads hamlet, "observe well the roads to Bull Run and Warrenton. Do not bring on an engagement, but keep up the impression that we are moving on Manassas." The head of Tyler's column marched into Centreville at about 9 A.M.[1]

Located at the junction of three important roads—the Warrenton Turnpike, Braddock Road, and the road to Chantilly—Centreville figured prominently in every military map of the era, and much ado had been made by the Federals about capturing it. Cheers rolled through Tyler's columns as the men tramped up the ridge to the crossroads. But for all its notoriety, Centreville was an eminently unimpressive place. "It looks for all the world," wrote a man in William T. Sherman's brigade, "as though it had done its business, whatever it was, if it ever had any, fully eighty years ago, and since then had bolted its doors, put out its fires and gone to sleep." Abandoned Confederate huts and a jumble of earthworks and redoubts rendered the crossroads and its decrepit houses even more homely to Yankee eyes.[2]

Few subordinate commanders of the war held their commanding officer in greater disdain than did Daniel Tyler. If his postwar memoir can be believed, he thought McDowell unqualified for his post and his rise to command the product of relentless efforts at ingratiation. Tyler called McDowell "an expensive ornament to the military service" and averred that his "courtier-like services in the salon have immeasurably exceeded his military services in the field." It is little surprise, then, that Tyler, commander of McDowell's lead division on July 18, greeted McDowell's orders for that day with disdain. McDowell ordered restraint. Tyler opted for aggression.[3]

As his troops entered Centreville, the fresh signs of retreating Confederates urged Tyler onward. He and his division did not linger long. Locals told him that Philip St. George Cocke's brigade of Virginians had retreated toward the west along the Warrenton Turnpike earlier that morning, toward the Stone Bridge. Milledge Bonham's brigade of South Carolinians, the larger force, had retreated southwestward toward Mitchell's and Blackburn's Fords. Israel Richardson's Federal brigade, accompanied by his wife and her honey-heavy beehive, quickly marched through the town and turned south on the road toward Manassas, marching a mile before stopping for water. Robert Schenck's brigade moved west of the village a short distance, while Sherman's brigade remained in the hamlet proper.[4]

Tyler himself remained in Centreville for about an hour, gathering what information he could, and then rode to join Richardson along the road toward Manassas Junction. Mindful of his orders to watch the roads toward Manassas, Tyler suggested to Richardson that they push ahead and make a reconnaissance. Richardson hunted up a makeshift battalion of forty men from each of his four regiments (the 2nd and 3rd Michigan, 1st Massachusetts, and 12th New York) and put them under command of Capt. Robert Bretschneider of the 2nd Michigan. He also gathered a squadron of cavalry and two 10-pounder rifles commanded by Capt. Romeyn B. Ayres. Shortly after 10 A.M., the expedition set out toward Blackburn's and Mitchell's Fords, on the direct roads to Manassas Junction.

Cautiously, Tyler and Richardson moved along for nearly three miles until they emerged from timber into the fields overlooking Bull Run. Directly in front of them, a farm path led to Blackburn's Ford, while the main road branched to the right, crossing Bull Run a mile distant at Mitchell's Ford. A quick look by Tyler revealed clearly that the Confederate position at Mitchell's was the stronger of the two. There, the approach to the ford passed over level ground commanded by a substantial ridge on the west side of the stream. The ground in front of Blackburn's Ford, on the other hand, seemed to be more favorable to the Federals, for there the rolling hills on the east bank fairly commanded whatever positions the Confederates might have on the west bank. Indeed, Tyler was, in his own word, "astonished" that the Confederates had not occupied in force this ground east of Blackburn's Ford. This he would seek to exploit.[5]

The ground the Confederates occupied had been carefully chosen by Beauregard on the presumption that McDowell would do exactly what he apparently was: move against Mitchell's Ford and the Confederate center. At Mitchell's, Beauregard had bolstered his line most impressively, for there stood the Confederate army's biggest, best-organized, and best-known brigade, commanded by Milledge Bonham, a former South Carolina congressman. Bonham's six regiments had the advantage of a well-prepared position; the right of his line, directly overlooking the ford, had the benefit of earthworks that had been erected weeks before. From the ford, his line extended a mile northward, almost to Island Ford. In front, across Bull Run, Bonham deployed three companies of Joseph Kershaw's 2nd South Carolina as well as two guns from Delaware Kemper's Alexandria Artillery. These were to sound the alarm in the event of a Federal advance.[6]

To Bonham's right, Bull Run bowed sharply northeastward. Near the apex of this bow, a rutted country road crossed the stream at Blackburn's Ford, where Brig. Gen. James Longstreet's brigade nervously stood watch. As Tyler had observed, the ground at Blackburn's did not favor Longstreet. The Confederate shore of Bull Run here was largely flat, "rising with a very gradual slope and undulations back to Manassas," reported Beauregard. The eastern bank, on the other hand, rose more steeply, creating, he noted, "an admirable natural parapet." Heavy brush and timber covered the east side of the stream opposite Longstreet's right. Opposite his left, the ground was clear, punctuated only by tangles of cedar.[7]

Longstreet charged the 1st Virginia with the immediate defense of the crossing on the right of the ford and the 17th Virginia with the left. Longstreet deployed these regiments in two lines, the first holding the brush-covered stream bank and the second in the open field back of the stream. To the 17th Virginia's left, connecting with Bonham's skirmishers at Mitchell's Ford, was Lynchburg's 11th Virginia. As for artillery, Longstreet had only two 6-pounder guns of the Washington Artillery at his immediate disposal. These he located in the open field to the right of the farm road and, because of their limited range and firepower, gave them orders to retreat as soon as "it was ascertained that our pieces were commanded by those of the enemy."[8]

Three brigades guarding McLean's and Union Mills Fords farther to the south stood ready for Beauregard's summons, should it come. D. R. Jones's brigade, with two guns of the Washington Artillery, held McLean's Ford. The brigade of bald-headed Richard Ewell, supplemented by four companies of cavalry and four howitzers from the Washington Artillery, guarded Union Mills Ford (where the Orange and Alexandria crossed Bull Run). Ready to act as Beauregard's sole mobile reserve, former Unionist-turned-ardent-Confederate Jubal Early and his hodgepodge brigade of Virginians, Mississippians, and Louisianans waited with three rifled guns of the Washington Artillery (rare machinery for the underequipped Confederate army). On the morning of July 18,

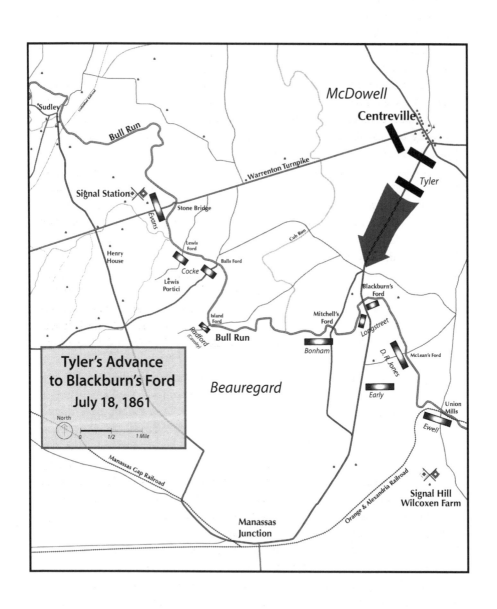

McDowell

Centreville

Tyler

Sudley

Bull Run

Warrenton Turnpike

Signal Station

Stone Bridge

Evans

Lewis
Ford

Henry
House

Cocke

Balls Ford

Cub Run

Lewis
Portici

Blackburn's
Ford

Island
Ford

Radford
(Cavalry)

Bull Run

Mitchell's
Ford

Longstreet

Bonham

D. R. Jones

McLean's Ford

**Tyler's Advance
to Blackburn's Ford**
July 18, 1861

Beauregard

Early

Union
Mills

North

0   1/2   1 Mile

Ewell

Manassas Gap Railroad

Orange & Alexandria Railroad

Signal Hill
Wilcoxen Farm

**Manassas
Junction**

Beauregard ordered Early to move to a more central position near Wilmer McLean's house, Yorkshire, about a mile back from the stream and roughly equidistant from Mitchell's, Blackburn's and McLean's Fords. Beauregard himself located his headquarters in McLean's house and directed his medical staff to set up shop in McLean's barn, just south of the road to Blackburn's.[9]

Heavily defended though his position may have been at Mitchell's and Blackburn's Fords, Beauregard in no way begged the Yankees onward—not yet. His much-needed help, Johnston's army, still meandered in the Shenandoah Valley 60 miles away. Nor had Beauregard had sufficient time to prepare his planned counterattack against the Union left. If McDowell insisted on pressing against the center, Beauregard had no choice but to make do with what he had.[10]

From their command post at the Butler house a mile and a half away, Tyler and Richardson could see little of Beauregard's position—only a Confederate battery and a few skirmishers. Tyler suspected there must be more. As Tyler pondered the matter, Maj. John G. Barnard, McDowell's chief engineer, joined him and reminded him of McDowell's orders not to bring on battle that day. But, Barnard said, if Tyler wished to make a demonstration, he could. Tyler needed no more encouragement. To provoke the Confederates into revealing their positions, Tyler ordered Bretschneider's makeshift battalion to move to the front as skirmishers and ordered forward R. B. Ayres's two rifled cannon. Perhaps hinting at grander aspirations, Tyler also sent orders back to Richardson's brigade, and later to Sherman's, to move toward Blackburn's Ford from Centreville in case something bigger developed.[11]

Ayres's guns rumbled forward and unlimbered at the edge of the wood line near the Butler farm. They opened fire first on Kemper's Alexandria Artillery in the direction of Mitchell's Ford, and then on the guns of the Washington Artillery behind Blackburn's. To Tyler's chagrin, the response from the Confederates was half-hearted, revealing nothing of the Southerners' positions. Kemper's men held their fire until they detected some movement among the Union guns, when they fired feebly, their cannonballs falling far short of their targets. After only six shots, Kemper hitched his guns and, under cover of Kershaw's skirmishers, hustled back across Mitchell's Ford. Longstreet's two guns did not wait so long. As ordered, they withdrew at the first shots from Tyler.[12]

Ayres's gunners continued to fire, but Longstreet's and Bonham's men bore the Federal iron silently. "All nerves were strung to a high tension," wrote one of Longstreet's Virginians, who made particular note of the first shell fired his way. It came, he said, "making a noise that cannot be described; it was more like the neigh of an excited or frightened horse than anything I can compare it to; a kind of 'whicker, whicker, whicker' sound as it swapped ends in the air." The shell whistled overhead, exploding harmlessly but "making the dirt fly, and tearing a hole in the ground, as some of the boys said, 'Big enough to bury a horse in.'"[13]

Though novel, the Union artillery fire did little damage and provoked no response from the Confederates, momentarily defeating Tyler's hope that the Confederates would reveal their positions and strength (or lack thereof). Tyler decided if the artillery could not get the Confederates to reveal their positions, surely the infantry would. Major Barnard, now joined by Capt. James B. Fry of McDowell's staff, begged Tyler not to escalate the affair; he would exceed orders, they said, and risked bringing on an unplanned major engagement. But Tyler didn't heed them, and shortly before noon he ordered Richardson to take his brigade forward, "scour" the ground in front, and flush the Confederates.[14]

Richardson deployed Bretschneider's collection of infantryman 500 yards in front of Ayres's guns. To bolster the skirmish line on the left of the road, Richardson trotted out three companies of the gray-clad 1st Massachusetts commanded by Lt. Col. George D. Wells. Barnard watched all this helplessly, still trying to talk Tyler out of provoking anything more serious, but for naught. Finally accepting that Tyler would do as he pleased in any event, Barnard directed one of his engineers to accompany the Federal advance and see what he could learn.[15]

As the Federals pushed toward Bull Run at Blackburn's Ford, Longstreet's skirmishers tumbled back, giving the alarm. "Immediately every man was on his feet, gun in hand," recalled Pvt. Alexander Hunter of Company A, 17th Virginia, guarding the ford. The men slid cartridge boxes to the front of their belts and formed into battle line. Officers moved among the men, telling them in quiet tones, "Remember boys, fire low." (Soldiers of all eras have had a tendency to fire over the heads of their foes, and this was a popular refrain on Civil War battlefields.) Of the hundreds of Confederates near Blackburn's Ford, only a handful had been shot at before, and nerves brought most to a physical and mental state they had never experienced. "I saw many pale faces," recorded one soldier of the 11th Virginia. "I don't know how I looked, but [I] felt rather pale."[16]

Colonel Wells's Federals moved forward cautiously through the woods south of the road, unable to see anything. The firing began as an occasional *pop, pop, pop*, and grew gradually until it sounded like the irregular rattle of a bad spoons player. As the Bay Staters, dressed in gray uniforms, crested the ridge bordering the stream, the Confederates suddenly opened fire with more earnestness, and "bullets screamed over our heads like a hornets nest," remembered a New Englander. Wells reflexively—naively—ordered his three companies to charge.[17]

His paltry force swept down the wooded slope toward the ford and Longstreet's nervous Virginians. They stood largely in the open, screened only by brush along the bank of the stream, while the ground to the east rose steadily— clearly placing the Virginians at a disadvantage. Alexander Hunter of the 17th Virginia remembered, "every man acted for themselves, most stood and gallantly delivered their fire . . . though we couldn't see a thing, but away we fired as fast as we could load, blazing away in every direction." Some Southerners ran at the

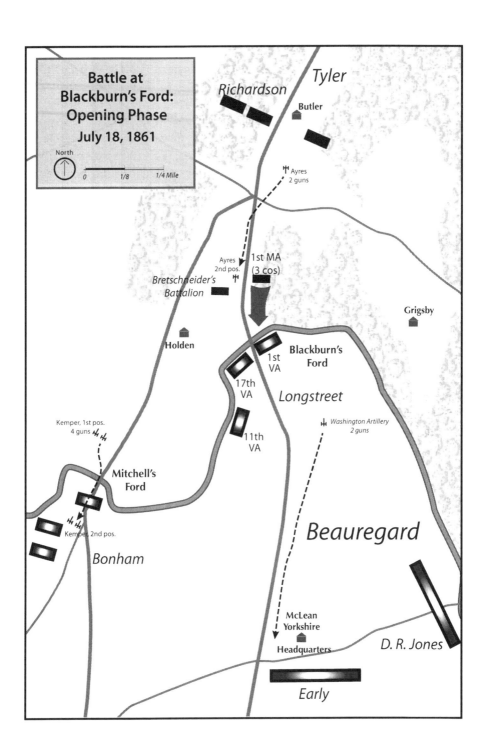

Battle at Blackburn's Ford: Opening Phase
July 18, 1861

North

0   1/8   1/4 Mile

Tyler

Richardson

Butler

Ayres
2 guns

Ayres
2nd pos.

1st MA
(3 cos)

Bretschneider's
Battalion

Grigsby

Holden

1st
VA

Blackburn's
Ford

17th
VA

Longstreet

11th
VA

Washington Artillery
2 guns

Kemper, 1st pos.
4 guns

Mitchell's
Ford

Beauregard

Kemper, 2nd pos.

Bonham

McLean
Yorkshire

Headquarters

D. R. Jones

Early

first Federal fire, finding refuge in distant timber. They huddled behind trees, pet-rified, and "fired at the sun . . . in a most valorous manner." But enough Confed-erates held their places to make things uncomfortable for Wells and his men, and the Federals yielded. A second charge by the Federals met the same fate.[18]

On the right of Wells's line, Lt. William Smith of the 1st Massachusetts dis-covered what he supposed was the enemy. But the opposing line, like he and his men, appeared in gray uniforms, and Smith had seen enough of his own multi-colored army to know that uniform color would mean nothing on this battlefield. The lieutenant ordered his men not to fire and ran toward the distant line yelling, "Who are you?" The Confederates responded in kind: "Who are you?" Smith, faithfully demonstrating the hope and trust of a rookie soldier, yelled back, "Massachusetts men." The Confederates instantly leveled their guns and fired a volley at the hapless lieutenant, "which laid him dead upon the spot."

Wells and his men resumed their position on the crest of the ridge and for nearly an hour contested the Confederates single-handedly. By late-war stan-dards this affair was merely a brush, but to these men the pace and intensity of this fight seemed frantic. Even officers left their places to join the men in the ranks and get a "dab" at the Rebels. "Lieut. Col. Wells fought like a common soldier," wrote one soldier. "He rushed from man to man, grasping their muskets and firing them, and shouting for another loaded one. So did our captain, and the men, encouraged by their example, fought like devils."[19]

While the fighting seemed stiff enough to the Massachusetts men, Tyler, with his artillery back near the Butler farm, viewed the Confederate response as inconclusive. He had challenged them with only three companies and he could not yet say with certainty that the Confederates held the ford in strength. So the general became bolder and upped his commitment. He ordered Captain Ayres to take his two howitzers—guns well suited to short-range work—and put them into position alongside the road, about 500 yards from Bull Run. The general deepened his commitment to this slapdash affair by ordering two companies of cavalry to support Ayres's guns. At the same time, Richardson recommended his entire brigade move forward to the wood's edge and be ready to charge the enemy's batteries on the far bank, if the opportunity presented itself. Tyler, despite the entreaties of those around him, agreed.

Moving these commands took nearly a half hour. Richardson personally accompanied the 12th New York on the left of his line. "Fighting Dick," as he would become known, rode in front of the 12th: "Move forward New Yorkers," he yelled, "and sweep the woods." Richardson then rode to the right, putting in place the 1st Massachusetts, 2nd Michigan, and, on the extreme right, the 3rd Michigan.[20]

Meanwhile, Ayres's guns rolled into position near the road, unlimbered, loaded with canister, and fired a thundering volley—probably the first such vol-ley of the war. The iron balls zipped over the heads of Longstreet's men along the stream, showering them with branches and twigs and making them feel, as one man recorded, "decidedly uncomfortable." Still, Longstreet's men responded vigorously, and the entire creek bottom erupted in gunfire. "It appeared to me that there were 5,000 muskets fired at once," said Tyler.[21]

With that first Confederate volley at the ford, Tyler had learned what he came to learn—the crossing was strongly defended by alert Confederate infantry. The general, much to the relief of Barnard and Fry, seemed inclined to break off the engagement and fall back toward Centreville. But by the time Tyler decided to close the engagement, Richardson and the New Yorkers had advanced so far as to engage Longstreet's infantrymen behind the ford, rendering it too late to pull out now. His good sense overcome by lack of tactical control, Daniel Tyler's battle would continue.[22]

The advance of Ayres's guns and Richardson's brigade forced Longstreet to strengthen his line at the ford. He ordered reserve companies of the 1st and 17th Virginia in the woods behind the ford to move to the firing line, which they did with enthusiasm. "We sprang to our feet like one man," wrote Frank Potts of Company C, 1st Virginia. Maj. Frederick Skinner, six and a half feet tall, waved his sword overhead and wailed, "Charge boys, and drive the dogs back." But, Potts admitted, "the dogs were too smart to come on," and Skinner and his men simply joined in the firefight. Longstreet also sent for more distant help, requesting Colonel Early, whom Beauregard had directed to be ready to assist wherever needed, to move forward as support.[23]

The newly intensified fire from Longstreet caused havoc among the Federals. Near the ford, Ayres's gunners fled from one of their pieces, according to Colonel Wells. Captain Brackett, commander of the cavalry supporting Ayres's guns, frantically rode around, looking for someone to save the guns from what he felt was certain doom. Dressed in citizen clothes with appropriate shoulder straps simply pinned into place, Brackett found Col. Ezra Walrath of the 12th New York and pleaded with him to move forward and save the guns.[24]

Walrath was one of upstate New York's preeminent drillmasters before the Civil War, but had never maneuvered men under fire. He led his New Yorkers into the woods to the left of Ayres's guns. Low, thick pines and brush "veiled everything in front beyond a few paces," he recalled, and the 12th stumbled on until they came within view of Bull Run. Suddenly the bushes in front "seemed to be alive with rebels," wrote Walrath, and just as suddenly those bushes exploded with a "murderous fire" that raked his line. Walrath made the expedient move and ordered his men to lie down and fire—something the men had never practiced. One man's gun went off in his face when smoldering sparks prematurely ignited the charge in the barrel.[25]

On the Confederate side of the stream, among the bushes, Frank Potts of the 1st Virginia fired wildly at Walrath's men. "I fired twice at random," Potts wrote in his diary, "and then growing cool, I loaded deliberately and waited, with piece

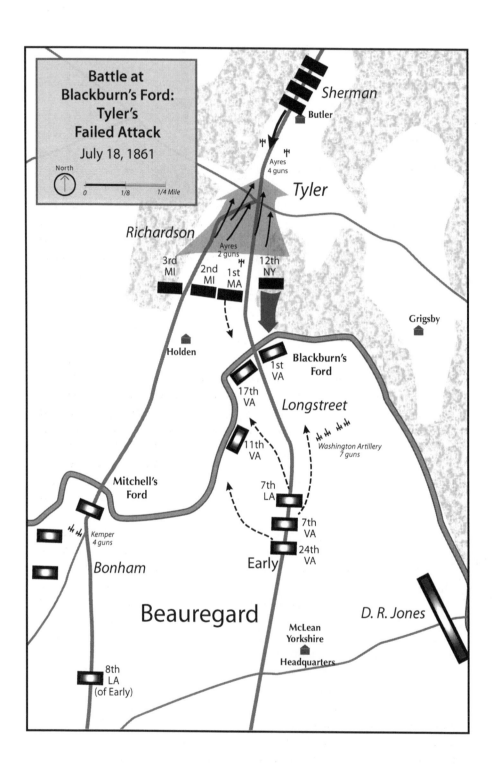

**Battle at
Blackburn's Ford:
Tyler's
Failed Attack**

July 18, 1861

North

0   1/8   1/4 Mile

Sherman

Butler

Ayres
4 guns

Tyler

Richardson

Ayres
2 guns

3rd
MI

2nd
MI

1st
MA

12th
NY

Grigsby

Holden

1st
VA

Blackburn's
Ford

17th
VA

Longstreet

11th
VA

Washington Artillery
7 guns

Mitchell's
Ford

7th
LA

Kemper
4 guns

7th
VA

Bonham

Early

24th
VA

Beauregard

McLean
Yorkshire
Headquarters

D. R. Jones

8th
LA
(of Early)

at 'a ready' for a sure shot. At length I was rewarded." Potts watched a blue-clad fellow stealthily creeping forward. He had, Potts noted, a "black hat like my own and a glazed cloth haversack. I came to aim, steadied my piece, and aiming at his breast, I fired. I saw him no more, God have mercy on him." Potts had never killed a man before. Tinged with guilt, he explained, "The distance was about 70 yards, and I could not miss him. Well, I was fighting for my home, and he had no business being there."[26]

With Walrath's advance the battle came to its climax. Wrote Private Hunter of the 17th Virginia, "It was no longer volleys rattling up and down the bank, but a roar, not a dull sound, but precisely like the crackling of the woods when a forest was on fire." In a letter home, another man explained, "There is something very grand in the whizzing of balls and the bursting of shells, but it is not such as I like." Two newly minted lieutenants from West Point, Emory Upton and Patrick O'Rorke, served on Tyler's staff, and the two young men decided, as O'Rorke put it, to ride to the firing line "to see how it felt to be under such a fire." General Longstreet, a cigar stump clamped between his teeth, had his horse shot from under him. Still he stayed with his men. "He is a good soldier and brave man," one soldier wrote in a letter, "and won the hearts of the men on all sides."[27]

Beside the road, in the midst of the Alexandria Rifles, stood a regal old tree of considerable girth—4 full feet in diameter. With bullets and shells—especially the shells—whizzing about, raw soldiers simply could not resist the protection offered by this stately tree. As the battle progressed, more men edged behind the tree, forming a line of about fifty men. Wrote one Virginian: "As a shell from the battery on our right would come whistling through the air, the whole line would run around and place the tree between them and the shells. All at once another battery opened on the left, and as the balls came from that direction, the men would hang on to each other and run on the opposite side, and so they kept shifting to and fro."[28]

The battle continued in this manner for perhaps twenty minutes. Colonel Walrath's New Yorkers effectively returned the Confederate fire until one of the captains, either through misunderstanding or fear, gave the order to retreat. At that, the 12th disintegrated. Walrath rode among his men, trying to rally them around the colors, but the retreat could not be stemmed. The hapless colonel later admitted being trampled by his own frightened men, and some newspapers accused Walrath of panicking right along with them. The two adventurous lieutenants on Tyler's staff, Upton and O'Rorke, also tried to stem the break in the 12th New York. "We appealed to their pride and to their manhood," wrote O'Rorke. "We begged them for the honor of our state and of our flag to reform, and make another stand—but without effect." Richardson, too, tried rallying the 12th. Fighting Dick found two companies of the regiment retreating in good order, but these men claimed the rest of the regiment "were all killed." Richardson spurred his horse farther to the left, where he found the rest of the 12th in confusion. "What are you running for?" he yelled. "There is no enemy here. I cannot see anybody at all. Where is your Colonel?" Walrath could not be found, and despite Richardson's queries, the retreat continued. Richardson sent word to Tyler of the 12th's travails. "Let them go," Tyler replied.[29]

The retreat of the 12th New York came at precisely the moment Longstreet's line teetered under the Federal pressure. Rather than watch his line fall back, Longstreet ran to his men and ordered those who could hear him to charge. Two companies splashed over the ford. "Like a pack of hounds after a fox, we got across," wrote Private Hunter. But the Confederate advance was little more organized than the New Yorkers' retreat, and it soon slowed. Still, the retreat of the New Yorkers exposed the left flank of the 1st Massachusetts, 2nd Michigan, and 3rd Michigan north of the road, and the few Confederates who managed to cross the stream created considerable Union consternation by lapping around the flank of the 1st Massachusetts. The 1st found itself in a virtually indefensible position, and its colonel ordered the men to lie down to avoid the fire. Pvt. Charles Jackson of the 1st Massachusetts saw his friend Thomas Harding leaning on his gun against a tree. Harding called for a sergeant, Jackson wrote a few days later, "told him he was shot, shook hands with him, and fell over dead." To the right of the 1st, the 2nd Michigan suffered similarly, while on the extreme right of the line the men of 3rd Michigan, well out of danger, took some time to pick blackberries.[30]

Tyler had had enough. He rode to his beset brigade commander, Israel Richardson, and found that even the near destruction of one of Richardson's regiments had not dissuaded the Michigander from his notion that his brigade could force a crossing at Blackburn's Ford. Though the 12th New York had broken, Richardson pointed out, his three remaining regiments still held their ground. The colonel suggested he form the 12th as a support and move with the Massachusetts and Michigan regiments against the enemy's batteries across the run. Tyler politely told his pugnacious subordinate that the intent of the affair had been fulfilled, "that it was not a part of the plan of battle to do anything more . . . than a mere demonstration." Besides, Sherman's brigade, marching from Centreville, had not yet arrived. Tyler ordered Ayres's guns and Richardson's infantry to pull back again to the Butler farm.[31]

Though Tyler could not know it, the timing of his withdrawal was propitious, for the Confederates opposite were growing in strength by the minute. As the Federals fell back, two guns of the Washington Artillery (the two that had been supporting Longstreet at the beginning of the fight) returned and unlimbered in the field behind the ford. Following the artillery came three regiments of Early's brigade. Early deployed his regiments quickly: the 7th Louisiana moved directly to the ford, the 7th Virginia to the right of it, and the 24th Virginia to the extreme left of the line. As the Virginians moved into position, they saw some of Longstreet's skirmishers lying quietly in a neat row in the distant broomsedge. Someone yelled, "Good God, look at the dead men!"

"Now boys, if you don't run, the Yankees will," Early told his men. He yelled orders to load, and a captain strode in front of the line and directed the men to follow the nine-step process of loading, according to regulations. Early saw no time for formalities. "Load in nine times?" he growled. "Hell and damnation! Load in the most expeditious manner possible." By the time Early's men arrived, however, the musket fire had started to fade. The Federal infantry had done all the fighting it had a mind to do, and was busily withdrawing.[32]

Longstreet's men who had crossed north of the stream did not let the Yankee infantry go without a few final shots. Private Hunter, opposite the 1st Massachusetts, wrote, "They . . . seemed to be lost among the woods, [and] all we had to do was shoot them down." The Northerners ran from tree to tree, dodging bullets that kicked up dust and leaves around them. "It was glorious," said Hunter. The Federals made a brief stand in the Holden farm buildings, then scampered out of sight. "All of our dead were left," remembered one Union soldier.[33]

Longstreet briefly considered launching an organized attack against the retreating Unionists, but his own disorganization and the bad roads east of the stream dissuaded him. He recalled his infantry, and the fight reverted to an artillery duel. Behind Longstreet's infantry, five additional guns of the vaunted Washington Artillery joined the two guns already in place. (Before the battle, these Louisianans were the subject of considerable bluster and had built themselves a reputation unmatched in the Confederate army. Now they had an opportunity to earn it.) They rolled their guns into position in spectacular style, whipping the horse-drawn limbers in wide arcs. Amid bursting shells from Ayres's battery, the cannoneers unlimbered the pieces flawlessly and each man rushed to his appointed post. From left to right the guns opened, booming in rapid succession. Then the battery fired "at will," the men firing as fast as they could. Shells burst around the guns, but the cannoneers never lost their precision; neither did a man fall nor run. Indeed, their composure contrasted mightily with the frantic, almost frightened pace of the infantry fight. "They loaded and fired their guns with as much coolness and military regularity as they would on the parade ground," wrote one admiring onlooker. This was war as most of these green soldiers had imagined: impersonal, exciting, and bloodless.[34]

As the artillery duel raged, the last of Tyler's troops, Sherman's brigade, arrived on the field. Sherman and most of his men had very much wanted to be part of the day's battle, but when they arrived amid the wreckage of the 12th New York and the retreating throngs of the rest of Richardson's brigade, they knew their 3-mile dash from Centreville had been for naught. Instead of glory, Sherman's men received thankless orders to relieve Richardson's command in support of the artillery. Instead of sweeping forward in an unabated wave, as most of the men had fully expected, Sherman's men silently dodged cannonballs and exploding shrapnel.[35]

Dodging bullets and artillery shells drove many commanders to distraction, for it swiftly disheveled neat battle lines. As Sherman's men moved into position, the colonel quickly became exasperated with his men, who seemed to duck and dodge at every hostile sound. He rode in front of them, striding his horse slowly up and down the line—bullets whizzing all around—and urged them to "keep cool." Ducking was no use, Sherman told his men. Once you heard the bullet, it was already by you—the danger passed. The men listened intently, and just as Sherman finished his little speech, an artillery shell crashed into the trees just over his head. Instinctively, the colonel ducked down on the neck of his horse. Sherman, no doubt sheepishly, raised his head to find a line of young faces grinning widely at him. "Well boys," he said, breaking into a smile of his own, "you may dodge the big ones."[36]

For forty-five minutes Tyler and the Confederates continued to paw at each other at a distance. Tyler recorded that his eight cannon fired exactly 415 shots during the battle. The Confederates kept less precise count, but took greater satisfaction than the Federals when, about 4 P.M., the Federal guns gradually ceased firing. The battle came to a close.[37]

The war's first blood had been spilled, and as nearly everyone south of Baltimore had predicted, it flowed in the name of Southern victory. It mattered not to the Southern soldiers that the affair at Blackburn's Ford was a small one with no great results. It was victory enough. One of Longstreet's staff officers proclaimed, "[We] repulsed them most gloriously." As Tyler's men disappeared toward Centreville, the Confederates cheered wildly and staged a makeshift rally around the victorious guns of the Washington Artillery. (The artillerymen even had to fend off the over-enthused foot soldiers. "They actually wanted to hug us," recorded one gunner.) This, at last, was war, and though dead and wounded dotted the banks of Bull Run, it had been the sporting type of affair most Southerners had envisioned. "It was," concluded a soldier of the 1st Virginia, "the most decided down-right whipping the Yankees ever received on Virginia soil."[38]

Chapter Three

PLANNING A "WATERLOO"

M cDowell, who arrived at Centreville as the battle at Blackburn's Ford came to a close, soon learned of Tyler's junket, which he saw as nothing less than a sorry mistake. Like Beauregard, McDowell had carefully planned his campaign, and like Beauregard, he had calculated that any battle fought would be a premeditated affair. Instead, the first battle was a haphazard collision, and a losing one at that. The eighty-three men lost (nineteen killed) would, McDowell feared, have a "bad effect on the men."[1]

For this, McDowell and his loyal supporters blamed Daniel Tyler. They steadfastly contended that Tyler, McDowell's senior by twenty years, sought only to upstage his underqualified army commander. In McDowell's eyes, Tyler had grossly exceeded his orders in an attempt to single-handedly win the war by forcing a crossing at Blackburn's. In the acrimonious debate that followed the war (when hindsight made tactical judgment an easier matter), Tyler, to his own discredit, did little to quell such suspicions, claiming, "I think my four brigades could have whipped Beauregard before sundown." But Tyler's actions on the battlefield that afternoon suggest that bad tactical control, not glory-seeking, led to the bruising his division received.[2]

In the aftermath of his field command in Virginia in 1861 and 1862, McDowell would expend immense energy trying to guide the public and historians to a judgment in his favor. For McDowell, Tyler's actions at Blackburn's Ford emerged as a major misstep. He doubted Tyler's motives, and more than that, he greatly exaggerated the effect of Tyler's repulse on the army and McDowell's plans. True, the affair discomfited some of Tyler's units, especially the 12th New York. (The 12th, however, blamed Richardson, not Tyler, for their losses. It seems that before the battle Colonel Walrath had been paying inordinate attention to

Mrs. Richardson. The men of the 12th surmised that Colonel Richardson's jealous rage compelled him to send Walrath and his regiment forward to be butchered.) But the rest of the army sloughed off the battle's outcome as the result of incompetence. Certainly their commanders would not be so foolish in the coming battle. Certainly they would not run ignominiously in the face of the Rebel rabble.[3]

Hoping to put the best face on this mismanaged affair, McDowell ordered Tyler to retain his position along the Centreville–Manassas Road. But either through misunderstanding or pure discouragement, Tyler instead pulled his division back to Centreville, adding to McDowell's displeasure. In response to the fight at Blackburn's Ford, McDowell also changed orders for the army's march that day. Instead of allowing his brigades to dally near Fairfax to await the arrival of provisions, McDowell now ordered them, empty bellies notwithstanding, to support Tyler at Centreville.[4]

McDowell's complaints about the fight at Blackburn's Ford obscured a critical fact: it gave him valuable information that materially affected his plans for fighting the coming battle. While Tyler's involvement at Blackburn's may have been excessive, it did demonstrate beyond a doubt—at least to McDowell—the strength of the Confederate line along that section of Bull Run. McDowell would not repeat Tyler's mistake by attacking the Confederates headlong.

That meant, of course, that McDowell would have to find a way around one of the Confederate flanks. His initial intent had been to force the Confederates out of their line along Bull Run by moving past the Confederate right, but his examination of the ground south of the Orange and Alexandria Railroad revealed roads that amounted to little more than twisted woodland trails, insufficient for the large-scale movement needed. Now, McDowell concluded to move by Beauregard's left, which rested where the Warrenton Turnpike crossed Bull Run on a weathered stone bridge. To make such a movement, though, McDowell had to find well-screened, suitable crossings upstream from the Stone Bridge. No one in the army knew that ground, and whatever maps the staff carried included scant information about the road network heading to the upper crossings of Bull Run. Filling that void of information would be the job of McDowell's chief engineer, John G. Barnard. While the army rested and fed itself on July 19, Barnard would undertake the most important military task in the land. Assuming he found a crossing and mapped the roads leading to it, the climactic movement would take place July 20.[5]

While McDowell lamented the events of July 18, 5 miles away at Wilmer McLean's house Beauregard reveled in the first substantial Confederate success of Virginia's new war. So, too, did his men. In letters home, they described the battle in terms later reserved for places like Gettysburg, Chickamauga, and Spotsylvania. They claimed the enemy numbered anywhere from 5,000 to 15,000, and that the Union dead and wounded lay strewn in every direction, numbering, one man claimed, in excess of 1,000. The Confederates, meanwhile, had lost only 15 killed and 53 wounded. The theory that one Southerner could thrash three Yankees seemed confirmed.

Slight disappointment came for Beauregard only because the fight at Blackburn's came too soon—before he and Johnston could coordinate the bold offensive thrust the Creole calculated would win him the campaign. Beauregard envisioned Johnston marching part of his command overland from Winchester via Ashby's Gap in the Blue Ridge. Assuming McDowell advanced through Centreville, Johnston, coming through Aldie, would slash at the Union right flank. As Johnston struck McDowell's right, Beauregard would advance frontally, wedging the Federals between two presumably irresistible forces. It was the type of grandiose plan Beauregard relished (and just the sort of thing that looked marvelous on paper but presented obstacles impossible to surmount). That evening, he sent his chief of staff to Johnston to reveal the design.[6]

Johnston reacted coolly to Beauregard's plan, and rightly so. Johnston surely realized the complexities of bringing two armies then 50 miles apart together against a moving target (the Union army) with any kind of precision or timing. As Beauregard's senior, Johnston would ultimately set his own course. At 1 A.M. on July 18 he had received orders from Richmond to move, "if practicable," to Beauregard's assistance at Manassas Junction. The Virginian, reading his opponent Robert Patterson well, instantly deemed such a move practicable and ordered his army, led by Thomas J. Jackson's brigade, to move immediately eastward. But the army would not move by foot, as Beauregard envisioned. Instead, Johnston directed his entire command except his artillery and cavalry to march to Piedmont Station (modern-day Delaplane) and take the Manassas Gap Railroad to Manassas Junction. The artillery and cavalry would march overland.[7]

On the morning of the nineteenth, Johnston and his troops started to load onto the trains at Piedmont for the 35-mile ride to Manassas. Moving the army was slow work, for Johnston had only one locomotive at his disposal and extreme care had to be taken to ensure it remained in working order. Jackson's brigade loaded first that morning, crowding into and onto the handful of available cars. Then came the slow, hours-long ride to Manassas Junction. That tedious trip also proved excruciating for those of Johnston's men left behind. They idled nervously near Piedmont Station awaiting the train's return, fearful that they might miss the battle entirely.

General Jackson and his brigade arrived at Manassas Junction late in the afternoon of July 19. Jackson bounded off the train and rode directly to Beauregard's headquarters at the McLean house. There he found Beauregard huddled with his brigade commanders. At the moment Jackson arrived, Beauregard was explaining his plans for the morrow—Johnston would march overland and fall on McDowell's right flank. Jackson's surprise appearance disrupted Beauregard's meeting. Surely the rest of Johnston's command would be marching overland, Beauregard insisted. No, Jackson said, Johnston would bring his entire army by rail.

Jackson's disclosure, if true, would dash Beauregard's plans, for those depended on Johnston marching, not riding, to the field. The Creole quizzed Jackson further and concluded that Jackson simply must be mistaken (he knew little of this taciturn man from the Shenandoah Valley and could hardly adjudge his reliability). Beauregard remained satisfied that Johnston would do as he had requested. To the assembled subordinates, he outlined the rest of his plan.

By Beauregard's calculations, Johnston would arrive on McDowell's right the next morning. McDowell, certainly, would be so impressed by Johnston's attack that he "would not know what to think of it." Beauregard reckoned that McDowell would reflexively wheel his army to face Johnston squarely. At that, Beauregard's brigades would sweep forward across Bull Run and assail the hapless Federal general's left and rear. The outcome, Jubal Early recorded Beauregard as saying, could not be doubted. It would be "a complete rout, a perfect Waterloo."[8]

McDowell, meanwhile, worked to forge a Waterloo of his own, but as of dawn on July 19 his aspirations lay entirely in the hands of Chief Engineer Barnard, an accomplished professional, systematic and thorough (later he became chief engineer for all Union armies). In seeking a crossing of Bull Run above the Confederate left, he knew he had no room for error; should the Confederates learn of his search, any plan might be foiled. He started, then, by looking to his maps. Tracing Bull Run north from Mitchell's Ford, he spotted several fords (Island, Ball's, and Lewis), but the roads that led to each were little more than cart paths, inadequate to carry the better part of any army across the stream. Nor would they pass the Confederate left. North of Lewis Ford stood the Stone Bridge, which carried the macadamized Warrenton Turnpike across the run. Clearly this was the best crossing, but Barnard's information correctly indicated the Confederates defended the place with both infantry and artillery. Moreover, locals wrongly claimed the Confederates had placed explosives or mines on the structure, set for detonation should the Union try to cross.[9]

By all accounts, the Stone Bridge marked the left of Beauregard's defenses. Two miles north of the bridge, Barnard's maps showed a ford marked "Sudley." Barnard focused his attention here. Intelligence held that the ford was suitable for passage and defended by only one or two companies of infantry. Doubly reassuring was word that the stream above the ford might be passable by wheeled vehicles almost everywhere. And a mile below crossed another ford (known locally as Poplar or Red House Ford) that might be useful.

Having identified the fords, could Barnard find the roads that led to them? Unconfirmed reports indicated that beyond Cub Run a farm road branched off to the north, by which, as Barnard wrote, "opening gates and passing through private grounds we might reach the fords." But this would have to be verified. That morning, joined by the governor of Rhode Island, William Sprague, Barnard took a company of cavalry to find the route by which McDowell's army could outflank the Confederates.

Barnard and company rode from Centreville westward along the Warrenton Turnpike nearly two miles until they crossed Cub Run. Just west of the stream Barnard turned north, following the stream valley, until he reached a road that seemed to head off in the direction of the ford marked "Sudley Spring" on his maps. He followed its winding course in and out of woods and farmers' fields, but after going only a short distance he encountered Confederate cavalry. "As we were most anxious to avoid attracting the enemy's attention to our design," Barnard recalled, "we did not care to pursue the reconnaissance further."[10]

Barnard decided to send out parties at night to scout the roads anew, but this too failed. In the end, Barnard's efforts produced little more information than McDowell already possessed—a fact that clearly irked McDowell. The army commander suggested a reconnaissance in force to clear the way to the crossings, but his subordinates talked him out of that. Instead, McDowell contented himself with a negative conclusion: nothing in Barnard's reports indicated that the move envisioned by McDowell might be impractical. This apparently satisfied Irvin McDowell. At midday on Saturday, July 20, he decided to mount his offensive by way of Sudley Ford the next morning, though no one in the army could yet say how to get there. Such were the vagaries of war on the eve of its first battle.[11]

During the two days Barnard hunted for a crossing, the Federal camps in Centreville hummed with activity, excitement, and novel scenes. From Washington came senators, congressmen, and cabinet members, all loaded with delicacies and opinions. When not hovering around McDowell's headquarters, they swarmed through the camps, giving speeches and handing out cigars. Soldiers provided a few spectacles themselves. Maj. George Sykes's Regulars—the only infantry Regulars in the army—roared at seeing a volunteer trudging along with apparently all his worldly goods packed on his back. "As he passed by with pots, dippers, etc., rattling he turned a jolly red face toward the column and exclaimed, 'Lord Gee! but I wish't I was a mule!' The roars of laughter that followed seemed greatly to refresh and speed him on his way." Others marveled at the sight of the first Confederate prisoners. "They attracted a good deal of attention," recorded one soldier, "and we discussed among ourselves whether we should shoot or hang them."

The bursts of laughter and ever-present chords of brass bands contrasted mightily with the strained efforts of officers trying to extract discipline from their men. On the morning of the nineteenth, the Regular battalion, as well as several volunteer regiments, formed a square to witness the flogging of two deserters. Officers dragged the two unfortunates into the center of the square, where a raw-boned sergeant administered fifty lashes. Then each accused suffered a branding—a "D" burned into his flesh. "It was a sickening, disgusting sight," wrote a shocked volunteer, "the blood flowing from every blow of the whip."[12]

The desertion of two men, however, seemed trifling compared to the impending exodus—entirely legal—of two of McDowell's units: the 4th Pennsylvania Infantry and Varian's New York battery. Like several others, these two units had enlisted for ninety days shortly after Fort Sumter; now, on July 20, those enlistments expired. McDowell, mindful that he would need every available man and gun, appealed to the men's patriotism. He wrote to the Pennsylvanians, "the departure of the regiment at this time can only be considered an important loss to the army." But at least to the Pennsylvanians, the war had lost its luster, and a deal was a deal. They, along with the New York artillerymen, left for Alexandria on the very eve of battle. If McDowell did not move soon, more troops would follow.[13]

By midday, McDowell had settled on a plan for his offensive. While part of his army demonstrated in front of the lower crossings of Bull Run, McDowell would march nearly half his command to the crossing Barnard had earmarked at Sudley, beyond the Confederate left. From there, McDowell's leading brigades would sweep southward along the west bank of Bull Run, uncovering crossings at the Stone Bridge and other fords as they went. As additional troops crossed, the lead troops would bear right to make room. Some would be sent west along the Warrenton Turnpike to Gainesville to sever the Manassas Gap Railroad, the connective artery between Johnston and Beauregard.[14]

McDowell's earlier plans for the campaign—articulated in June and only discarded after the march had begun on July 17—had not called for him to sever the rail connection between Manassas Junction and the Shenandoah Valley himself. Instead, McDowell had envisioned turning the Confederate right flank (south of Manassas), leaving the job of detaining Johnston's Confederates in the Shenandoah Valley entirely to Gen. Robert Patterson. But on July 20, for the first time, McDowell added the task of severing the Manassas Gap Railroad to his own set of orders. He never explained why, but almost certainly the plan to destroy the railroad emerged from McDowell and his subordinates' growing belief that at least part of Johnston's army was already en route to Manassas. The effort to cut the railroad at Gainesville made perfect sense.[15]

No doubt, the prospect of Johnston's arrival rendered McDowell's job more complex. After the battle, McDowell wove an explanation for failure that laid blame on his counterpart in the Valley confronting Johnston's Confederates. Patterson, a bedraggled veteran of the War of 1812 and friend of Winfield Scott, had the job of, at the very least, holding Johnston and his 11,000 Confederates in the Valley and away from Manassas. So long as that was accomplished, McDowell would outnumber Beauregard about three to two. But Patterson proved unfit for the task. He magnified Johnston's strength fourfold and searched mightily for reasons not to advance against his foe. Indeed, on July 17 Patterson actually

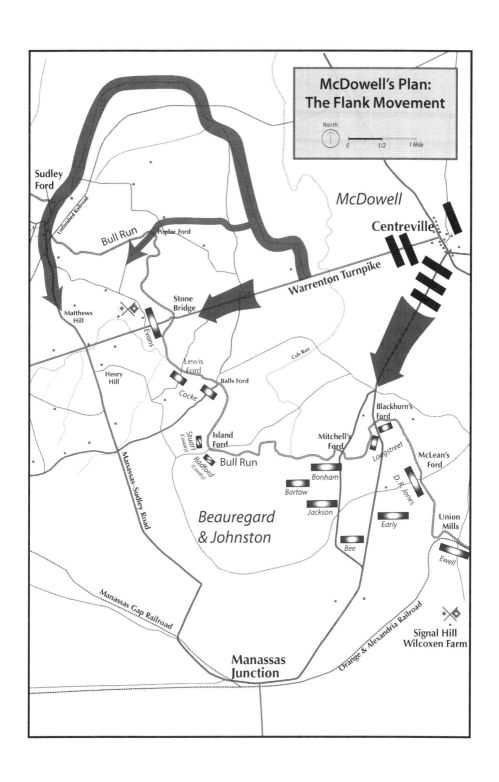

McDowell's Plan: The Flank Movement

North

0   1/2   1 Mile

Sudley Ford

Unfinished Railroad

Bull Run

Poplar Ford

McDowell

Centreville

Warrenton Turnpike

Stone Bridge

Matthews Hill

Evans

Lewis Ford

Cub Run

Henry Hill

Cocke

Balls Ford

Blackburn's Ford

Stuart (cavalry)

Island Ford

Mitchell's Ford

Longstreet

McLean's Ford

Radford (cavalry)

Bull Run

Bonham

D. R. Jones

Manassas–Sudley Road

Bartow

Jackson

Early

Union Mills

Beauregard & Johnston

Bee

Ewell

Manassas Gap Railroad

Orange & Alexandria Railroad

Signal Hill Wilcoxen Farm

Manassas Junction

retreated 7 miles farther from Johnston. At that, Johnston slipped away. Even then, as Johnston's men prepared to board the trains at Piedmont Station to assist Beauregard, Patterson wrote to General Scott, "The enemy has stolen no march on me. I have kept him actively employed, and by threats and reconnaissances in force caused him to be reinforced. I have accomplished more in this respect than the General-in-Chief asked or could well be expected." On July 22, one day after Johnston's troops played a major role in defeating Irvin McDowell, Robert Patterson was relieved of command and retired from service.[16]

Patterson's poor performance made him an easy scapegoat for the Union failures that followed, and after the battle McDowell seized the chance to shift blame. In explaining the defeat at Bull Run to Congress later that year, McDowell and others pointed to Patterson as the architect of failure. Much of the fighting done on July 21 was by regiments in Johnston's command. If only Patterson had done his part and detained them in the Valley, McDowell and his subalterns claimed, the battle along Bull Run might have been won by the Union. That may have been true, but the accusation also carried the implication that McDowell could not have succeeded unless Patterson detained Johnston in the Valley. That simply was not so. Since the first articulation of his plan for the campaign (in June), McDowell had anticipated that his army would likely confront a number of Confederates that equaled the size of his own army. Nothing that had happened since the Union army arrived on the east bank of Bull Run contradicted that belief. Starting on July 19, Union officers reported the sound of trains arriving at Manassas Junction. Many in the army suspected those trains carried Johnston's men (some did, but others came direct from Richmond with additional troops reporting directly to Beauregard). When McDowell reported to Washington on July 20, he noted rumors that "Johnston had already joined Beauregard." Later, McDowell testified that he based his plans "not so much on what [the Confederates] had here, but what they would bring here." That evening, when Daniel Tyler queried McDowell, "What force have we to fight tomorrow?" McDowell replied, "You know, general, as well as I do." Tyler agreed; they'd been hearing the trains come in. "General, we have got the whole of Joe Johnston's army in our front." In fact, not all of Johnston's men would get to Manassas in time (and McDowell surely *hoped* none of them would), but the first hour of battle on July 21 proved that enough had come to matter.[17]

There can be little doubt that had Patterson managed to detain Johnston in the Shenandoah Valley, McDowell's chances of victory along Bull Run would have increased. But a stark fact remained: even with Johnston on the field with Beauregard's men, McDowell had the resources and numbers at hand to defeat the Confederates. The fight near Manassas Junction would be between armies almost equal in numbers (about 35,000 each). Patterson's failure in no way assured that McDowell's would follow.

McDowell's two-day delay at Centreville gave Johnston the time to move most of his troops to Manassas Junction, to Beauregard's army. After delivering Jackson's 2,500-man brigade on July 19, the lone locomotive chugged back to Piedmont, where Barnard Bee's and Francis Bartow's brigades piled on. Bartow and Bee arrived at Manassas on the twentieth. Late on the same day, the locomotive churned back to Piedmont Station yet again. By then, everyone expected the battle to commence on the morning of July 21, so as the men of Arnold Elzey's brigade climbed aboard the train in the predawn hours, they embarked on a race to the field. Whether they would arrive in time to fight depended quite simply on how long the battle lasted.

In addition to Johnston's army, other reinforcements sped to Beauregard's aid. From Fredericksburg marched Col. Theophilus Holmes and his brigade, which arrived July 20. And from Richmond came Col. Wade Hampton and his Legion of South Carolinians. Amid rumors that a "terrible battle" was then raging along Bull Run, the 600-man Hampton Legion did not even begin its journey until the evening of the nineteenth. The train chugged along at a slow pace—a few miles an hour—and often had to idle on sidings to allow other trains bearing wounded from the Blackburn's Ford fight to pass. Almost twenty-four hours later, the train reached the Orange and Alexandria at Gordonsville, turned northward, and six hours later steamed into Manassas Junction. Tired, but armed to the teeth with equipment their prominent colonel had supplied them, they discovered that, "thank God," they had not missed the battle. They stopped in their places and fell fast asleep.[18]

Joseph Johnston arrived at Manassas and Wilmer McLean's house at midday on July 20. As senior in rank, he assumed command of the fast-consolidating armies. He did not, however, usurp Beauregard, for Johnston realized that the Creole's familiarity with the ground and the enemy's options would serve him well. Johnston's arrival, of course, fulfilled Jackson's prediction and wrecked Beauregard's fading hope for a combination of the two armies on the battlefield under fire. After discussing matters with his new chief, Beauregard fell back once again to the plan he had developed July 8, to attack the Federals at Centreville and try to cut off their retreat toward Washington. That evening he presented his plan to Johnston for approval.

Johnston fully expected that Patterson would shadow his movement out of the Valley and probably join McDowell on July 22, so, as he saw it, the need for immediate offensive action was acute. Johnston readily assented to Beauregard's plan (that it depended to an extent on the arrival of troops still at Piedmont Station was only a minor concern to the commander). Then, inasmuch as he had been without rest since July 17, Johnston "begged" Beauregard to attend to preparing the written orders for his signature while he retired to a nearby grove for some sleep.[19]

Before Beauregard could get the orders on paper, however, he received information that led him to change his plan substantially. First, he learned that as many as 5,000 of Johnston's troops (E. Kirby Smith's brigade, Arnold Elzey's brigade, plus regiments of various commands) would not arrive at Manassas in time to carry out their assigned roles. Secondly, and more importantly, the Creole learned "from reliable sources" considerably more about McDowell's strength and intentions.

According to Beauregard's informants, McDowell had 55,000 men at hand (he actually had 35,000), largely concentrated along the Warrenton Turnpike between Centreville and the Stone Bridge. Given that McDowell had already (as Beauregard saw it) suffered "signal discomfiture" against the Confederate center at Blackburn's, the Confederate general correctly surmised that McDowell would attack the Confederate left, perhaps as early as the morrow. This presented a real challenge to Beauregard, for the Confederate left was, as Beauregard admitted, "weakly guarded." Only Nathan "Shanks" Evans's 1,100-man brigade and two artillery pieces defended the Stone Bridge. His nearest support was a half mile away at Lewis Ford, where Philip St. George Cocke's brigade of Virginians milled behind low earthworks.

Given such circumstances, the instinct of most men would have been to brace for the attack by strengthening the threatened area. Beauregard did not consider so mundane a response. He decided instead to relieve his left by attacking the Federals at Centreville with his right. The grandiose plan required some matching language as accompaniment: "By such a movement I confidently expected to achieve a complete victory for my country by 12 [noon]," he exclaimed.[20]

The order Beauregard delivered to Johnston at 4 A.M. on July 21 outlined his new plan. Upon Beauregard's signal, the entire right of the line would cross Bull Run. Ewell would cross at Union Mills Ford, move to the Union Mills–Centreville Road, and from there be ready to join the attack on Centreville or move along the railroad eastward toward Sangster's and Fairfax Stations to separate the Federals from the railroad. D. R. Jones at McLean's Ford would do likewise, as would Longstreet, supported by Jackson, at Blackburn's.

In Beauregard's plan, Bonham's and Francis Bartow's brigades would spearhead the advance toward Centreville. These two units, joined by Cocke's brigade on the left, would cross Bull Run at Mitchell's Ford and assail Centreville directly. Barnard Bee's brigade (much to Bee's chagrin) would act as the army's mobile reserve. To each of the foremost brigades Beauregard assigned two or three companies of cavalry and two batteries of artillery.[21]

Johnston again agreed to Beauregard's design, with some modification, insisting Beauregard pay more heed to his left and the possibility of a Federal attack in that area. Johnston argued that Bee and Jackson should be detached from the attack and sent to the left to support Evans and Cocke. Beauregard assented, and indeed he did Johnston one better by ordering Hampton's fresh-off-the-train Legion to the left, too. Beauregard issued the needed orders. All was ready. Daylight would bring action and, every Confederate was certain, victory.[22]

The Federals mirrored the Confederates' confidence in victory. That night, about 8 P.M., McDowell called his division and brigade commanders together, spread a map on his tent's dirt floor, and explained their assignments in the next day's climactic movements.[23] Like Beauregard, McDowell planned to move against his opponent's left on July 21; he would do so through a coordinated, three-pronged operation. McDowell intended the two southernmost prongs to merely occupy the Confederates' attention. Israel Richardson's brigade, supported by one of Dixon Miles's brigades, would repeat its appearance of the eighteenth in front of Mitchell's and Blackburn's Fords. This time, rather than rushing headlong at the Confederates as he had done that day, Fighting Dick would demonstrate in front of them with just enough energy to feign attack. Meanwhile, the rest of Tyler's division would advance along the Warrenton Turnpike to the Stone Bridge, where it would open the battle at daylight. But McDowell harbored no illusions that Tyler could force a crossing at the bridge—he believed it to be mined and heavily defended. McDowell hoped a simple demonstration by the three brigades at the Stone Bridge would suffice to occupy the Confederates' attention while the main Union column followed Barnard's uncertain route to the ford above.

At 13,000 strong with five batteries, the flanking column represented McDowell's major effort. It would be led by Col. David Hunter's division of two brigades, followed by Heintzelman's division. Hunter would follow Tyler and then turn northward along Barnard's looping route to Sudley Ford over Bull Run. There he would turn southward along the Manassas–Sudley Road, cross Catharpin Run at Sudley Springs Ford, and head for the Confederate rear.

As Hunter crossed at Sudley and moved down the west bank of the stream, Heintzelman was to break off from the column about mid-march and head for Poplar Ford, midway between Sudley and the Stone Bridge. Hunter's sweep down the west bank of Bull Run would presumably force the Confederates away from the stream and out into the open. When Hunter uncovered Poplar Ford, Heintzelman would cross and form on Hunter's left. Together, the two divisions would press forward to the Warrenton Turnpike, forcing the Confederates to abandon the Stone Bridge and allowing Tyler to cross and join the movement. In addition, a party would be dispatched westward to Gainesville to destroy the Manassas Gap Railroad. That done, McDowell reasoned, Beauregard would be both outflanked and cut off from those men of Johnston's command still in the Shenandoah Valley. Significantly, McDowell's plan did not use the words "attack" or "assault" (in this it differed dramatically from Beauregard's mirror-image plan), though he clearly realized the possibility of combat. Instead, McDowell's movement constituted a bold-but-uncertain challenge to a foe whose response he could not, at this stage of the war, predict. Would the Confederates collapse and yield the cause at the mere appearance of the Union army? Or would his old West Point cadet-mate Beauregard come out and attack McDowell? McDowell's plan allowed for both outcomes, and clearly he thought either would bring the success the nation so desperately sought.

To his credit, McDowell had few illusions about his plan. It was risky and complex to be sure, and depended on the timely flow of Tyler's division and the flanking column. (Tyler was to march at 2:30 A.M., and the flanking column was to cross at Sudley by 7 A.M.) Few in the army expected the Confederates to turn tail and run without a fight, and while McDowell hoped for the former, he prepared for the latter. "The troops," McDowell warned his commanders, "must be held in order of battle, as they may be attacked at any moment." Like his soldiers, McDowell saw the coming day in historic terms: "These movements may lead to the gravest results," he warned. "There must be no failure."[24]

Shortly after 8:30 on the evening of July 20, the army's division and brigade commanders left headquarters to prepare for what would surely be an historic day. If the meeting had buoyed their spirits, the same could not be said for their commander. That evening, Congressman Elihu Washburne—riding with the army since July 17—found his way to McDowell's headquarters at Centreville, where he had "quite a conversation with" the general. Two days later he described the meeting to his wife: "I never had much an opinion of him as a general, and I left his tent with a feeling of great sadness and a sort of prescience of coming disaster." McDowell, Washburne recorded, "seemed discouraged and in low spirits, and appeared very doubtful of the result of the approaching conflict. That was a bad symptom." McDowell might have been the only discouraged soul on either side of Bull Run that night.[25]

For a half century, men of all stripes had dreaded the coming of civil war. Now, on the eve of that war's first major battle, they heralded its arrival. In Washington, livery stables emptied as politicians and everyday civilians hurried to the front to watch the battle. One civilian already with the army that night was John Taylor, an aspiring politician from New Jersey, who had come out from Washington early to witness history. The future state senator watched the Union army assemble that night at about 2 A.M. It was, he wrote, "one of the most inspiring and impressive sights of my life time." From the fields on either side of Braddock Road and the Warrenton Turnpike, hundreds of soldiers tumbled from their camps and into column. Writing of the scene thirty-two years later, Taylor wistfully remembered that the cadence of the troops seemed to be measured "by the unison of those hearts beating stoutly for their country's salvation."[26]

One of those soldiers wrote with appropriate sense of drama, "We are all well and feeling first rate, longing for the drum to sound that bids us on to victory or death. We shall take Manassas or die before tomorrow night. . . . I never felt better in my life. I fear death as much as I fear the sting of a bee."[27]

In the moonlit camps and in nearby farmhouses, few could sleep. Instead, men quietly moved among the thousands of campfires, writing letters or gathering in little groups to whisper of tomorrow's events.[28] Hamilton Branch of the 8th Georgia, which camped that night without tents behind Mitchell's Ford, concluded a letter to his mother with the sad admonition, "Give my love to everybody, tell them that [if] I never see them again to try and forgive me if I have ever done them any harm." Col. Francis Bartow stopped at the camp of the 8th Georgia to offer his men a few words of encouragement, telling them he had secured for the regiment the honor of opening the battle. He felt certain the regiment would do its state proud. With that honor, though, came risk. "Remember boys, battle and fighting mean death, and probably before sunrise some of us will be dead." One of the young soldiers listening to Bartow remembered, "As I lay on my blanket, when all was hushed and still, and looked up at the starry vault, and thought of the morrow and the last words of Bartow, I confess I was a bit homesick."[29]

Local civilians felt the moment, too. Some had already fled the approach of the Union army. At Robert Carter Weir's home near Sudley Ford, more than twenty refugees huddled that night without any idea the Union army would be among them in the morning. Nannie Leachman, who lived near Groveton, remembered her mother led two calves into a swamp to keep them away from the Yankees (after the battle, she named them "Jackson" and "Early"). The pastor of Sudley Church, Alexander Compton, lay ill in bed that night, coughing up blood. His wife hovered over him and worried too about their son serving in the 8th Virginia Infantry, bivouacked just 3 miles away near Lewis Ford. Indeed, families throughout the neighborhood went to sleep that Saturday night acutely aware of the danger looming for their loved ones the next day. One of the neighborhood soldiers, John Thornberry, left his wife, Martha, and children behind in a simple house only 100 yards from both Bull Run and Sudley Church. That evening, his brother-in-law, James Wilkins, checked on the family and suggested that Martha evacuate to safer quarters at his house, about a mile away. Martha agreed: "If you think so, I will get the children's clothes ready for Sunday school and I will go."

Wilkins responded, "They will not need any clothes for Sunday School for there will be no Sunday School tomorrow."[30]

Chapter Four

"YOU ARE TURNED"

The last night of bloodless war ended with the bustle of Union troops preparing to march. In Tyler's camps between Centreville and Cub Run, preparations went smoothly, and at 2:30 A.M., as scheduled, Schenck's and Sherman's brigades fell into column on the Warrenton Turnpike and started their march westward, toward the Stone Bridge. (Erasmus Keyes's brigade, camped near Centreville, started earlier but was delayed and did not catch up with the rest of the division until midmorning.) Much depended on an expeditious march by Tyler, because for the flanking column to reach its turnoff west of Cub Run, it too had to use the Warrenton Turnpike. By allowing Tyler's diversionary force (barely three miles from the Stone Bridge) to take the road first, McDowell ran the risk that the main attacking column, which must cover 10 miles to reach its destination, would not reach Sudley by its assigned time of 7 A.M.

From the start, Tyler's march crawled along at a maddening pace. While the Warrenton Turnpike itself was macadamized and uncommonly wide,[1] the weathered suspension bridge over Cub Run proved to be a considerable bottleneck. Narrower than the road itself, the bridge creaked and groaned under the weight of the wagons and thirty pieces of artillery, including Lt. Peter Hains's 3-ton, 30-pounder Parrott rifle. McDowell ordered some impromptu structural work on the span to ensure its survival (work that might have been done in the prior two days of inactivity). Probably ninety minutes passed as Sherman and Schenck filed across, but even after, the pace of Tyler's march improved but slightly. "The country between Cub Run and Bull Run was supposed to be occupied by the enemy," Tyler later explained. He asserted it was imperative for his division, "being without cavalry, and with no knowledge of the country, to move slowly." That it did. General Schenck, an Ohioan commanding Tyler's leading brigade,

41

carefully threw out 500 skirmishers and inched along at a pace that covered barely a mile and a half in three hours.[2]

Meanwhile Hunter's and Heintzelman's divisions—the flanking column—stacked up in the road, waiting for Tyler to cross Cub Run and clear the road north leading toward Sudley. By the first hint of daylight, Heintzelman's division, which had camped along the Braddock Road southeast of Centreville, should have been well on its way to Sudley Ford but had not even cleared Centreville. Still, this stop-and-go marching in pitch darkness did little to diminish the enthusiasm of these buoyant volunteers.

At 5:30 A.M., the rear of Tyler's column finally cleared the Cub Run Bridge, and Hunter's and Heintzelman's divisions began their march in earnest. On the steep slope leading to Cub Run, batterymen had to chain the wheels on their limbers and caissons, lest the vehicles overrun the horses leading them. At the bridge itself, the cannons and wagons progressed slowly, each waiting until the one in front had completely cleared the rickety bridge. After crossing Cub Run, Hunter's column moved along the turnpike for several hundred yards until it reached the house of Mrs. Spindle. There, Hunter turned to the right onto the country road Major Barnard had discovered. That road, Hunter found, was but a cart path, and its narrow, winding course rendered Ambrose Burnside's pace-setting march, in Andrew Porter's words, "slow and intermittent." Twenty-five axe men of the 2nd New Hampshire led the march, clearing obstructions, hacking at brush, and chopping at stumps.[3]

Behind the pioneers marched the 2nd Rhode Island, followed in order by Capt. William Reynolds's Rhode Island battery, the 1st Rhode Island, the 2nd New Hampshire, and the 71st New York National Guard, which tugged along two naval boat howitzers by hand. Riding with Colonel Burnside at the head of the column, determined to have a hand in the moment, was the Honorable William Sprague, governor of Rhode Island. Sprague was rich, cultured, eligible (he would later marry Washington's foremost belle, Kate Chase, daughter of the Treasury secretary), and ambitious. The governor took seriously his titular post as commander of the Rhode Island State Militia and had dressed that day in the uniform of the 1st Rhode Island.[4]

Behind Burnside marched Col. Andrew Porter's brigade, which included the army's lone battalion of Regulars, the fancily bedizened 14th Brooklyn, and Charles Griffin's Battery D, 5th U.S. Artillery, the oldest continuously serving battery in U.S. service. Following Porter marched Heintzelman's division of ten regiments and two batteries. All told, the flanking column comprised nearly 13,000 men and 20 cannon—one of the largest attack forces the nation had ever seen.

While the column began its fitful march north, the rest of the army prepared to demonstrate along the crossings of Bull Run. For his part, Tyler managed to arrive in front of the Stone Bridge only an hour late. Unlike his performance at

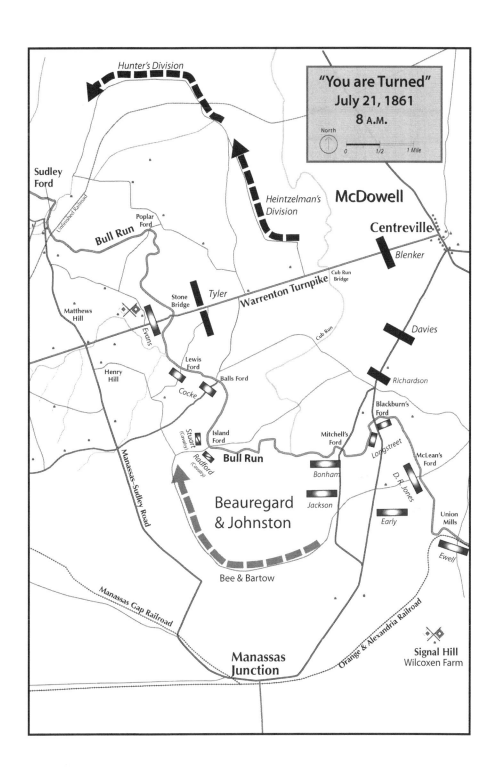

Hunter's Division

"You are Turned"
July 21, 1861
8 A.M.

North

0   1/2   1 Mile

Sudley
Ford

Unfinished Railroad

Heintzelman's
Division

McDowell

Poplar
Ford

Bull Run

Centreville

Blenker

Cub Run
Bridge

Matthews
Hill

Evans

Stone
Bridge

Tyler

Warrenton Turnpike

Cub Run

Davies

Henry
Hill

Lewis
Ford

Balls Ford

Richardson

Cocke

Blackburn's
Ford

Stuart
(Cavalry)

Island
Ford

Mitchell's
Ford

Longstreet

McLean's
Ford

Radford
(Cavalry)

Bull Run

Bonham

D. R. Jones

**Beauregard
& Johnston**

Jackson

Early

Union
Mills

Manassas-Sudley Road

Bee & Bartow

Ewell

Manassas Gap Railroad

**Manassas
Junction**

Orange & Alexandria Railroad

Signal Hill
Wilcoxen Farm

Blackburn's Ford two days before, this time Tyler paid considerable attention to positioning his troops before he opened fire.

As the column reached the ridge overlooking the Bull Run bottomland, about 1,000 yards from the Stone Bridge, Schenck deployed his three Ohio regiments in the fields south of the turnpike, encountering no Confederate resistance. Sherman's troops deployed too, filing into line along a wood line atop the ridge. From there Sherman could see little, so he decided to ride forth and examine the supposed Confederate position. What he saw on the other side was hardly intimidating. Only a handful of men stirred on the far bank, and he saw "plenty of trees cut down, some bush huts, such as soldiers use on picket guard, but none of the evidences of strong fortifications we had been led to believe" were present.[5]

Sherman saw only what his opponent, Nathan "Shanks" Evans, let him see. Evans had learned of Tyler's advance early when at 3 A.M. pickets of the 4th South Carolina reported muffled commands in the distant woods. At 4 A.M., some of Evans's pickets fired about a dozen shots at Tyler's vanguard. At that, Evans roused his command and ordered them into line. The 4th South Carolina, commanded by Col. J. B. E. Sloan, deployed behind the eastern edge of Van Pelt Hill, just left of the turnpike. Maj. Rob Wheat's "Tigers" from Louisiana—hard men inclined to brawn and brawl—fell in on Sloan's left, largely screened by woods. Evans's only artillery, two Virginia cannon commanded by Capt. George S. Davidson, unlimbered under cover on a hill just south of the turnpike, 600 yards from the bridge. All too aware of the inadequacy of his small command to defend against a crossing at the bridge, the normally pugnacious Evans decided to keep his regiments—and hence his weakness—under wraps. Meanwhile, he sent word to Beauregard of the growing Federal menace.[6]

The apparent paucity of the Confederate defenses at the Stone Bridge mattered little to Tyler at the moment, for he had come there only to threaten, not to do battle. That he could do as well (and more safely) with artillery as with infantry. So as Schenck's and Sherman's brigades took position astride the turnpike, Tyler rolled out his artillery. Most conspicuous among that artillery was Hains's 30-pounder Parrott. It had required a herculean effort just to get the gun to the battlefield (uphill had been backbreaking effort, while downhill was a high-speed adventure), but the immense effort placed the men assigned to this gun—a coveted assignment—on the cusp of history. The Confederates would surely cower at the behemoth's first roar. Appropriately then, Tyler chose Hains to open the battle. Hains would later call this task a "sacred duty."[7]

At about 6 A.M., Hains manhandled his beloved gun—called the "Baby Waker" by some Wisconsin troops—into place on the Warrenton Turnpike several hundred yards from the Stone Bridge. He ordered it to be loaded with a percussion shell that would explode upon impact. Lacking any discernible military targets across the stream, Hains trained the gun on Abraham Van Pelt's large white house, a mile away on top of the ridge behind the bridge. Hains surmised it "was some general's headquarters. . . . It was sufficient that it stood out large and white, a target for my gun which I could hardly miss." Hains sighted the piece carefully, then announced all was ready. "The men grinned their delight," he remembered. The lieutenant stepped back from the cannon, probably paused for some dramatic effect, and then yelled "Fire!" "The reverberation was tremendous," remembered a nearby reporter, "shaking through the hills like the volley of a dozen plebeian cannon."[8]

The historic First Shot whistled over the Confederates' heads and, according to Hains, crashed into poor Mr. Van Pelt's house. Hains followed that shot with two others, one of which collapsed the tent of Beauregard's chief signalman, Capt. Porter Alexander (he had been ordered to Wilcoxen's Hill only a few minutes before and hence was not present). Though Evans's men noted these historic shots, to the Federals' disappointment they did not cower or run. Nor did they respond. Tyler's opponent, Colonel Evans, determined to give him as few targets as possible. His ceremonial role fulfilled without real effect, Hains limbered his gun and lugged it into the nearby fields, where he joined the four guns of J. Howard Carlisle's battery. Carlisle joined in the barrage, but still the Federal artillery could not provoke any response from Evans.

For Tyler, the Confederate quiet was but a repeat of Longstreet's initial response at Blackburn's Ford. Once again, the silence compelled Tyler to do more. He ordered Colonel Schenck to push his three regiments south of the road toward the bridge, hoping for a reaction from the Confederates. Schenck's lines of battle moved slowly, taking advantage of each roll of the ground and every fence line. Soon, however, Schenck's regiments came within sight of Bull Run. His Ohio infantrymen fired the first scattering shots of the battle.[9]

Evans had no choice except to meet Tyler's challenge, but he did so in kind, with just a portion of his troops. He detailed four companies of the 4th South Carolina and one company of Wheat's Battalion as skirmishers. Two companies of the South Carolinians, including the "Calhoun Mountaineers," deployed on either side of the bridge, while Wheat's lone company scrambled into position farther upstream. Evans held the two remaining companies of the 4th in reserve at the base of Van Pelt Hill, about 200 yards from the stream.[10]

Schenck's skirmishers closed to within about 100 yards of Evans's men. South of the bridge, Pvt. B. B. Breazeale spotted two of the Federals coming unwarily toward them. Breazeale and one of his buddies ran to the fence along the stream, laid their guns on the top rail, and fired. As Breazeale jumped up on the fence to see the fate of the two Federals, a bullet zipped by his ear. "This was the first intimation I had that a Yankee would shoot if he had a chance," Breazeale admitted, "and I lost no time in getting down from the fence and getting under cover."[11]

For the next two hours, Schenck's and Evans's men skirmished, and a scattering rattle of musketry, punctuated occasionally by the boom of Federal artillery, echoed across the Bull Run valley. After the first few minutes of excitement—once it became obvious the Confederates at the Stone Bridge had no intention of responding with any vigor—Tyler's men settled in to do what soldiers do most: pass the time. More than a few climbed trees for a better view. Some slept. In the 79th New York, a few confronted the gloomy prospect of battle by writing their wills. A Nova Scotian serving with the 79th bequeathed his boots and hats to one friend, but to another less favored, "I left all my bad debts."[12]

Booming guns from elsewhere along the line soon joined the rising chorus. At Blackburn's and Mitchell's Fords, another of Tyler's brigades, Israel Richardson's, moved into place. (On this day Richardson was attached to and supported by Col. Dixon Miles's division.) Like Tyler, Richardson had learned something from his battle at Blackburn's on July 18 and this time also deployed his command more carefully. He placed six guns under the command of Maj. Henry J. Hunt, supported by the 1st Massachusetts and 3rd Michigan, astride the roads leading to the fords, covered his flanks with skirmishers, and kept two full regiments in reserve. Soon, Richardson heard the distant rumble of Hains's 30-pounder Parrott at the Stone Bridge. This was his signal. Hunt's guns opened fire, followed quickly by Richardson's skirmishers. The Confederates along Beauregard and Johnston's 8-mile-long line could not doubt that the day would bring decisive action. But where? Neither Longstreet at Blackburn's nor Bonham at Mitchell's responded to the Federal provocation with any vigor.[13]

At least for the moment, the noisy Federal demonstrations against his left at the Stone Bridge did nothing to dissuade Beauregard from his intention to take the offensive. Indeed, as Beauregard saw it, McDowell's actions that morning dovetailed nicely with Confederate hopes for the day. "The most effective method of relieving that flank was by a rapid attack with my right wing and center on the enemy's flank and rear near Centreville," the Creole later wrote.[14]

Beauregard's superior, Joseph E. Johnston, bore caution as easily as a horse does hair, and he evinced more anxiety about McDowell's activities than did Beauregard. Johnston would not yet squelch Beauregard's plan for an attack, but he did insist additional troops be sent to support Evans near the Stone Bridge. At about 7 A.M., he ordered Beauregard to get Bee's, Bartow's, and Jackson's brigades and the Hampton Legion (newly arrived from Richmond) moving toward the left. Bee and Bartow (with Bee in overall command) would support Evans at the Stone Bridge; Hampton would follow Bee; Jackson would move leftward so he could support either Cocke at Lewis and Balls Fords or Bonham at Mitchell's Ford. Four guns of John Imboden's Staunton Artillery accompanied Bee; five guns of the Washington Artillery moved with Jackson.[15]

Bee chafed at his orders to move to the left. Like Beauregard, he believed the battle would be fought and won by a Confederate assault from the lower crossings of Bull Run. Bee had rushed his command from the Shenandoah Valley to be part of such a victory, but now his orders cast him and his command in the role of a mere safeguard on what Bee believed would be the fringe of the battle-field. When Imboden protested that his men had had nothing to eat for twenty-four hours, a disgusted Bee snapped, "You will have plenty of time to cook and eat, to the music of a battle in which we shall probably take little or no part."[16]

With Bee and Jackson en route to bolster the left of his line, Beauregard once again turned his attention to the offense. Despite McDowell's rumblings at the Stone Bridge and at Mitchell's and Blackburn's, the orders authorized by John-ston at 4:30 A.M. still remained in effect. Bonham would spearhead the attack against Centreville. Longstreet, Jones, and Ewell would join the attack on the right, pivoting to their left to sweep northward. Probably about 7 A.M., with Johnston's assent and with great expectations, Beauregard dispatched orders for the attack to begin. That done, he and Johnston vacated the headquarters at McLean's house and rode to a more central position on a hill behind Mitchell's Ford to wait for Confederate victory.[17]

The wait seemed interminable, for the orders Beauregard issued that morning were both unclear and, in one most important instance, undelivered. Beauregard left the attack to his brigade commanders, failing to provide them with either a signal or a time to begin a concerted move; he merely advised his commanders to "establish close communication with each other before making the attack." Apparently Ewell, on the extreme right, was to open the attack, but he never received such an order.

Of course, the rest of the attacking force had no knowledge of that. Shortly after 7 A.M., Longstreet received his orders and dutifully marched his brigade across Blackburn's Ford to confront Richardson's Federals. Surrounded by the bloated Union dead from the fight of the eighteenth, he formed his command in a dense mass: two regiments in front supported by two in rear. Richardson's artillery raked Longstreet's men, but they withstood it quietly, preparing to charge the guns and silence them (a task one of Longstreet's green soldiers "regarded with a feeling of horror"). They waited only for the attack to open far-ther to the right.[18]

At McLean's Ford, D. R. Jones did likewise. Shortly after 7 A.M., he hustled his brigade across the stream. But what Beauregard intended for him to do once he got across could hardly have been clear to him. The order Jones received from Beauregard was a model of bad grammar. Strictly construed, it called for Jones to attack Ewell, not the enemy. Jones overlooked his commander's literary short-comings and moved to the Union Mills–Centreville Road. From there, theoreti-cally, Jones could either move directly on Centreville, veer to the left against Richardson in front of Blackburn's, or steer to the right toward Sangster's Station and the Union rear.[19]

Beauregard's plan, however, depended most on Richard Ewell, whose move-ment would prompt Jones to join the attack. But at 8 A.M. Ewell's brigade still waited for orders, his command still stationary at Union Mills. What happened to the courier assigned to carry the orders from Beauregard to Ewell is not known. Beauregard later admitted, "Our guides and couriers were the worst set I ever employed." Whatever the cause, the result was clear: the miscarriage of Ewell's orders wrecked Beauregard's plan, left two brigades sitting idly under fire east of Bull Run, and put the initiative squarely in Irvin McDowell's hands.[20]

Beauregard could not know that the immense reality of the moment had given Irvin McDowell pause. The Union general felt unwell, bothered apparently by an upset stomach. The anxiety he had expressed the night before to Congressman Washburne had only been intensified by the specter of an attack by Beauregard against his relatively weak left flank. McDowell's suspicions heightened when Tyler opened at the Stone Bridge and drew no response. McDowell explained, "We expected the Stone Bridge to be a strong point, with batteries in position, regular works, etc." He surmised, correctly, that the Confederate silence at the bridge indicated their primary strength lay elsewhere. Doubts about whether Hunter and Heintzelman would reach the upper crossing at all also seized him. His fear that Beauregard would assail his left inspired him to forego traveling with his own flanking column. Instead, McDowell hung back with O. O. Howard's brigade at a blacksmith shop on the Warrenton Turnpike, fearful he would have to conduct a defensive battle south of Centreville against Beauregard's flanking column.[21]

While McDowell betrayed concern about his plan, his flanking column still trudged toward the crossing of Bull Run at Sudley. The road Major Barnard had deemed sufficient two days before was in reality barely passable. The march amounted to four hours of starts and stops as the vanguard of pioneers cleared the way. Frustrating though it may have been for this column of tenderfoots, the frequent pauses did provide enough time for water, blackberry picking, and even short naps that offered welcome refreshment.[22]

By 6 A.M., when the guns opened opposite the Stone Bridge, the march of the flanking column was two hours behind schedule. The incompleteness of Barnard's reconnaissance on the nineteenth and twentieth now haunted the column. Barnard and McDowell had impressed a local man, Mathias Mitchell, to guide the column to Sudley Ford. As the column moved along, Mitchell insisted that the route envisioned by Barnard—an unobstructed course across open land—would expose the column to enemy batteries, and hence detection. The guide proffered an alternate route, longer but more secure. Hunter had no choice; his column took the longer route. A timetable two hours behind schedule now lagged even further behind.[23]

Mitchell had another surprise for Barnard. According to McDowell's plan, Heintzelman's division would break off from Hunter's column halfway to Sudley Ford and take another country road to Poplar Ford, about a mile above the Stone Bridge. Heintzelman would cross there after Hunter swept down the far bank. But Mitchell knew nothing of a supposed road to Poplar Ford, and

Heintzelman's staff officers could not locate one either. After what must have been considerable fretting, Heintzelman had no alternative but to continue following Hunter. That meant, quite simply, that rather than entering the fight concurrently with Hunter, Heintzelman would follow him into battle—still more hours behind schedule.[24]

Mindful of the delays, Hunter and Heintzelman hurried their divisions along. To Heintzelman's 11th New York went the order: "Forward double quick." The 11th had developed quite a reputation for pugnacity during its stay in Washington, but apparently paid less attention to drill. Normally, a member of the 11th explained, a regiment moving at the double quick was "a very pretty movement." Not so with these New York firemen. The maneuver, he wrote, was executed "in a manner not set down in our tactics. Anyone who has seen a closely contested race between two fire engine companies down Grand Street can form a pretty good idea of what double quick was with us." As the New Yorkers rushed along, they and other soldiers tossed blankets and other equipage to the side of the road to lighten their loads.[25]

As the head of Hunter's column neared Sudley Ford, the country path brought Burnside's brigade past a more densely populated area. Civilians occasionally appeared on the roadside or on porches to watch the Yankees pass. Absent guns, the civilians contented themselves with hateful glares and words. One woman later admitted she spent the day "holding up for our cause the best we could in our bearing toward the 'Yanks.'" More than a few Federals noted the bad attitudes. One remembered a "a very frowzy and dirty personage" who emerged from a rundown log hovel to assail the column with a verbal tirade. There were Confederates ahead, she taunted, enough to whip all the Yankees in the world, and her husband was among them. The soldiers scoffed at the old woman, but one later admitted (with perfect hindsight), "Despite her disreputable appearance, it must be conceded she had fine military judgment."[26]

As the sun rose and everyone's plans seemed to be going awry, control of events shifted from the army commanders to the army's subordinates—brigadier generals, colonels, and even captains. Primary among the Confederates who found themselves with unforeseen responsibility, at least on that bright morning, was Col. Nathan G. Evans. He was as crude and conceited a man as the Confederacy possessed. A South Carolinian and graduate of West Point (where his fellow cadets called him "Shanks" because of his extraordinarily skinny legs), he drank far too much; indeed, everywhere he went a Prussian orderly tailed him with a gallon jug of whiskey—his "barellita," Evans called it. But Evans was also brave, brash, and fiercely independent. That was good, because in his position defending the Stone Bridge he was alone, and events around him were building fast.[27]

At 8 A.M., the halfhearted skirmish and cannon fire at the Stone Bridge extended into its third hour. Since the beginning, Evans knew the enemy outnumbered him significantly, so he had steadfastly refused to open fire to better conceal his weakness. If the Yankees had been serious about crossing at the Stone Bridge, they likely would have increased the pressure. Instead, their fire continued only at its former rattling pace. Evans concluded that the Federals opposite the Stone Bridge had no intention of forcing a crossing. But that raised a critical question: If the main Federal attack would not be made here, then where?

One advantage Evans had over his fellow commanders on the Bull Run line was immediate access to the signal station on Mr. Van Pelt's farm. From here Evans could communicate quickly with the two other working stations at McLean's farm and Wilcoxen's Hill, near Union Mills, 8 miles away. Capt. E. Porter Alexander commanded these stations, and that morning, much to the signalman's disgust, Beauregard had ordered him to take to the station at Wilcoxen's Hill. Dutifully, Alexander assumed his post and began scanning the distant stations at McLean's and Van Pelt's.

A half hour after Alexander arrived at Wilcoxen's Hill, the station at Van Pelt's churned out a message. Alexander focused his glass to receive it. As he watched the distant signalman, Alexander spotted a brief flash of metallic glint in the lush green fields and pastures that served as a backdrop to the Van Pelt Hill station. "I recognized it at once as the reflection of the morning sun from a brass field piece," he later remembered. Ignoring the message being sent, Alexander changed his focus to the glinting metal beyond Van Pelt Hill. A closer look revealed not just a cannon, but also musket barrels and bayonets. Alexander had spotted the Union flanking column, heading toward the Bull Run crossings above Evans's left.

There could be no mistaking the import of this. Even before notifying Beauregard and Johnston, Alexander quickly sent a message to Evans: "Look out for your left, you are turned." Then he scribbled a note to Beauregard: "I see a body of troops crossing Bull Run about two miles above the Stone Bridge. The head of the column is in the woods on this side. The rear of the column is in the woods on the other side. About a half mile of its length is visible in the open ground in between. I can see both infantry and artillery."[28]

Evans had been diligent about watching the crossings on Bull Run above the Stone Bridge (as Barnard's frustration in reaching the crossings on the nineteenth and twentieth demonstrated), and that morning his pickets and scouts delivered important information again. At the same time he received Alexander's ominous message, Evans received the same warning from his outposts near Sudley. Identical intelligence from two sources at almost the same moment highlighted the danger Evans faced and emboldened him to act quickly. In this, he reaped the greatest benefits of having kept most of his command under cover that morning, invisible to the Yankees opposite the Stone Bridge. He left in place only the four companies of the 4th South Carolina the Yankees could see and made off with all of Major Wheat's Louisiana battalion and the remaining six companies of the 4th to confront the Union flanking column. (It would be hours before Tyler realized that 900 of the 1,100 Confederate troops defending the Stone Bridge had gone.) Evans's management of his troops and the Stone Bridge and his quick movement to confront McDowell's column was perhaps the boldest, most important decision made by a subordinate commander on the battlefield that day.

Evans sent word to Colonel Cocke (a half mile downstream at Lewis Ford) that he intended to weaken the defenses at the Stone Bridge. Then he led his 900 men leftward a quarter mile, along the road leading from Van Pelt's house to Pittsylvania, the now-rundown former estate of Landon Carter (and likely birthplace of elderly Mrs. Judith Carter Henry, whose farm sat atop Henry Hill). Wheat's battalion led the way, and upon nearing the house, the major deployed a company, the "Catahoula Guerrillas," as skirmishers into the yard. Following Wheat came Sloan's six companies and the two guns of George Davidson's Lynchburg Artillery that had been with them at the bridge. These deployed on Wheat's right.[29]

In taking position on the farm road near Pittsylvania, Evans presumed that after crossing at Sudley the Federals would hew close to the west bank of Bull Run as they moved south, heading directly toward the Confederate left at the Stone Bridge. Evans miscalculated. Rather than march along the west bank of Bull Run, the Union column had stayed along the road leading directly south from Sudley. By doing so, they threatened to outflank Evans's men near Pittsylvania and gain the Warrenton Turnpike, directly in Evans's rear. Evans quickly adjusted and rushed his command across fields to the farm of Edgar Matthews. Again Wheat's Louisianans moved first, taking position on the southern slope of what would ever after be known as Matthews Hill, not far from Matthews's small farmhouse. Sloan and his South Carolinians followed, taking position on Wheat's left rear, their flank resting on the road from Sudley to Manassas Junction. In front of the Louisianans, Wheat again threw out the Catahoula Guerrillas as skirmishers. Sloan also deployed a company into the thicket that separated the Carolinians from Wheat's men. Davidson's two guns unlimbered behind them all, just north of the turnpike, about a mile east of the Stone Bridge, covering from a distance the right of Evans's position.[30]

As Sloan's skirmishers moved into position, they saw figures in the open ground beyond. Inclined at this point to shoot at anything that moved, the South Carolinians opened fire—on the Louisianans. These Louisiana men came from rough neighborhoods in New Orleans and were "not afraid of God or man," wrote one of Evans's soldiers. They were disinclined to accept untoward treatment from anyone, be they South Carolinians or New Jerseyans, and when Sloan's men opened fire, the Louisianans simply turned and fired back at them. The Carolinians realized their mistake, and after some frantic yells back and forth, the firing between countrymen stopped. Evans completed his deployment on the slopes of Matthews Hill at about 9:30 A.M. His men now awaited the Union advance.[31]

The geometry of Evans's move made perfect sense—his small command stood boldly in front of the Union flanking column. But the geography of his new position remains a puzzle to this day. Matthews Hill was a high point on one of the many generally north–south ridges that roughened the area—the only significant geographic feature between Sudley and the Warrenton Turnpike and, it would seem, highly defensible. Evans, however, did not occupy the crest of the hill. Instead, he placed his command in a swale on the south slope, about 150 yards from the crest. Perhaps Evans calculated he could surprise the Federals as they crested the hill. Or perhaps he thought the lower ground offered some security for his small, untried command. In any event, this was no position of strength. Directly in front, the Federals would hold ground 30 feet higher than his own. Likewise, to Evans's left (west), the heights of John Dogan's farm dominated the Confederate line, wrapping around its left flank. Only hard fighting that begot time enough for reinforcements to arrive would allow Nathan Evans to hold this position.

While Evans did not occupy a position of particular defensive strength, he did possess one of some depth. Behind Sloan's and Wheat's regiments, Evans had the two guns of Davidson's Lynchburg Artillery. One of these, commanded by Lt. Clark Leftwich, moved to support the infantry directly from a position on Buck Hill, a lower elevation only 300 yards behind the infantry. The other, supervised by Captain Davidson, went into position farther to the right, just north of the Warrenton Turnpike.[32]

There was more. As Evans prepared to throw his meager command at the head of what one of his men called "Lincoln's horde of northern barbarians," the reinforcements Evans so desperately needed arrived on Henry Hill. Barnard Bee had grumbled at being ordered away from the Confederate center that morning, fearful he would miss the fight altogether. When Bee's column reached the Lewis house, Portici, behind Lewis Ford, battery commander John Imboden reported that he could see the Union flanking column from a nearby knoll. Bee immediately diverted his lead regiment, the 4th Alabama, to the left, toward Mrs. Henry's farm. Driven, as one man said, by a "chance to get a dab at the Yankees," Bee's men ran "through pine thickets and cedar hammocks, over ditches, gullies and briar patches, fences, swamps, hills and valleys," until they reached Henry Hill. As they broke through the wood line on the southwest edge of the hill, the broad vista of Henry Hill, Matthews Hill, and, to the right, Van Pelt Hill opened up. When Bee saw that, he exclaimed to Imboden, "Here is the battlefield, and we are in for it! Bring up your guns as quickly as possible, and I'll look round for a good position." Bee would not miss the battle after all.

Soon the first rattling musketry echoed from Matthews Hill. Bee led the 4th Alabama, 11th Mississippi, and 7th and 8th Georgia to the field and orchard around old Widow Henry's small house on the northern edge of Henry Hill, about 700 yards behind Evans's line. He ordered Imboden's four 6-pounder guns into position on the northern edge of the hill behind a convenient swell of ground, overlooking the valley of Young's Branch, the Warrenton Turnpike, and the Stone House. In the distance, Bee, Imboden, and their men could see Evans's 900 men in position on the southern slope of Matthews Hill. White smoke marked the battle's first serious volleys. Six Union cannon rolled into position less than a mile away, and soon their shells tore the ground around Imboden's guns and Bee's infantry near the Henry house. Imboden, overmatched but well protected by the swell of ground in front of his guns, responded by ricocheting solid shot and shell on the hard, smooth slopes beyond the Stone House, into Union lines. Imboden remembered, "The effect was very destructive to the enemy." Destruction indeed would be the theme for that Sunday morning.[33]

Chapter Five

MATTHEWS HILL

O n Sunday morning, July 21, 1861, about twenty women—many of them refugees—gathered on the porch of Robert Weir Carter's house north of Sudley Church, anxious for the day's events to unfold. They had not long to wait. Union skirmishers soon appeared in the fields to the east, near Sudley Ford on Bull Run, moving gracefully through freshly cut wheat. Mrs. J. K. McWhorter noted that as the Union soldiers passed each shock of wheat, one of them "ran a bayonet through it to be sure it did not contain a hiding rebel." These were the first Yankees any of these women had ever seen. The sight, McWhorter wrote, provoked "feelings that would be hard to describe." Following the skirmishers marched the head of the Union column, "a dark line of blue, with glittering bayonets" that "came slowly winding down in front of us." One of the thirsty Union soldiers broke from ranks to ask a woman on a porch for some water. "She gave me a gruff and insolent answer," the artilleryman remembered, "and I turned away with feelings not the kindliest imaginable." Another woman bid the Union soldiers onward with the hope that they all might be killed before nightfall.[1]

At 9:00 A.M., hours behind schedule, Hunter's division at the head of the Union flanking column reached Sudley Ford on Bull Run and then, a few yards beyond, Sudley Springs Ford on Catharpin Run. Racked by thirst, the men of his leading brigade, Burnside's, swarmed into the streams, churning them into an unpalatable murk. Those who could not—or would not—drink collapsed on the ground for some rest. In the distance, the boom of Tyler's guns sounded at the Stone Bridge. Mindful of the need for haste, Hunter's officers tried in vain to get the men back into ranks, but many minutes passed as the column refreshed itself under the warm morning sun.[2]

While the men lolled, officers of all stripes flocked to the high ground east of the ford to scan the scene in front of them—the ground that led to the Confederate rear. Colonel Porter's adjutant, William Averell, recalled, "A low cloud of dust in that direction attracted our attention, and, mounting a fence I could see with a glass a long, moving column of troops and discern their glistening bayonets and mounted officers. It was moving in a direction which would cross our line of march." Chagrined, Averell reported his observations to Colonel Hunter, then lunching with Burnside at the head of the column. Hunter ordered Averell and Capt. Amiel Whipple to reconnoiter. Averell and Whipple rode south on the Manassas–Sudley Road, and from some high ground east of the road they could distinctly see the approaching column and its flags. There could be no mistaking it: the Federal flank march had been found out. McDowell's hopes for surprise were lost.[3]

That revelation added still more urgency to Hunter's movement, for success depended on reaching the Warrenton Turnpike before the Confederates could "assemble a sufficient force to cope with us," as engineer Barnard put it. Hunter directly ordered an end to the midmorning halt. He told Burnside to throw out five companies of the 2nd Rhode Island as skirmishers and resume the advance. As the 2nd splashed across the stream, followed by the six-gun battery of Captain Reynolds, the rest of the brigade gradually reassembled into column and made ready for battle.[4]

After crossing Bull Run, the column turned sharply southward, crossed Catharpin Run at Sudley Springs Ford, and followed the road past Sudley Church, where there would be no Sunday services that day. After crossing the bed of an unfinished railroad, the column entered a shaded area. Woods crowded in on the left. On the right the ground was more open, but still the men could see little that suggested danger—certainly no Confederates.

Soon after Burnside started his march anew, General McDowell reached Sudley. He could see his plan had gone awry, at least insofar as time was concerned, and warned all within earshot that "the enemy is moving heavy columns from Manassas." Officers should have their men ready, "for we shall soon have to meet the enemy in large force," McDowell said. The morning's delays, and the attendant Confederate buildup in front of the flanking column, also meant that McDowell's plan to have Hunter's division uncover the crossings at Poplar Ford (which had not yet been found anyway) and the Stone Bridge would have to be scrapped. Instead, he would have to use force to reach the Warrenton Turnpike and clear the Stone Bridge. To Tyler went orders to force a passage, "to press the attack with all vigor." If Tyler could cross at the bridge, and if Hunter could overcome the promised resistance in his front, the day and the cause might still be salvaged.[5]

Colonel Hunter and Governor Sprague led Burnside's brigade as it pushed southward on the Manassas–Sudley Road (it's likely that no governor since has led his own constituents into battle). The five companies of the 2nd Rhode Island acting as skirmishers fanned out on either side of the road, feeling their way cautiously. A mile from Sudley, the woods on the left of the road ended, and the skirmishers emerged into the open. To their left front, about 300 yards from the road, stood the Matthews house, while to their right front, about a half mile away, the men could see the John Dogan house. In front of them, the ground rose gradually to the crest of Matthews Hill. There, huddled behind a flimsy rail fence, the skirmishers of Nathan Evans's brigade waited.

Evans's men fired the first volley. "The sensation caused by the first shower of bullets around one's head is very strange," observed one of the Rhode Islanders, who returned the fire, then instinctively fell on their backs to reload. Colonel Hunter ordered them to push forward and drive the Confederates back. As they rose, another Southern volley whizzed over their heads, but the Rhode Islanders rushed ahead and forced Evans's skirmishers away from the fence line. Indeed, Evans apparently had no intention of holding that line anyway and yielded easily.[6]

"They are driving in the pickets!" exclaimed an excited member of Reynolds's battery, and soon all of Burnside's column stirred. Burnside rode up to the five undeployed companies of the 2nd Rhode Island and yelled, "Forward!"

"Every man seemed to move at once," wrote an onlooker, "and all threw off their haversacks and blankets . . . and away they went on a quick run over the hill." As the regiment filed out of the woods into the open field to the left of the road, a ragged Confederate volley flew well overhead. "I remember that my first sensation was one of astonishment at the pecular [sic] whir of the bullets," wrote Elisha Rhodes of the 2nd, "and that the regiment immediately laid down without waiting for orders." The 2nd's commander, Col. John Slocum, ordered the men up again and yelled, "By the left flank—March!" and the regiment started across the field toward the crest of the hill. In doing so, the men had to clamber over a fence, from which one tumbled rather ungracefully, breaking his bayonet. "This caused some amusement, for even at this time we did not realize that we were about to engage in battle," Rhodes recalled.[7]

"Yelling like so many devils," Slocum's men rushed across the open field. As they crested the hill, Evans's 900 infantrymen and two cannon threw up a wall of metal that belied their small numbers. "A perfect hail storm of bullets, round shot and shell was poured into us, tearing through the ranks and scattering death and confusion everywhere," remembered Pvt. Sam English of the 2nd. Though shaken, the New Englanders maintained their line. With something less than drill-ground precision, they aimed down the slope and opened fire on Evans's men.[8]

The 2nd fought alone atop Matthews Hill for only a few minutes. Immediately behind them rumbled Captain Reynolds's battery of six brass James Rifles. Though the Confederate infantry stood only 150 yards from the Union line,

Burnside ordered the artillery to the firing line. (Using massed artillery at close quarters was a favorite tactic of Napoleon, and one that would be exhibited at Bull Run but rarely thereafter.) "Forward the battery," he yelled to Reynolds. The captain hesitated. "In what position?" he asked. Burnside had no time for such details. "Forward the battery!" he repeated. The batterymen quickly mounted the teams of horses and whipped them into a run along Sudley Road. Nearing the firing line, the battery stopped long enough for some infantrymen to clear away the fence along the left of the road. "Forward into line of action, front," hollered Reynolds, and the six guns bounded off the road into the field and up to the crest of the hill, now shrouded in billows of white smoke.[9]

As they wheeled their limbers in the wide arcs needed to get their guns into position, the gunners found themselves under a nasty fire. Men tumbled from horses that fell dead or wounded in their traces, dragged along by the onrushing teams. "It was rather nervous business for one who had never seen anything but 'muster day' encounters to find the balls flying round his head, perfectly regardless of whom they might hit," admitted one artilleryman.[10] The gunners went to work but, according to Robert Carter of the Regulars, to little effect. "They did no execution," Carter wrote. "I did not see the elevating screw touched. . . . They would fire, allow the guns to recoil, load again, push them back up to the crest of the hill, and pull away in the direction of the enemy." The artillerymen, of course, saw it quite differently. One claimed the battery fired 250 rounds that day. Certainly the Confederates saw the battery as a frightening presence, for they could see that the Rhode Island guns dominated the field. One member of the battery wrote, "How they ever let us get on top of the hill is more than I can imagine."[11]

At this precise moment, Shanks Evans may indeed have regretted giving the Federals that position atop Matthews Hill. No matter now, for it was too late to do anything except fight hard and buy time enough to allow reinforcements to arrive. His men proved most willing. Roberdeau Wheat's Louisiana battalion, after regaining its skirmishers, opened on the 2nd Rhode Island as soon as the New Englanders crested the hill. After five volleys by Wheat, J. B. E. Sloan moved his 4th South Carolina into the swale on the Louisianans' left and joined in. Along a 300-yard front the two sides blazed away.[12]

This was far deadlier business than most of these untried soldiers had expected. The enemy fire seemed so tremendous that one Federal proclaimed the Confederates numbered no fewer than 80,000 men. The masses of Confederates seemed a fat-enough target even for green soldiers: "Every shot dropped one man," boasted another Yankee. Yet many Federals fell, too. Colonel Slocum, crossing the rail fence on top of the hill, tumbled with a bullet through his head. His men carried him quickly to the nearby Matthews house. So too, fell Maj. Sullivan Ballou—who days earlier had foretold his death to his young wife—his leg torn off by a shell. Division commander Hunter also fell, wounded in the

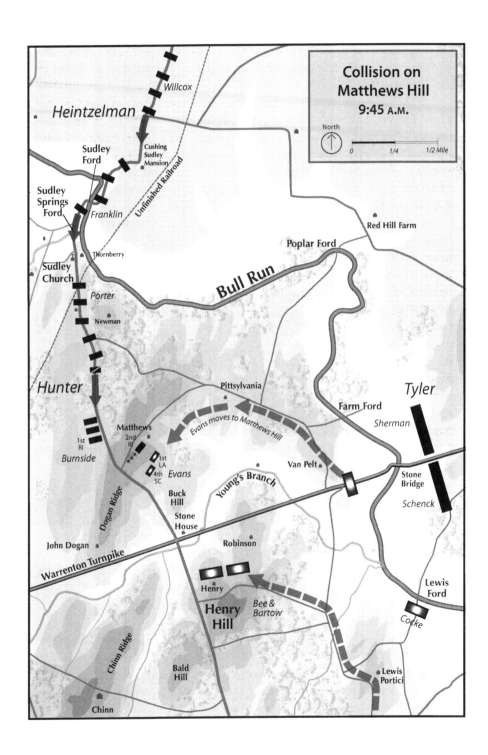

Collision on Matthews Hill
9:45 A.M.

North

0   1/4   1/2 Mile

Willcox

Heintzelman

Sudley Ford

Cushing
Sudley
Mansion

Sudley
Springs
Ford

Franklin

Unfinished Railroad

Red Hill Farm

Poplar Ford

Thornberry

Sudley
Church

Bull Run

Porter

Newman

Hunter

Pittsylvania

Tyler

Farm Ford

Evans moves to Matthews Hill

Sherman

Matthews

1st
RI

2nd
RI

Burnside

1st
LA

4th
SC

Evans

Van Pelt

Stone
Bridge

Schenck

Dogan Ridge

Buck
Hill

Young's Branch

Stone
House

John Dogan

Robinson

Warrenton Turnpike

Henry

Henry
Hill

Bee &
Bartow

Lewis
Ford

Cocke

Chinn Ridge

Bald
Hill

Lewis
Portici

Chinn

neck. As he rode to the rear, he met Burnside. "Burnside," he said, "I leave the matter in your hands. Slocum and his regiment went in handsomely, and drove the scoundrels."[13]

Before his wounding, Hunter had managed to foul up his division's deployment so severely that it jeopardized its cohesion, if not its existence. For some reason, Hunter held back Burnside's three unused regiments (the 1st Rhode Island, 2nd New Hampshire, and 71st New York National Guard) and instead told Col. Andrew Porter to take his brigade onto the field to assist the 2nd Rhode Island and the battery. But Porter apparently misunderstood the order (indeed it was an illogical directive), and instead of passing Burnside's three regiments, he deployed his brigade behind them, even farther from the front. Hence, thirty minutes into the fight the 2nd Rhode Island and the Rhode Island battery fought alone, despite the nearness of probably 4,500 men.[14]

That would soon change. With Hunter wounded, brigade commanders Burnside and Porter asserted themselves. Burnside, for his part, rushed to aid his men engaged on Matthews Hill. He rode back to the 71st New York and 2nd New Hampshire and ordered them into the fight. But the 2nd New Hampshire at first advanced on the right of Sudley Road and did little, while the 71st fumbled its deployment so badly that Burnside felt compelled to order up his fellow Rhode Islanders of the 1st Regiment instead. "Forward 1st Rhode Island!" he yelled, and the regiment crossed Sudley Road, where it found the 71st New York still struggling with its formation. "Lie down, 71st, and let the Rhode Islanders pass to the front," Burnside ordered (to the New Yorkers' embarrassment). Swept by fire from Davidson's guns and John Imboden's newly placed battery on Henry Hill, the 1st Rhode Island hurried up the slope toward the left of the 2nd.[15]

While Burnside attended to the burgeoning fight on Matthews Hill, fellow brigade commander Andrew Porter took a broader view of the battlefield. Instead of throwing his troops into the growing cauldron on Matthews Hill, Porter focused his attention on Dogan Ridge to Burnside's right and opposite the vulnerable Confederate left. Porter intended to place four of his five units there, plus Griffin's storied Battery D, 5th U.S. Artillery. But inexperience foiled Porter's noble intent. Stray Confederate shells and bullets discombobulated his battalions and made moving them a slow matter. The move to Dogan Ridge was an excellent idea, but it would take some time for his men to get there.[16]

While Burnside and Porter untangled their brigades from their awkward, initial deployments, the Rhode Islanders continued their battle with the Louisianans and South Carolinians on the southern slope of Matthews Hill. By now Reynolds's Union battery and Imboden's and Davidson's Confederate guns were fully involved, and the boom of cannon and explosion of shells punctuated the pealing musketry. Undoubtedly, Evans sensed that, despite the current stalemate, more Federals must be at hand. Without a quick, decisive offensive stroke or substantial reinforcements, he would soon be overmatched.

At probably just after 10 A.M., Evans and Wheat spotted an opening—what they thought was a softness in the Federal line. Instantly, Wheat ordered his battalion of 400 to charge. One of Wheat's sergeants wrote days later, "Our blood was on fire, life was valueless, the boys fired one volley, then rushed upon the foe." Wheat's fire knocked down cannoneers and horses and crippled some of Reynolds's gun crews. The Louisianans swept up the slope toward the Union cannon, wielding clubbed muskets and drawn Bowie knives (one man even asserted that some men threw away their muskets altogether, trusting entirely to the big knives). The Louisianans later claimed the charge "struck terror into the [Yankees'] souls," but Burnside's Rhode Islanders held their ridgetop.[17]

"This seemed to me to be the most terrible moment of this terrific contest," remembered a man of the 2nd Rhode Island. Many Federal muskets became so foul the men resorted to banging ramrods against fence posts to get the charges down. Other men had expended their forty rounds and groped among the dead and wounded for cartridges. Those who could blasted away from behind any available cover. One group of Yankees took shelter behind one of Matthews's haystacks, only to be showered with hay when a Confederate shell obliterated it.

Wheat's men mistimed their charge. Whatever the "softness" Wheat and Evans thought they had detected in Burnside's line, they soon discovered that the 2nd Rhode Island intended to go nowhere. Worse still, the 1st Rhode Island was just arriving to assist its sister regiment. The Louisianans charged to within 20 yards of the battery, only to be brought to bay by the intensified Union fire. Then the two Rhode Island regiments "gave a most hideous scream" and raked the Southerners anew. Wheat's men staggered, then gave way, much to the glee of the beleaguered cannoneers. "Never will I forget how that rebel flag looked as it bobbed out of sight under the hill," wrote one.[18]

Wheat's men tumbled back not to their former position, but rather across Sudley Road on Sloan's left, where they took refuge among the haystacks and outbuildings of John Dogan's farm. That meant, of course, that Evans's right was shorter, and hence more vulnerable, especially with the arrival of the 1st Rhode Island on the Union firing line. Evans needed help, and he rode to Henry Hill to ask Bee for reinforcement. For some time, Bee had been watching the battle from afar and could see the difficulty of Evans's position on the slope of Matthews Hill. Bee suggested that Evans retreat to his position on Henry Hill. Evans, however, was in no mood for such talk. He could hold the ground if he could get some help, he insisted. Bee yielded. He had been looking for a fight all morning. Now he had found it.[19]

For as long as Evans had been resisting the Yankees on Matthews Hill, Barnard Bee and the four regiments of his own and Francis Bartow's brigades had been on Henry Hill, silently withstanding the fire of Reynolds's Rhode Island guns. The first shots from the Federal battery flew harmlessly overhead, startling a handful of men who had climbed one of Mrs. Henry's apple trees for brunch. "The boys dropped from the trees like shot bears," remembered an onlooker. But soon the Rhode Islanders bettered their aim, and shells burst in and around the regiments, wounding a few men and spattering nearly all with clods of dirt. Bee's and Bartow's men, like the rest, were rookies, and this business of an artillery barrage was something they had not foreseen. "I felt I was in the presence of death," wrote a man from Bartow's 8th Georgia. "My first thought was, 'This is unfair; somebody is to blame for getting us all killed. I didn't come out here to fight this way; I wish the earth would crack open and let me drop in.'"[20]

About 10:15, Bee galloped up Henry Hill and hunted for the 4th Alabama, commanded by Col. Egbert Jones. "Up Alabamians," Bee yelled, waving his hand toward the battle raging across the valley. The Alabama soldiers could clearly see their task. Clambering over one of Mrs. Henry's fences, the 4th led the procession of Bee's regiments into the fight. The Union guns turned their fire on the fat column. Past Imboden's guns the Alabamians ran, down the northern slope of Henry Hill to the valley below where, thankfully, the ground shielded them from the Federal fire. Passing Young's Branch, the Warrenton Pike, and the Stone House, the regiment started up the steep slope of Buck Hill (in reality the southern, somewhat lower shoulder of Matthews Hill). As they reached the crest, they came under Federal fire again. In front of them, about 300 yards away, billowed the white smoke of the battle.[21]

Reynolds's guns pelted Colonel Jones and his regiment as it moved toward the firing line. The lone gun of Davidson's battery located on Buck Hill did little to diminish the Federal fire. Bee ordered the Alabamians to veer to the right toward the cover of a thicket beyond Sloan's flank. Once in the woods—filled with dead and wounded from Wheat's battalion—the 4th Alabama deployed into line of battle. Beyond the woods stood a cornfield, and beyond that, along the fence atop the hill, stood the Federal line of battle. Jones led the 4th out of the timber and up the slope toward the Federal line. Swept by bullets, halfway up the rise—within 100 yards of the Federals—the line stopped. Jones ordered the men to lie down and open fire.[22]

Even these rookie soldiers, only a handful of whom had ever been shot at before, could see the Federals held most of the advantages. The ground in front of the Alabamians rolled, and here and there along the front swells of ground made it virtually impossible for some companies to return fire. The left of the line fronted the cornfield, which further obscured the 4th's field of fire. Most ominously, the Alabamians could see more Union soldiers forming into line on the high ground in front, extending the Union line still farther to the Confederates' right. "It was a critical moment," wrote Chaplain James G. Hudson of the 4th, "and a fearful position for a handful of men."[23]

Bee had sensed this would be a difficult position to hold (hence his hesitancy in going there in the first place), but he said he would help Evans and was not inclined to halfhearted efforts. Soon after the 4th Alabama moved into position,

Bee sent back to Henry Hill for the rest of his command: the 7th and 8th Georgia, the 2nd Mississippi, and two companies of the 11th Mississippi.

Receiving orders to advance from Colonel Bartow (a nominal brigade commander who had been largely superseded by General Bee), the other regiments hopped to their feet, happy at the prospect of finally being able to shoot back at the Yankees. Before starting out, Col. W. M. Gardner of the 8th Georgia walked in front of his regiment. "Men, I am no orator," he said. "I shall not attempt to make you a speech. Keep your ranks, do your duty, and show you are worthy of the state from which you came! Right Face, double quick, march!"[24]

As soon as the Confederates started, Reynolds trained his six rifled cannon on the column. "The whole air sounded as though a large Aeolian harp was hung over, around and about us," an 8th Georgian wrote afterward. "Gracious! How the shot came." Driven in part by a desire to silence the battery, the three regiments moved on the double quick across the valley to Buck Hill. There, Bee met them and ordered them to their places, where possible picking for each a thicket of pines that might provide them some cover. He directed the Mississippians to move into place between the 4th South Carolina and 4th Alabama. The 7th Georgia moved to still another thicket to the right of the 4th Alabama, and the 8th Georgia took a position on the extreme right—one Bee hoped would be on the flank of the enemy.[25]

Bee's hope that the 8th Georgia might get on the Union flank succumbed to more fast-arriving Union troops. Just as Bee worked to extend his line to the east, so too did the Federals, who had both more men and the advantage of position. After putting the 1st Rhode Island into the fight, Burnside ordered up the 71st New York, which slid into position on the left of Reynolds's battery (the other regiments moved to the left to make room). The New Yorkers brought with them two boat howitzers; since the regiment hadn't been able to secure horses for the two guns, they had dragged them by hand from the Washington Navy Yard. Now they manhandled the pieces into position in front of the 4th Alabama. Burnside also moved up his last remaining regiment, the 2nd New Hampshire, as a general reserve.[26]

Now the fighting exploded along a 700-yard front. John Ellis and four of his brothers fought with the 71st New York National Guard that day. "The cannon balls were ploughing up the earth all around," Ellis wrote. "Shells were bursting and crashing through the trees directly in our rear, and the Minie balls were battering and humming in all directions." The New Yorkers' boat howitzers flailed the Alabamians in front of them, "doing fearful execution . . . completely cut up the Alabama regiment." Wrote another New Yorker, "We could see them fall one after another very fast. They returned our fire with great activity and killed many of us, and wounded some thirty of our boys."

The Alabamians struggled to maintain their foothold on the hillside, standing only to fire through Matthews's waist-high cornfield. Colonel Jones, massive on a 6-foot-3-inch frame, was "as calm as a statue, giving orders as they came," until a Union bullet knocked him from his horse. "Our brave men fell in great numbers," wrote a company officer to his homefolk, "but they died as the brave love to die—with faces to the foe, fighting in the holy cause of liberty."[27]

The 7th and 8th Georgia battled on the right of the 4th Alabama, hoping to take the Federals in flank but suffering increasing pressure themselves. The Georgians took cover in a pair of pine thickets, their line facing northwest, at an angle to the Alabama regiment. In front of them bluecoats crowded into the Matthews farmyard. "They were in the shrubbery in the front yard, down through the horse lot, behind the stables and barns and haystacks," wrote Georgian Berrien Zettler. "Seemingly a thousand rifles were flashing and the air was alive with whistling bullets." The Federal fire blistered the Georgians' line. Dozens fell, some gasping or groaning, others in perfect silence. "It is only surprising that any of us escaped," another man told his hometown paper—an assertion often repeated by men on both sides. Still, the Georgians held their position. "Most of the men were as cool as cucumbers—each would load, pick his man, and take deliberate aim."[28]

Despite what they viewed as overwhelming numbers, Bee's men fought Burnside's brigade to a standstill. "The scene was terrible," remembered a member of the 1st Rhode Island. "Shells were exploding and the cannon roaring made such a noise that the cry of the wounded could not be heard." Governor Sprague had two horses shot from under him, certainly the only sitting governor in American history to suffer that distinction. Men took cover wherever they could find it. One wrote, "I was standing on top of the hill waiting for the cowards to show themselves, when I felt a commotion between my legs, and a man was deliberately firing away, using my legs as a port hole." Another man watched in horror as first one of his buddies fell, and then a shell decapitated another, and then a third had his leg ripped off, splattering everyone around with blood. "I felt so badly that I almost fainted," he admitted, "but I rallied immediately, and clenching my teeth went in, and every shot that I fired made it tell. . . . I saw five rebels fall dead."[29]

The position of the 7th and 8th Georgia in the pine thicket threatened the left of Burnside's line, forcing the Rhode Island colonel repeatedly to push the 2nd Rhode Island farther to the left. But the move failed to dislodge the Georgians and further weakened Burnside's line near Reynolds's Battery. Probably twenty minutes after the Georgians arrived, Burnside realized he needed help. "We must have the Regulars," he said. Burnside sent an aide to Porter to get them.[30]

Much was expected of Maj. George Sykes's eleven companies of Regular army infantry. In this army of buoyant volunteers, the Regulars were perceived to be an anomaly. Most presumed the battalion to be composed of hard-bitten, well-drilled veterans. In reality, much of it consisted of greenhorns who had rarely fired a musket. Its strength lay in its officer corps; the colonel to the lowest lieutenant had virtually all graduated West Point. Most of McDowell's army, including, apparently, Burnside, regarded the battalion as little less than a magical force whose mere presence would rout the enemy. One officer wrote, "The volunteers expected much of the regulars."[31]

The aide dispatched to bring up the Regulars was evidently too slow to suit Burnside, and soon the beleaguered colonel rode off to see Colonel Porter for himself. His horse foaming, Burnside encountered Porter as he was putting his own brigade into position on Dogan Ridge. Burnside yelled, "Porter, for God's sake let me have the Regulars. My men are all being cut to pieces." Porter, now in command of the division after Hunter's wounding, seemed miffed at Burnside's urgency. "Colonel Burnside, do you mean to say that the enemy is advancing on my left?" he asked. "Yes," said Burnside, "and you will be cut off if you can't stop him." Porter was not keen on losing the Regulars, but huffed and consented.[32]

Major Sykes barked out the orders. The Regulars fell out of column and moved off toward Burnside's line, wading through the flotsam of battle as they marched. Diarist Robert Carter remembered, "The first thing I saw was a man stretched out dead, with his hand nearly shot away." Such ghastly sights produced only silence, not pause. Still the Regulars' pace was too slow for Burnside, who rushed back again to hurry them along. "Good God! Major Sykes," blurted the exorcised colonel, "you regulars are just what we want: form on my left and give aid to my men who are being cut to pieces!" The Regulars hardly needed such a beckoning, but their pace quickened.

Tradition holds that the Regulars rushed to the left of Burnside's line and delivered a fatal blow to the Confederate position—that, clearly, is what Burnside had in mind when he summoned them. But in fact, the Regulars stopped far short of the Union left and instead went to the direct support of Reynolds's six cannon, still blasting away after an hour. Once at the battery, the Regulars veered right into line of battle and lay down in support of the guns. Some of the Rhode Island batterymen saw the Regulars lying there and berated them as cowards: "What are you lying down there for?" (The Rhode Islanders failed to understand exactly what infantry support for a battery meant.) After many minutes, the Regulars did indeed rise and open fire. They had drilled often in anticipation of this moment, but here, when it counted, many men simply forgot what to do. "Our men fired badly," admitted Carter. "They were excited, and some of the recruits fired at the stars." One of the wild-firing culprits explained, "I did my level best to fire as fast and often as possible," but "it does disconcert one's aim to be under the direct fire of cannon and musketry."[33]

The fire of the Regulars, irregular though it might have been, coincided with the arrival of new troops on the Union left—the vanguard of Tyler's division. Tyler and his officers had spent the morning of battle rather leisurely, fulfilling their role as a diversion and waiting patiently for the Union advance west of the

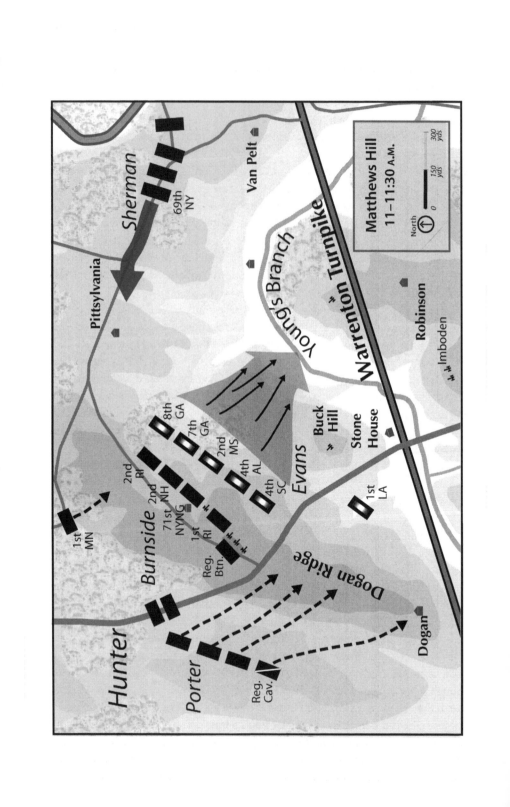

Hunter

Sherman

69th
NY

Pittsylvania

Van Pelt

Young's Branch

Warrenton Turnpike

Burnside

2nd
RI

2nd
NH

1st
MN

71st
NYNG

1st
RI

Reg.
Btn.

8th
GA

7th
GA

2nd
MS

4th
AL

4th
SC

Evans

Buck
Hill

Stone
House

Robinson

Imboden

1st
LA

Porter

Reg.
Cav.

Dogan Ridge

Dogan

Matthews Hill
11–11:30 A.M.

North

0   150   300
      yds   yds

stream to clear the way for a crossing at the Stone Bridge. He and his officers seemed more intent on climbing trees to watch the developing battle than on preparing for any movement that might be ordered. Not so William Tecumseh Sherman, who had been nothing but inquisitive since first light. Repeatedly, he had ridden or walked out to examine the Confederate position, looking especially for some place his brigade might cross Bull Run if need be (everyone confronting the bridge, including Sherman, still believed the span to be mined). About 9 A.M., while Sherman studied the ground, two horsemen rode along the far bluff, then suddenly descended and crossed the stream, riding toward Sherman and his entourage. "You damned black abolitionists, come on," they taunted, waving a gun defiantly. Sherman's skirmishers fired on them ineffectively, and the Confederates escaped. The Confederates' obnoxious display interested Sherman far less than precisely where the Confederate horsemen had crossed the stream. He marked the spot in his mind.[34]

When Tyler received McDowell's orders to cross at the Stone Bridge and "press the attack," the junior general flinched. Tyler's orders envisioned the flanking column uncovering the bridge for him; he had not prepared to force a crossing himself. Sherman, however, had. When Tyler ordered Sherman and Keyes to cross, Sherman headed for the farm ford revealed by the obnoxious Confederate riders earlier that morning. His men splashed across and encountered no resistance. Sherman's five regiments—3,400 men—mounted Van Pelt Hill and tramped toward Pittsylvania. Beyond, Sherman could see the battle. Indeed, the flank of the Confederate line lay directly in front of him.[35]

The Irish 69th New York led Sherman's march across the plateau. Lt. Col. James Haggerty rode at the front of the regiment. Some newspapers had reported him killed at Blackburn's Ford a few days before, and as he rode forward this day he joked to a reporter that he "felt very warlike for a dead man." Beyond Pittsylvania, the 69th spotted some Confederates falling back across the fields. Haggerty brashly rode ahead without orders to try intercept their retreat by himself. Sherman watched as a Confederate stepped out of ranks, confronted Haggerty at short range, and fired. He fell from his horse, dead. The Irishmen of the 69th instantly opened fire, and for a few moments the brigade's first musketry battle of the war raged. Sherman soon called it off and directed the 69th—with flags flying conspicuously out in front to ward off friendly fire—to continue the march west to join with Hunter's division.[36]

Sherman's arrival on the battlefield—the convergence of disparate forces in the presence of an enemy—was no mean feat by nineteenth-century standards. For the Confederates, Sherman's arrival confirmed what had already become obvious: the position of Evans and Bee on Matthews Hill was untenable. In front of Sherman, the 7th and 8th Georgia now felt enormous pressure on their right flank. After the war, a man of the 8th Georgia remembered those fading moments of resistance on Matthews Hill: "Here were men, young men, healthy and strong and brave, shot down by the score. . . . They were all around me." The pine thicket that had given shelter to the 8th had become a place of horrors. "That pine grove and field was a terrible shock to me, for my friends were there and some of my kindred." Men in Civil War regiments often came from the same region, and heavy losses on a battlefield in Virginia could have a ruinous effect on a hometown. What happened that morning on Matthews Hill "startled a whole community, and the news of it carried from neighbor to neighbor until it was the talk of the whole county."[37]

On the Confederate left, opposite the Rhode Island Battery, the 4th Alabama and 2nd Mississippi confronted an ever-strengthening Federal line atop Matthews Hill as the Regular battalion lent its weight to the forward Union lean. Not even help from Sloan's 4th South Carolina, which moved to the right into the thicket to help Bee's men, changed the discouraging tenor of the fight. Matters only worsened for the Confederates when Porter's brigade and Griffin's battery of artillery moved into place on Dogan Ridge, overlapping the Confederate left flank as well. There, the Confederates had only Wheat's decimated battalion to do battle. The Louisianans did what they could from behind the cover of fences and haystacks until Wheat fell seriously wounded and the disorganized little band gave way, leaving the Confederate left bare and vulnerable.[38]

With both of the Confederate flanks menaced, and with no reinforcements in sight, Evans and Bee had no choice but to retreat. Orders to fall back went down the line, but in fact they were hardly necessary. The 8th Georgia had lost nearly 200 men—it "appeared annihilated," wrote one man—and the ranks had already started to crumble. "I saw it was all up with us," remembered Pvt. Berrien Zettler, "and as everyone about me seemed to be dead or wounded, I determined to take my chances of saving myself by getting away as fast as I could." Others shared the view, but enough of them maintained their organization that the Georgians could conduct some semblance of a fighting withdrawal, though at heavy cost.[39]

The Mississippians, South Carolinians, and Alabamians did likewise. Under heavy fire, Colonel Jones's 4th Alabama (probably the last regiment to leave) slowly pulled back out of the open field into the thicket. As they did so, Reynolds's battery and the New York howitzers opened on them with canister, which rattled into the trees and ripped into bodies indiscriminately. Colonel Jones fell wounded. Gasping, he yelled, "Men don't run!" Few did, but still they left the colonel behind and followed the rest of Bee's and Evans's commands across the fields toward Henry Hill.[40]

Initially, the Confederates' exodus seemed more a source of relief than joy to the Federals. Burnside immediately requested permission to pull his command back from the firing line for some rest. Only the Regulars mounted anything resembling an immediate pursuit, rushing down the slope. Dead and dying littered the fields and thickets. One of the wounded held aloft a white handkerchief on a sword. It was Colonel Jones, mortally wounded. The Regulars gave him a drink of water. The colonel asked his enemies what they intended to do. Whip the Confederates, they asserted. But Jones had a warning. "Gentleman," he said, "you have got me, but a hundred thousand more await you!"[41]

The Federals scoffed at such talk, and with good reason. Retreating Confederates covered the slope of Matthews Hill and soon appeared streaming up onto the heights of Mrs. Henry's farm. Though the battle left Burnside's brigade battered and longing for shelter, thousands more Union troops were now on the field. Porter's brigade bristled atop Dogan Ridge. Griffin's and Ricketts's batteries, which totaled ten rifled pieces and two howitzers, pounded Henry Hill. Their fire made things decidedly uncomfortable for John Imboden and his four overmatched pieces near the Henry house. The Federals chuckled with glee as Imboden's gunners scattered "like ants from an ant hill" every time a Federal shell burst near them. Heintzelman's Union division (except Howard's brigade, which was still en route) was now entirely across Bull Run, too; flushed with a victory they had had no part of, the men impatiently waited for someone to tell them where to go and what to do.[42]

Success had repaired McDowell's flagging spirit. As the 3,000 Confederate defenders of Matthews Hill retreated, McDowell had nearly 18,000 men on the ground. The general and his staff galloped among the brigades, waving their hats and shouting. McDowell rode by Reynolds's six cannon, still hot from firing more than 250 rounds. "Well done, Rhode Island boys!" he yelled. McDowell's staff officers galloped among the infantrymen. "They are running!" "Victory! Victory! The day is ours!" It seemed so. On the distant slopes of Mrs. Henry's farm, McDowell and his soldiers could see scattered knots of Confederates, some running, others simply milling about, and mounted officers trying unsuccessfully to bring order to the retreating rabble. The Confederate army—at least what could be seen of it—appeared to have disintegrated. The only lament among many Federals: the Confederates had fled too fast, and the battle might end before the fresh Union troops on Matthews Hill had a chance to inflict damage of their own. "Give us a chance at them, general, before they all run away," one man yelled to McDowell. The young soldier quickly received a whack from one of his sidekicks, who admonished him with a tremor: "Shut up your damned head; you'll get chances enough, maybe, before the day is over."[43]

CHASING VICTORY

One great question hovered over this first battle of the war that distinguished it from all others: What, exactly, would victory look like? Would the rebellion collapse at the mere appearance of the Union army? Or the first shot? Thoughtful Unionists had answered "no" to those questions weeks before, and certainly the day's events had borne out their obvious wisdom. But now, at 11:30 A.M. on July 21, 1861, as retreating Confederates streamed up the slopes of Henry Hill, the question arose in pointed form: Was *this* victory? Would the Confederate army continue its retreat—perhaps simply disintegrate? Would the South give up the rebellion altogether in the face of imposing Union might? The four years of war that followed rendered the answer to these questions obvious enough to historians and distant observers, but in the fading battle smoke of that Sunday morning no question loomed larger. *Was this victory?* When McDowell's staff officers (and perhaps even McDowell himself) rode along the lines proclaiming "Victory!" and "The day is ours!" they almost surely saw the moment in absolute terms. This *must* be what victory looks like.

They could not know then what four years of war would demonstrate in deadly form: the outcome of individual battles (even decisive victories or defeats), though heavy with implications for military operations in the field, often moved the needle toward war's end slightly indeed. The process of learning that lesson—learning exactly what absolute victory required—began just before that July 21 noon on the fields west of Bull Run.

For the Confederates, the battle—the war—was only two hours old. Could it be lost already? It certainly seemed so to those Confederates close enough to see anything of the fight for Matthews Hill. Bee's and Evans's brigades streamed back from the Matthews farm, across the Warrenton Turnpike, and up the slopes of Henry Hill. Occasionally a ragged Confederate battle line formed and unleashed a scattered volley or two—in one instance into their fellow Confederates—but mostly the Southerners retreated without stopping. Soon the beaten and bloody remnants of five Confederate regiments—a tangled mob—swarmed the fields between Widow Henry's house and the Robinson house. Of the 600 men who had marched with the flag of the 8th Georgia earlier that morning, only 60 gathered around the standard on Henry Hill at midday. South Carolinians mingled with the Georgians; Mississippians fell in with Louisianans. Officers rushed back and forth, pleading with the men to join their regiments, to rally around their flags. These were good men who would become good soldiers, but their introduction to battle proved more than they could manage at the moment. Many dazed soldiers merely continued toward the rear. They had seen enough fighting for a lifetime, much less a day, and they simply drifted toward a place of safety. Soon, the last of the beaten Confederate regiments, the 4th Alabama, plodded up the hill. The rout seemed complete. All six regiments that had seen combat that morning—nearly 3,000 men—were in some measure disorganized and defeated. It had been, wrote one man, "an appalling hour."[1]

Worse, it seemed nothing could prevent the Federal army from pursuing—15,000 men thrilled with apparent victory. If they moved quickly, then surely the war would be over soon. Irvin McDowell need only get his regiments moving forward from Matthews and Buck Hills, down across the Warrenton Turnpike and Young's Branch, and up the northern slopes of Henry Hill, where a quick, sharp attack would probably send the relative handful of Confederates into final, disastrous retreat. Even to military greenhorns—and these fields were full of them—the Federal task seemed so simple.

To survive, the Confederates needed additional men and the time to put them someplace useful. Some of the men were on the way: the Hampton Legion and Jackson's brigade of Virginians had been on the road for hours and now neared the battlefield. But their commanders would need time to understand the battlefield and position their men. That time would either have to be bought—at a fearful price, no doubt—or given to them by McDowell.

It was perhaps fortunate that neither Johnston nor Beauregard knew much of the disaster that had befallen their armies. Until nearly 11 A.M., both remained on the hill behind Mitchell's Ford. They knew of E. P. Alexander's earlier warning of the Federal flanking column and could hear the intensifying fire on the left of the line. But until 10 A.M., Johnston and Beauregard adjudged the threat against the left to be nothing more than Bee, Evans, and Jackson could handle. Instead, both generals continued to hope that their attack, not McDowell's, would shape the battle that day. From their knoll near Mitchell's Ford, they waited for the sound of guns that would mark the opening of Beauregard's grand stroke against Centreville and the Union left.[2]

By 10:30, those plans for attack had run amok. Beauregard received a note from D. R. Jones stating that although his own command had moved into position, Ewell's brigade had not yet crossed Union Mills Ford. What was the problem? The answer came moments later from Ewell himself: he had not received his expected orders to advance. Somehow, the directive had miscarried. No doubt exasperated, Beauregard's hope for a climactic Confederate assault by his right wing yielded to the pressure of time. This attack had to succeed before McDowell could win the day against the Confederate left, and clearly McDowell's assault was already well underway. Wedded to the offensive though he was, Beauregard could not take the risk.[3]

At 11 A.M., the firing on the Confederate left grew louder. Johnston also received reports from his scouts at Blackburn's and Mitchell's Fords that the Federals were felling trees—signaling clearly that those forces had no offensive intentions. At least to Johnston, the situation now seemed clear. The Federals had the initiative, and the battle would be fought on the left, the weakest part of the Confederate line. "The battle is there," he told Beauregard, "I am going."[4]

Beauregard went, too, but before leaving, he issued a spate of orders that would strip the right of all but the minimum needed to defend the lower crossings of Bull Run. Under the new orders, Ewell and Jones were to make only a strong demonstration on the right. Early and Theophilus Holmes, meanwhile, were to abandon their positions in support of the southern crossings and move quickly up Bull Run to the left. Bonham also would send two of his South Carolina regiments and Kemper's battery. With those orders dispatched, Beauregard and Johnston mounted their horses and made haste toward Henry Hill.[5]

For Capt. John Imboden, whatever help Beauregard and Johnston might send could not arrive soon enough. Imboden's four 6-pounder smoothbores had been in position 150 yards north of the Henry house for about an hour. Despite his fire in support of the Confederate troops on Matthews Hill, the battle lines there had collapsed. An hour ago, Bee had told Imboden, "Stay until you are ordered away." No orders to leave had come, and now Imboden found himself— along with two guns of the Washington Artillery and one gun of the Lynchburg Artillery to his right—the only organized Confederate force standing between the Federals and victory, "alone in its glory," he said. Just a few hundred yards in front of him, beyond the Stone House, he could see the Federal infantry gathering for what looked to be an all-out attack. A half mile to his left-front, on Dogan Ridge, Griffin's and Ricketts's Federal batteries pounded his position and the disorganized infantry to his right. But a swell of ground offered Imboden's guns some protection. Most Union shells buried themselves harmlessly before exploding. "The ground," said Imboden, "looked as though it had been rooted up by hogs."[6]

While Imboden's cannoneers held out north of the Henry house, the first inkling of Confederate hope arrived on the field. Near the Lewis house (Portici), 600 handsomely clad men of Hampton's Legion formed into line of battle. Their commander, Wade Hampton III, bore a military lineage few Carolinians could match: his grandfather fought in the Revolution and his father fought against the British in the War of 1812. The most recent iteration of the Hampton name had not pursued a military career—he was a planter, lawyer, and politician, though the war would demonstrate that he had indeed inherited the military instincts of his forebears. At the outbreak of war, Hampton had enlisted as a private, but no one imagined him staying in the ranks for long. Soon the governor appointed him a colonel, and Hampton purchased with his own funds weapons enough to outfit a regiment—one he soon commanded.

Leaving his six companies of infantry behind for the moment, Hampton, followed by a bevy of officers and overeager enlisted men, rode ahead along the woods road leading from Portici to Mrs. Henry's farm. What he saw when he arrived did not inspire him. Disorganized Confederate troops covered Widow Henry's fields and those of her neighbor, a freedman named James Robinson. On the heights beyond them loomed the Federals; "their bayonets flashed like silver in the bright sunshine," one of Hampton's foot soldiers wrote. Shells from the Federal artillery on Matthews Hill and Dogan Ridge screeched wildly overhead, whistling, said one man, "like a flock of blackbirds." A solid shot slammed into the ground beneath the belly of Hampton's horse, covering the colonel and all nearby with red Virginia clay. Even a military novice like Hampton could recognize a crisis like this. He ordered his curious enlisted men to return to the ranks and the officers to assume their posts.[7]

At probably 11 A.M., Hampton received his orders: move forward and support one of the disorganized Georgia regiments. The South Carolinians hustled along the woods road and then down the hill to the hollow southeast of the Robinson house. There they found some of Bartow's Georgians and lay down along a fence just in front of them. Hampton rode forward to the top of the rise, and as quickly rode back. "Men of the Legion, I am happy to inform you that the enemy is in sight," he said. The Legion climbed the fence and started up the slope.[8]

As the South Carolinians reached the level ground around the Robinson house, they came under enemy fire. Again shells whizzed nearby. Bullets whined. Suddenly there came a loud *thwack*, and the first man tumbled from the ranks, his brass buckle mangled by a minié ball. Swarms of dazed Confederates passed the Carolinians, heading to the rear. Off to the left, near the Henry house, Hampton's men could see Imboden's cannoneers working their pieces feverishly. The gun that had supported Evans's men from Buck Hill now took position near the Warrenton Turnpike, just in front of the Robinson house. The Carolinians rushed past the house and down the lane leading to the turnpike. There they halted, took meager cover behind a lattice fence bordering the driveway, and opened fire on the still-distant Yankees. Federal shells and bullets whistled overhead, and the men dodged, ducked, fell down, and jumped up in an almost comical fashion. "I suppose they thought the dodging was a help," wrote one officer,

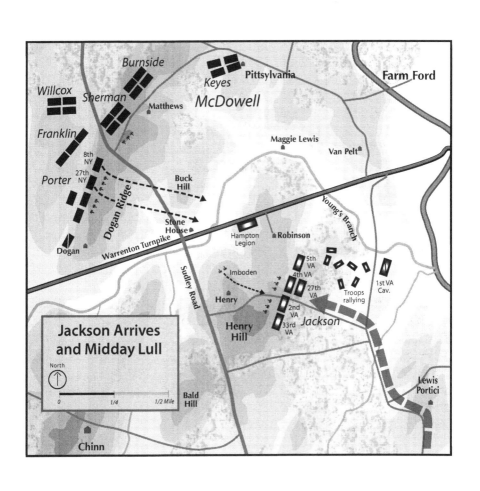

Burnside

Willcox Sherman Keyes Pittsylvania Farm Ford

Franklin Matthews McDowell

8th
NY Maggie Lewis Van Pelt
27th
Porter NY Buck
Hill Young's Branch

Dogan Ridge

Stone
House Hampton Robinson
Dogan Warrenton Turnpike Legion

Sudley Road 5th
VA 1st VA
Imboden 4th VA Cav.
Henry 27th Troops
VA rallying
2nd
Jackson Arrives VA Jackson
and Midday Lull Henry 33rd
Hill VA
North

Lewis
Portici
0   1/4   1/2 Mile Bald
Hill

Chinn

who lamented the disruption: "We could never keep orderly ranks so long as the men persisted in dodging."[9]

Hampton's arrival coincided with the first spasms of activity from the victorious Federals north of the Warrenton Turnpike. After their success on Matthews Hill, instinct told many Federal officers to keep moving, even without guidance from McDowell or other leaders. Col. Andrew Porter's brigade of Hunter's division stood next in the queue behind Burnside's exhausted men. While the Confederates had retreated from Matthews Hill, they had not been swept away. A few pockets of Alabamians and Georgians remained in the space between the Union guns atop Matthews Hill and the Confederate cannon (Imboden's and Leftwich's) on the forward edge of Henry Hill. More of them rallied along the banks of Young's Branch. As the 27th New York of Porter's brigade arrived on the field (just after the Confederate collapse on Matthews Hill), a staff officer instantly ordered it forward. "You will find the enemy down there somewhere," the officer said, waving in the direction of the Stone House intersection. The New Yorkers hustled along Sudley Road toward the Warrenton Turnpike and Imboden's and Leftwich's guns above. Col. Henry W. Slocum bid his regiment along: "Come on boys, let us silence that battery—come strike for your country and your God." As the 27th New York rushed along, fire from Confederate artillery struck nearby. "Here I saw the first man killed," remembered William Westervelt of the 27th. "Private Wesley Randall of Binghamton, who was marching just in front of me was struck with a grape shot over the left eye. He gave an unearthly screech, and leaping into the air, came down on his hands and knees, and straightened out dead."[10]

As the New Yorkers rushed into the valley, pockets of retreating Confederates rallied along the banks of Young's Branch, just below Imboden's guns. Parts of the 4th Alabama stood along the stream, while three companies of the 2nd Mississippi (refugees from the Matthews Hill fight from Bee's brigade) arranged themselves nearby. Soon, the battle line of the 27th New York appeared, veering down the hill toward the stream. Though the Yankees wore the "full United States uniform," someone among the Mississippians raised "a silly clamor" over their identity. Capt. Hugh Miller put an end to the debate by ordering the Mississippians into the calf-deep waters of Young's Branch, where they used the stream bank as a breastwork. Soon, Miller reported, the three companies opened fire, and "the dead bodies found on the hillside afterwards attest[ed] to the effect of our shots."[11]

At the same time the Mississippians fought from their watery breastwork in Young's Branch, a few hundred yards behind them Wade Hampton's men rushed over Mr. Robinson's flimsy fence and through his garden to the cover of the well-worn Warrenton Turnpike. Bullets passing overhead sounded to one man like "clouds of mosquitoes" in a Carolina swamp. Instantly, instinctively, the Carolinians fell to their knees, leveled their guns on top of the road cut, and fired a disorganized but apparently effective volley. One man new to battle attributed his calm demeanor to absolute resignation: "At this time I made up my mind for the worst; the sickening feeling which at first came over me when beholding the wounded wore away. I saw we had a terrible struggle before us and [I] could have met death calmly."[12]

Confronted by Hampton's Legion in the Warrenton Turnpike and by Alabamians and Mississippians along Young's Branch, the men of the 27th New York paused. "We did not know at first whether they were enemies or not," wrote one man. The uniforms of the distant men matched the gray outfits of the 8th New York State Militia, which had been next in column behind the 27th. Slocum rode toward the Confederates—probably the 4th Alabama—to within 80 yards: "What regiment are you?" he yelled. One of the gray-clad soldiers waved a white handkerchief, approached the 27th New York, and proposed that the regiment surrender. Behind him, the Confederates unfurled a flag and loosed a wicked volley. "Give it to them, boys," Slocum yelled to his men. The New Yorkers opened fire. One enraged soldier rushed the handkerchief-toting Confederate and ran him through with a bayonet.[13]

The exchange prompted a wholesale melee as the Mississippians and Alabamians, 600 men of Hampton's Legion, Leftwich's gun in the Warrenton Turnpike, and Imboden's guns on Henry Hill all pelted the New York regiment. Hampton, Lt. Col. Benjamin Johnson, and Capt. James Conner nervously paced up and down the embankment overlooking the line, yapping orders and encouraging their men. Hampton's horse fell from a wound. A bullet passed through Johnson's head, killing him instantly. Despite the losses, the Carolinians gave the best of it. "They thinned out our ranks terribly," conceded a New Yorker. Colonel Slocum ordered his New York regiment to withdraw back up the slope of Buck Hill. On the way, he fell wounded, too.[14]

Behind the Legion's left, near the Henry house, Imboden's battery stood in ragged form, the ground around the guns churned by Union artillery shells. The battery's limber chests were nearly empty, many of the horses had been killed (in some cases only two or three horses pulled limbers designed for six), and the Federal infantry on the distant heights looked increasingly more menacing. Orders or not, Imboden had no choice but to leave. With shells bursting on every side, the cannoneers hurriedly mated guns to limbers. A flash of teamsters' whips, and the battery rumbled across the fields, first directly south past Mrs. Henry's one-story frame home, and then southeasterly behind the house. The Federal shells followed, some striking the house, shattering shingles and boards and showering the Virginians with splinters. One shell thumped into one of the guns, breaking its axle and forcing Imboden to leave it on the field. Moving on, the Virginians headed for the southeastern edge of Henry Hill.[15]

The withdrawal of Imboden's guns might have signaled a major opportunity for McDowell and his army, if not for the confusion that still reigned on the slopes of Matthews and Buck Hills. The Hampton Legion and Leftwich's cannon and two more guns from the Washington Artillery—briefly in position between the Henry and Robinson houses—kept the open spaces on the Matthews farm dangerous. Moreover, some remnants of Bee's and Bartow's commands still huddled not just along Young's Branch but also in the pine thickets on the southern slope of Matthews Hill, firing at any Yankees who ventured near. Though Union batteries crowned the crest of Matthews Hill and the adjacent Dogan Ridge, the landscape between them and Henry Hill remained chaotic. McDowell refused to venture his army forth into that landscape of uncertainty.

Not so some of McDowell's junior officers. Col. William Averell, for one, had grown tired of seeing his men standing around idly. With Andrew Porter now in command of Hunter's division, Averell commanded Porter's brigade, including the ill-fated 27th New York. Averell recognized the importance of Henry Hill and saw that seizing that ground would deny the Confederates a place to rally and a strongpoint to defend. Consequently, he gathered his two most handy regiments, the 8th New York Militia and the 14th Brooklyn, and sent them down Dogan Ridge toward Henry Hill.

"They went down the hill in fine style," remembered Averell. "They were going so rapidly that the enemy could not keep the range." But when the two regiments reached the Warrenton Turnpike, rather than ascending Henry Hill, as Averell had ordered, someone redirected them. The 8th New York rambled along the turnpike toward Leftwich's gun and the Hampton Legion, and quickly broke. The regiment would not fight as a body again that day, though many men would join the ranks of other regiments. The 14th Brooklyn moved off course even more dramatically, circling back up the slopes of Buck Hill and Matthews Hill, where they suffered friendly fire from the 71st New York National Guard and hostile fire from the holdout Georgians and Alabamians in the pine thickets on Matthews's farm. In a few minutes, the Brooklynites too retreated back to Dogan Ridge. The disputed landscape between Matthews Hill and Henry Hill remained uncontrolled by either side.[16]

The Hampton Legion had been battling the Federal advance for nearly an hour. "By this time," wrote Pvt. John Coxe, "we didn't care much as to what happened. Our rifle fire sounded like the popping of caps, our throats were choked with powder, and we were burning up with thirst."[17] The Legion had won no important ground and had done little to reverse the disaster of the morning, but the sixty minutes of time they purchased with effort, blood, and sacrifice proved crucial to Confederate fortunes that day. While Hampton's men fought in the Warrenton Turnpike, behind them the fields of Robinson's and Henry's farms swarmed with activity. There, Beauregard and Johnston rode among the discouraged remnants of Bee's, Bartow's, and Evans's brigades. Regimental officers (many of whom had been local politicians before the war) resorted to speechmaking: "Strike for the green graves of your sires; strike for your altars and fires;

strike for God and your native land," a captain of the 4th Alabama told his troops. These efforts helped calm the bedraggled troops, and in time every Confederate regiment that had been battered on Matthews Hill would re-form. That was important, to be sure. But far more important was the time earned by the efforts of the Hampton Legion, Imboden's guns, and other stubborn Confederates, which allowed for the arrival on Henry Hill of Gen. Thomas Jonathan Jackson's five regiments of Virginia infantry—one of the largest brigades in the army.[18]

Jackson had begun the day near Mitchell's Ford, in the center of the Confederates' line along Bull Run. Johnston had then commanded his move to the Confederate left, along with Bee, Bartow, and Hampton. At about 11 A.M., Jackson pulled up at the Lewis house, not far from Lewis and Balls Fords, to support Philip St. George Cocke's brigade. But soon after he arrived, Jackson realized the emerging crisis was not at the crossings of Bull Run, but behind them, where Bee and Evans were locked in existential combat. On his own, Jackson redirected his brigade toward the sound of the guns.[19]

Few people outside his hometown of Lexington, Virginia, knew much about Thomas J. Jackson as he led his 2,600 men toward Henry Hill that morning. A West Point graduate and accomplished veteran of the Mexican conflict, he, like so many other soldiers, had faded to obscurity after the war. He taught at the Virginia Military Institute—and generally taught poorly, though with an earnestness and rigor that both faculty and students at least appreciated. With the outbreak of war, opportunity came to him anew, and he quickly found a place in the Confederate army as a brigadier general. In a year, he would be one of the most famous men in the world, but on July 21, 1861, his visage and carriage impressed no one. A young artillerymen saw him that morning: "A man of medium size wearing a shabby gray coat and on his head was an old blue cap. Across his shoulders was a strap made of calico and attached to the end of it a bag made of carpet, such as school boys use for their books. He wore also a pair of army boots—I should judge the size of them to be 9."[20]

Jackson's 2,600 men, four abreast, consumed about 600 yards of the narrow roads they traveled that day. Artillery from a variety of batteries followed. From Portici, they moved north along what is today called "Rocky Lane," then turned left onto the narrow farm road that linked the Henry and Lewis farms. The 5th Virginia infantry led the way, and as those Virginians marched onward, they encountered an increasing flood of fugitives from the morning's fighting. Some, remembered Charles Wight, hobbled along with wounds, and all of them were "tired and disheartened." Up and down the column, Jackson's men queried, "How goes the battle?" "It's a hard time, boys," said some. "We are whipped," said another. "The enemy is in overwhelming numbers, and our men are in full retreat." Another soldier of Jackson's command remembered, "Such talk was very inspiring to our troops. It was calculated to make a boy wish himself a thousand miles away and in the trundle bed at his mother's house."[21]

Soon the Virginians could see smoke rising. Artillery shells whipped over-head. "The shells pass over us with their strange hissing sounds," crashing through the thickets and blasting off the limbs of trees, wrote a Virginian. The number of wounded passing by increased. A few yelled out words of encourage-ment. One of Jackson's artillerymen recalled, "Our rapid motion and frequent running conversations with these men kept us from any grave reflections on the dangers into which we were venturing." After a mile's march, the head of Jack-son's column burst into the open on the southwest edge of Mrs. Henry's farm. "From the firing and smoke we now know that we are near the enemy," remem-bered Charles Wight of the 5th. His regiment, the first in column, turned to the right along the tree line bordering Mrs. Henry's fields. Other regiments turned left, and within a matter of minutes, Jackson's brigade stood on the rear slope of Henry Hill. Open fields undulated before them. The Henry house stood 400 yards distant, directly in front; the Robinson house stood a few hundred yards to the right. Beyond, a mile away, Union batteries boomed from Dogan Ridge and Matthews Hill.[22]

Among the retreating troops Jackson encountered during his advance were those of Barnard Bee. When Bee saw Jackson, he rode to him urgently. "Gen-eral, they are driving us," Bee said. "Sir," Jackson responded, showing the brutal determination that made him famous, "we will give them the bayonet."[23]

As Jackson and his column emerged from the narrow woods road onto Henry Hill, the general also met John Imboden leading his guns off the field. Imboden was piqued at having been left alone on Henry Hill for so long and filled Jack-son's ear with a long and profane diatribe on the subject. Jackson let the captain vent his disgust, then told him, "I'll support your battery. Unlimber right here." Imboden, however, had only three rounds left in the limbers, and he suggested heading to the rear for more ammunition. "No, not now," said Jackson. "Wait till the other guns get here." Though good for nothing more than show, Imboden's guns unlimbered on the southeastern edge of Henry Hill, 300 yards from the Henry house.[24]

When Jackson moved into position on Henry Hill, the urgency of holding the place was obvious; if Henry Hill were lost, the Yankees' path to the Confederate rear would be wide open. Consequently, Jackson chose his position on Henry Hill carefully, using the hill's contours to greatest advantage. The top of Henry Hill was fairly expansive, a gently rolling landscape large enough for two home-steads. Mrs. Henry's house, surrounded by a few fruit trees and a small cornfield, sat on the hill's northwestern shoulder, overlooking Young's Branch and the intersection of the Manassas–Sudley Road and the Warrenton Turnpike. Six hun-dred yards northeast of the widow's homestead, on the northernmost extension of the plateau, stood the small Robinson farmhouse. The gently rolling fields between the two houses were largely fallow, dotted with cedars and pines and crossed with rundown fences. (Mrs. Henry's husband, Isaac, had died years before, and the fields had not been consistently farmed in the interim). Occasional thickets covered the eastern and southeastern edges of the plateau, while mature woods lined its southern edge.

Jackson sized up the terrain quickly and chose as his defensive position the southeastern edge of the hill, a place of considerable advantage. Perhaps most importantly, the reverse slope and the pine thickets that covered it made his infantry virtually invisible to the Federals on Dogan Ridge and Matthews Hill. It also offered his raw men at least some cover from Federal artillery. At the same time, the slight swell of ground that protected Jackson's infantry offered great promise as an artillery position for his own guns. The gunners could fire from its crest and after recoil load under cover of the slope. Considering Jackson's background as an artillery tactics instructor at the Virginia Military Institute, the benefits this position afforded his artillery must have weighed heavily in his mind.

The position held other advantages as well. It offered Jackson an extensive field of fire. For the Federal infantry to reach his line, it would have to cross no less than 300 yards of open, undulating ground. Moreover, the terrain on the rear slope of the hill offered protection for Jackson's flanks. His right rested in a hollow near Young's Branch, while heavy woods on the south end of the field shielded his left. Finally, by choosing the reverse slope, Jackson avoided leading his troops through the disorganized pockets of Confederates still clogging the fields around the Robinson and Henry houses. He undoubtedly sensed that 500 retreating Confederates would discombobulate his lines faster than 5,000 attacking Federals.

The arrival of Jackson's troops coincided with a lull in the fighting, earned by stubborn Confederates along the Warrenton Turnpike and propitiously granted by Irvin McDowell. Jackson worked feverishly for the next hour establishing his line. First he placed the artillery he had immediately on hand: two guns of Standard's Thomas Artillery and Imboden's three "ornamental" pieces. Behind them, emerging from the woodland path, Jackson's infantry filed into place. On the extreme left went Col. Arthur C. Cummings's 33rd Virginia. On its right, the Valley men of the 2nd Virginia lay down in the broomsedge. The 4th and 27th Virginia took their places immediately behind the five guns. And holding down the extreme right, its own right resting in the hollow behind the Robinson house, stood Col. Kenton Harper's 5th Virginia.[25]

While Jackson formed his five regiments, Beauregard and Johnston arrived on the field. Along the way, the two generals had collected what artillery they could, and now they directed those guns to Jackson. The general released Imboden's three cannon and placed at least thirteen additional guns into line: four from Col. William Pendleton's Rockbridge Artillery; four from the Wise Artillery, that day commanded by a young lieutenant named John Pelham; and five from Squires's and Richardson's companies of the Washington Artillery of New Orleans. As fast as they arrived, Jackson put these guns on a swell of ground immediately in front of his infantry. The Washington Artillery held the left. The remaining batteries were largely intermingled, extending the line nearly to the front of the 5th Virginia Infantry on Jackson's extreme right.[26]

Jackson also worried about his flanks. Flitting about the prospective battle-field was Col. J. E. B Stuart with 300 cavalrymen. Jackson corralled Stuart and asked him if he would keep an eye out for his flanks, particularly his left, which at this point constituted the left flank of the entire army. Stuart split his force, sending half to watch the right while he rode with the other 150 men to guard Jackson's left. This was the first act in a productive partnership between Stuart and Jackson that would continue until the evening of Jackson's mortal wound nearly two years later.[27]

Jackson's line took its form while Johnston, Beauregard, and scores of others pitched in to rally the still-broken Confederate infantry in the fields to Jackson's right-rear. Beauregard wrote of the pandemonium: "Every segment of line we succeeded in forming was again dissolved while another was being formed; more than two thousand men were shouting each some suggestion to his neigh-bor, their voices mingling with the noise of the shells hurtling through the trees overhead, and all word of command drowned out in the confusion and uproar."[28]

From regiment to regiment the two generals rode, exhorting each to fall in. Johnston encountered the 4th Alabama first. The unit had lost all of its field offi-cers. Then Bartow rode up, his foot bleeding from a painful wound. "General Johnston," he exclaimed, "I am hard pressed on my right and I cannot hold my position without reinforcements." Johnston rode to the colors of the 4th Alabama and reached for them. The young color-bearer jerked them away. "Don't take them from me, General," he said, "just tell me where you wish them taken and I will carry them." Together the general and the young flag-bearer led the regiment into position.[29]

Meanwhile Beauregard, as was his wont, rode up and down the line exhort-ing his men. Arriving along the line of artillery, Beauregard yelled to Col. J. B. Walton of the Washington Artillery, "Col. Walton, do you see the enemy?"

"Yes," Walton replied.

"Then hold this position and the day is ours. Three cheers for Louisiana!" As Beauregard wheeled to ride away, a Federal shell exploded beneath him, dis-emboweling his mount. Covered with dust, the Creole calmly called for a nearby horse that was nibbling on some oats, mounted again, and dramatically rode off. Beauregard's theatrics worked magic. A man of the Hampton Legion recorded, "I cannot describe to you the effect of his appearance. Indeed all was changed in a moment. The men brightened up, dressed their ranks and gave [him] a rousing cheer."[30]

Thanks largely to Hampton's fighting, Jackson's arrival, and the influence of Beauregard and Johnston, by 1 P.M. conditions on the new Confederate front line had improved. Jackson's front now extended for more than a quarter mile along the southeast edge of Henry Hill, his 2,600 men protected on the downslope behind at least thirteen belching cannon. On the plateau southeast of the Robinson house, behind Jackson's right, the regiments that had done the fighting that morning re-formed, stacked one behind the other. Indeed some of the men in those regiments now spoiled for a fight again, anxious for a chance to redeem themselves (though redemption was hardly necessary). The flag-bearer of the 8th Georgia, Sgt. Charles Daniel, proudly held his banner aloft for all to see, friends and foes, attracting a shower of bullets and shells. "Put that flag down," someone yelled at Daniel. "They told me to hold it up when they gave it to me," Daniel retorted, "and I'll do it."

"Put down that flag," someone else yelled again, "they'll know we are here." Daniel flared, "That's what we want."[31]

With the situation stabilized, Beauregard once again asserted control. Manifestly, the battle would be fought on Henry Hill, and Beauregard wanted desperately for this to be his battle. He rode to Johnston and asked him to yield immediate command. He suggested that Johnston ride to Portici and assume the task of forwarding reinforcements to the field, while Beauregard would place them once they arrived. At first Johnston refused, but Beauregard reminded him that someone had to do it, and the job properly belonged to the commanding general on the field. Reluctantly, Johnston complied.[32]

A mile away, Union commander Irvin McDowell surely sensed that the landscape of battle had changed dramatically in the past hour and that the victory of the morning did not necessarily imply victory for the day. Though it is unlikely McDowell knew of Jackson's newly placed line of infantry on the rear slope of Mrs. Henry's farm, he could not have missed the appearance of the cannon massed in front of that line. While he surely could see the masses of retreating Confederates filtering across Henry Hill, he also witnessed the fierce resistance of the Hampton Legion in the Warrenton Turnpike and Bee's and Evans's men along Young's Branch. Those Confederates had badly damaged the only two of McDowell's regiments that had thus far been sent forward toward Henry Hill. While no one could say what victory on this battlefield would look like, McDowell had learned enough to know that *this* was not yet victory. He and his army had more work to do.

He had much with which to work. Sherman's and Keyes's brigades of Tyler's division had come across Bull Run, and in most respects the Union army's circumstance at midday was precisely as McDowell had outlined in his orders the day before: the army lay overlooking the Warrenton Turnpike, Union forces at the Stone Bridge had come across, and the road to Gainesville lay wide open, should McDowell wish to send forces west to cut the Manassas Gap Railroad. Only one of his own brigades, Burnside's, had been seriously bloodied in the morning fight. Two other regiments, the 27th New York and 8th New York State Militia, had suffered in the abortive advance toward Henry Hill and would henceforth sit out the battle. But behind these spent units, something approaching 15,000 men stacked up, ready for whatever the afternoon might bring.

In his orders issued before the battle, McDowell contemplated drawing the Confederates out and fighting on the defensive. The morning's emphatic defeat of the Confederates on Matthews Hill, however, rendered that idea moot. He could not now reasonably hope that the Confederates could or would come at him on ground of his choosing. Instead, victory would require McDowell to hunt them down on unfamiliar ground. Certainly, to anyone looking on the scene from Dogan Ridge or Buck Hill, an afternoon assault on Henry Hill offered the promise of a historic, complete victory.[33]

Or so it seemed. As the minutes and hours passed without orders from McDowell, euphoria over the morning's victory gave way to impatience and subtle confusion in the Federal ranks. The regiments, with few exceptions, stood in good order and high spirits, ready to go. But for two hours McDowell issued few orders. Circumstances on the ground surely contributed to his two-hour flinch. The dangerous uncertainty of the contested ground between Matthews Hill and Henry Hill—ground that had nearly ruined two regiments—surely inspired caution. And perhaps McDowell succumbed to the imaginings of what he could not see, filling, as some do, a void of information with assumptions that justified his fears. McDowell shared few thoughts that afternoon, leaving his subordinates to wonder at his plan, and even at his capacity. "There was a want of headquarters somewhere on the field," wrote Averell, and as a result 15,000 men spent the better part of two hours standing around with nothing to do.[34]

Meanwhile a sporadic, convulsive combat continued. The artillery of both sides maintained a persistent fire, though the Federals with their long-range rifles on Dogan Ridge and Matthews Hill gave vastly better than they received. One of Jackson's men remembered, "The bursting of shells, the shrieking of cannon balls, the crashing as they splintered the trees . . . would have filled the soul of a warrior with ecstasy. Not being a warrior but a plain citizen, I saw nothing especially entertaining in such a hubbub. . . . We lay as flat as flounders."[35]

Back on Matthews Hill and Dogan Ridge, Federal regiments also hugged the earth as Confederate shells flew overhead. "It was very laughable and amusing to see some of the men jump and squat down, trying to dodge, in all manner of ways, the cannon shots from the Rebel guns; and I was not slow at the dodging business myself," recalled one Minnesotan. "One of my company would constantly run out of ranks and up to the captain and say, 'Has the fight commenced yet?' He was not long in finding out when the fight did commence."[36]

Chapter Seven

TO HENRY HILL

At 12:30 P.M. on July 21, 1861, Erasmus Keyes's Union brigade arrived on the heights north of the Warrenton Turnpike, overlooking Henry Hill. Keyes had followed Sherman's five regiments across at Farm Ford, and the arrival of these two brigades gave McDowell six with which to make the battle's next move. (One more brigade, O. O. Howard's, would arrive soon.) The hurried march to the field certainly left Keyes's men from Connecticut and Maine hot and fatigued, but the adrenaline that attended making history rendered each man and each unit ready to go forward on McDowell's order. The problem was, McDowell had no orders to give. He may have thought the battle already won. Certainly his staff's oft-recorded proclamations of victory suggest they, at least, did. ("We have done it! We have done it!" shouted McDowell's aide James Fry.) Or perhaps McDowell still hoped to lure the Confederates into attacking him (though handing the initiative back to a defeated foe was hardly the stuff of great captains).

More likely, he simply grappled with a chaotic battlefield and an uncertain foe as the glow of morning victory yielded to uncertainty. The Confederates had blunted and bloodied the first Union attempts to sweep across the Warrenton Turnpike to Henry Hill, and Confederate cannon kept the landscape between Henry Hill, Matthews Hill, and Dogan Ridge dangerous. McDowell also could hardly judge just what forces might be waiting for him on Henry Hill. The thirteen or more guns on the back edge of the hill seemed obvious, but what lay behind them? McDowell confronted real problems and much uncertainty—much of it forged by the sudden, unexpected victory of the morning. But in yielding to uncertainty, he overlooked something else: every minute that passed worked to the Confederates' advantage.[1]

The crossing of Sherman's and Keyes's brigades cleared the way for their division commander, Daniel Tyler, to come across Bull Run as well. Though McDowell's subordinate, Tyler clearly felt emboldened to act on his own, as events at Blackburn's Ford had demonstrated. That and Tyler's slow march to the Stone Bridge that morning left the rival generals in disagreeable straits, a strained relationship that quick and total victory might resolve. Capt. James B. Fry of McDowell's staff greeted Tyler on the high ground north of Henry Hill with his proclamations of victory and vague orders to push ahead. That suited Tyler. He formed his brigade on Sherman's left—on the high ground around the old Carter mansion, Pittsylvania—and at about 1:30 started the dangerous march southward toward Henry Hill. The 1st Connecticut ventured out first. Confederate artillery on Henry Hill soon had the men dropping for cover ("Down boys, down!") and rising to run to the rhythm of the cannon blasts ("Rise up men! Up! Go!"). The regiment passed evidence of the morning fight. "We found a dead Georgian," wrote Capt. Joseph Hawley, "then a wounded one waving a white handkerchief, and told him he was safe." The sight of wounded barely distracted many others. They worried only that the battle might be over before they got into it. "We won't get a pop at them," men muttered as they quickened their step.[2]

Keyes's men approached the battlefield from a new direction—the northeast—and therefore seem to have attracted less attention from the Confederates on Henry Hill than did McDowell's main force on Matthews Hill and Dogan Ridge. Still, the four Union regiments occasionally collided with holdout Rebels in the thickets north of the Warrenton Turnpike. The encounters, which invariably resulted in Confederate flight, only encouraged the Union troops. They confidently moved toward Henry Hill but, at least at first, with an uncertain mission.

For generals on the battlefields of the Civil War, information about the enemy came in small glimpses and snippets. Sometime before 2 P.M., Tyler had spotted a Confederate battery on Henry Hill—almost certainly one of the batteries on Jackson's line. Tyler sent word to Keyes to capture it or drive it off. The two generals could see Confederate infantry near the guns, but they in fact had no idea that they had discovered the right of Jackson's new line—its most vulnerable spot. A stark fact illustrates just how little Keyes and Tyler understood the situation: they would undertake the greatest opportunity the Union army would have all day with just two regiments, the 2nd Maine and the 3rd Connecticut. Leaving Van Pelt Hill to their left, the two New England regiments marched directly south down the gentle slopes toward Young's Branch. Near the stream, the 3rd Connecticut encountered some Confederate cavalrymen who tried to screen Jackson's right flank. The Connecticut men quickly swept these away, and the two regiments splashed across Young's Branch and halted at the foot of Henry Hill. Hampton's South Carolinians held the Warrenton Turnpike above them.[3]

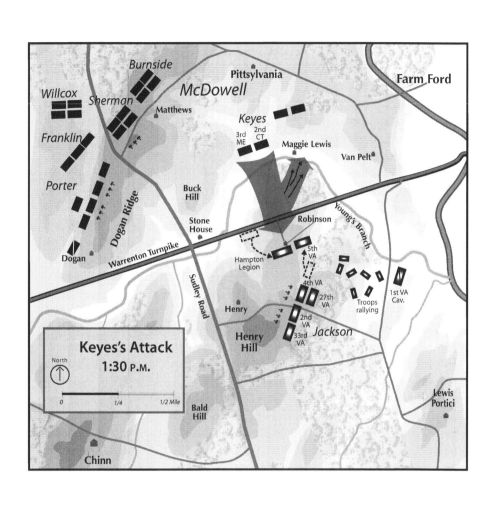

Burnside

Willcox

Sherman

Franklin

Porter

Dogan Ridge

Dogan

Warrenton Turnpike

Pittsylvania

McDowell

Matthews

Buck
Hill

Stone
House

Keyes

3rd
ME

2nd
CT

Maggie Lewis

Robinson

Hampton
Legion

Young's Branch

5th
VA

4th VA

Farm Ford

Van Pelt

27th
VA

Troops
rallying

1st VA
Cav.

Sudley Road

Henry

Henry
Hill

2nd
VA

33rd
VA

Jackson

Lewis
Portici

Bald
Hill

Chinn

Keyes's Attack

North

1:30 P.M.

0   1/4   1/2 Mile

Keyes placed the 2nd Maine on the left of the 3rd Connecticut and ordered a charge. Their double ranks extended for nearly 400 yards, and the New Englanders pressed up the bare slope of Henry Hill toward the Robinson house. After about 100 yards, the line stopped, under fire from the men of Hampton's Legion. Keyes ordered his men down, and for several minutes a musketry battle raged. The line of Yankees overlapped the Legion's right by a significant margin, and it seemed to one of the Carolinians that "we were in danger of being surrounded." Hampton ordered his men out of the road and back to the Robinson house: "Fall back in good order, men!"[4]

The Carolinians carefully gathered their wounded and executed a not-so-careful 100-yard retreat along the lane leading from the turnpike to the Robinson house, leaving one company in the road toward the bottom of the hill. That company fought entirely alone for many minutes, subject, as one man said, "to a raking fire." Soldiers wrestled with their weapons, repeating time and again the nine-step process of loading and firing. In the roadbed, Charles Hutson of the Legion loaded his gun, carefully put on his spectacles, took "good aim & fired my first shot." As he reloaded, he recalled, "a rifle ball struck me in the head, a little above the forehead; & the violence of the concussion felled me to the earth immediately." Hutson flung aside his glasses and attempted to reload, "But the blood was gushing over my face & blinding my eyes, [and] I found it impossible to do so." Fearing faintness from loss of blood, Hutson wrapped his head with a handkerchief, put his hat on, and wrapped that tightly with a silk cloth. By then, his company had started up the hill in retreat. Hutson followed, and again stopped to reload. This time a Union bullet shattered his rifle. Hutson gave up the effort and hurried to the Robinson house, Union bullets splattering the ground around him. He and the remainder of his company joined the rest of the Hampton Legion around the house and its several outbuildings. Lucky were the men who had a smokehouse or corncrib for shelter. After nearly two hours in combat, the Hampton Legion prepared for yet more. By this time, at least one man had found calm amid the mayhem. Days later, he explained, "I was not a bit more excited when I was in the battle than I am rite [sic] now."[5]

Hampton, Col. Kenton Harper of Jackson's 5th Virginia, General Bee, and many lesser officers cobbled together a line to confront the Yankees. Recalled a man of Hampton's Legion, "We got mixed up with many strange troops, apparently in panic and whom it was said that our fight at the Warrenton Turnpike had saved, but just how we did not know." The lull granted by Keyes's pause would be brief. Soon, the blue-clad soldiers wiped their sweaty faces, adjusted their cartridge boxes, loaded their weapons, and resumed their advance up Henry Hill.[6]

Keyes's two regiments surged across the Warrenton Turnpike (passing some of the dead and wounded of Hampton's Legion), and the opposing lines saw each other at once. Keyes's officers had never seen a Southern soldier dressed in any color, but they had seen several Northern units dressed in gray, and some of those officers, remarkably, presumed that these gray-clad men in front simply must be Federals. The Southerners flinched momentarily, too, fearful of firing on what might be their own men. But Keyes's troops continued to move toward them, and the Confederates quickly concluded that such a purposeful advance must be hostile. The jumbled line of Virginians, Carolinians, Georgians, and Alabamians—probably 1,100 men in all—leveled their muskets and loosed a volley that rocked Keyes's ranks. "We were staggered," admitted one Connecticut soldier. But still the New Englanders came on. The landscape around the Robinson house exploded in battle.[7]

Keyes had all the advantage of position, moving as he was on the Confederate flank, and his advance put the Hampton Legion and the 5th Virginia in dire jeopardy. It was, wrote Capt. James Conner of the Legion, "an awful fight." The Carolinians and Virginians took cover behind the Robinson house and its outbuildings. "It was terrible, and the men were falling all around, and fearing they would be surrounded," wrote Conner. "It was the only time in the day the men looked dashed." Some of Bee's and Evans's men, still trying to rally, rushed to join the Legion but were too few to make an impact. For a time the 3rd Connecticut claimed the Robinson house, but soon the 5th Virginia rallied and made life miserable anew for Keyes's two regiments. One Federal wrote of the Confederates, "They knew they had to fight or die, and so they went at it, and I tell you . . . they will fight when you get them penned." The Confederate fire became so hot, said Keyes, that "exposure to it of five minutes would have annihilated my whole line." Keyes ordered a retreat, first to the cover of the Warrenton Turnpike, and then by the left flank to the base of the hill. Keyes and his two regiments hovered there menacingly for some time and then filed quietly along Young's Branch toward the Stone Bridge. Though he would remain literally behind the right of the Confederate line on Henry Hill for the next two hours, Keyes was done fighting for the day. Jackson's line was safe, at least for the present. His men, though, had come to an inevitable realization: "We begin to think a battle is not so nice as some had imagined."[8]

The geometry of Keyes's attack—focused on the Confederate flank—hinted at its promise. But in fact no one in a blue uniform fully recognized that at the time. Keyes's attack amounted to an insufficient swipe at a portion of the Confederate line that was both visible and accessible. No one on Tyler's front seems to have understood the larger Confederate position, and thus the potential of this attack. McDowell, on the other hand, perhaps knew something of the Confederate position, but knew nothing of Tyler's attack until it tumbled back down the hill. Such lack of coordination would plague the Union army that afternoon. Keyes's misadventure was a mere foreshadow of the problems the Federals would confront in the coming hours.[9]

As Keyes's men filed down Henry Hill in unmolested retreat, quiet settled over the field for the first time in eight hours. "There was a calm—an indescribable calm," wrote one Northerner. "Every man on the field felt it. I doubt if anyone could describe it." Along Jackson's line, the men still willingly lay down, but the officers sat on stumps of trees or chatted in small groups. Jackson rode up and down his ranks, a wounded finger wrapped in a bloody handkerchief. His horse limped slightly from a wound in the thigh. A mile to the northwest, the batteries of Ricketts (Battery I, 1st U.S.) and Griffin (Battery D, 5th U.S., also known as the West Point Battery) stood mute, the men milling beside the guns, waiting for orders. Behind them thousands of Union troops filled the fields on John Dogan's and Edgar Matthews's farms, nervously hoping the battle over and won, but fearing it was not.[10]

It was not.

At about 2 P.M., after more than two hours of preparation, McDowell finally issued orders for a forward movement to Henry Hill. Those orders did not call for the sweeping final attack expected by men on both sides. Instead, McDowell summoned to headquarters his chief of artillery, William F. Barry, and directed him to move two batteries to Henry Hill. The army commander outlined no infantry attack—indeed, he did not even insist on infantry support for the batteries. Rather, like Hunter that morning, it seemed McDowell intended to follow the tactics of Napoleon: roll artillery to within a few hundred yards of the enemy line and blast away. But the small arms in the hands of Napoleon's opponents were different machines from those in the hands of many Confederates on July 21, 1861. Wellington's smoothbore muskets might hit something at 100 yards. Rifle-muskets in the hands of Confederates on Henry Hill had a range of more than 300 yards and could kill at a half mile. The two batteries—mostly rifled cannon with a range of well over a mile—would put themselves in a killing zone. More than that, the batteries would go first, without infantry clearing the way in advance. Clearly, McDowell envisioned no decisive attempt to destroy the Confederate position on Henry Hill. Rather, this was a partial, halting effort to learn something more about the Confederate positions on Henry Hill—to stare the Confederates down or, at worst, to understand better what victory on this field might require (if indeed it required anything more than this show). According to McDowell's plan, most of the 15,000 infantrymen he had worked so hard to bring to the field that morning would stand by and wait for developments.

Barry, who had been with McDowell's army for only three days, rode to Griffin and Ricketts and gave them the order. Griffin, who would emerge as one of the war's most efficient-but-truculent subordinates, protested vehemently. His battery had been firing at the Confederate cannons on Henry Hill for more than an hour, all the while at a distance easily reached by his rifled cannon but largely beyond the range of the mostly smoothbore guns on the Confederate line. Griffin could see clearly that the summit of Henry Hill was no place for batteries, especially without solid infantry support. Ricketts protested, too, sending an officer to headquarters. "I saw at a glance," Ricketts said, "that I was going into great peril for my horses and men." Their protests failed. The orders stood. The gunners limbered their pieces and trotted down the slope of Dogan Ridge toward Henry Hill.[11]

If McDowell did not see the need for infantry to accompany the artillery, at least Major Barry did. While Griffin's and Ricketts's batteries moved out, Barry rushed about hunting up infantry support. With the help of Gen. Samuel P. Heintzelman, he gathered five regiments in short order: the 14th Brooklyn and U.S. Marine Battalion of Porter's brigade, the 1st Minnesota of W. B. Franklin's brigade, and the 11th New York and 38th New York of Orlando Willcox's brigade. "Come on boys and show them what New York can do," yelled the officers of the Fire Zouaves (the 11th New York). "And with that," remembered one Zouave, "the pet lambs were led to slaughter."[12]

Before making his final move to Henry Hill, Griffin renewed his protest to Barry. "I went to Major Barry," he recounted, "and told him I had no support and that it was impossible to go there without support." Barry reassured him that the Fire Zouaves were ready to go. Griffin remained unsatisfied. "I told him," Griffin later testified, "I wished he would permit them to go and get in position on the hill—let the batteries . . . come into position behind them, and then let them fall back." Events would prove this to be a reasonable (and necessary) proposal, but Barry—no doubt feeling the pressure of a disapproving boss—refused Griffin's request. The beleaguered captain tried another tack: "I told him the better place for our battery was on a hill [Chinn Ridge] about 500 yards in rear of the one to which we were then ordered," out of immediate danger should the infantry support fail. No, said Barry. McDowell's orders were explicit. Henry Hill was the objective, and there they would go, with the artillery in the advance. Frustrated, Griffin insisted anew that the Fire Zouaves would not support the guns properly. "Yes they will," Barry retorted; "at any rate it is General McDowell's order to go there."

"I will go," Griffin said, "but mark my words, they will not support us."[13]

Griffin's five guns (three 10-pounder Parrotts and two 12-pounder howitzers)[14] led the eleven-gun column to Henry Hill. At a gallop they moved down the face of Dogan Ridge past the Stone House, across the ford over Young's Branch, and up Henry Hill along the worn bed of Sudley Road. "The horses had their noses and tails extended, and the drivers were lying low over their necks, yelling and plying their whips," wrote an onlooker in the 1st Minnesota. "It was a splendid, thrilling sight." As the Federals neared the top, an officer "hallooed" to Lt. Charles Hazlett, leading Griffin's battery, to take the guns not to the left but to the right, toward Chinn Ridge. Dutifully, Hazlett veered right. Surprised at the unexpected change in direction, Griffin rode quickly to the head of the column, stopped it, and ordered it onto Henry Hill. The turnaround took time, and meanwhile Ricketts's battery rumbled to the front, tore down the fence bordering

Sudley Road, and bore left into position just south of Mrs. Henry's house, only 350 yards from the Confederate line.[15]

As soon as Ricketts's cannoneers dropped the trails of their guns, bullets began to slap into the limbers and thud into the men and horses. Ricketts instantly realized that Confederate sharpshooters filled the Henry house, only about sixty yards from his left piece. He turned some of his guns toward the house and opened fire. "I . . . thoroughly riddled it," he said later. The sharpshooters scurried out and headed for safer ground. Ricketts could not know that the Confederate sharpshooters shared the house with its owner, virtually immobile eighty-five-year-old Judith Carter Henry, her daughter, and a slave. A shell from one of Ricketts's guns exploded in the house, wounding Mrs. Henry in three places. She died before nightfall, the only civilian to perish in the battle.[16]

The Confederate sharpshooters gone, Ricketts redirected the fire of his six 10-pounder Parrott rifles toward Jackson's line, just 350 undulating yards away. Meanwhile, Griffin's guns arrived on Ricketts's left and unlimbered just north of the Henry house, within 400 yards of the enemy. Griffin placed his pieces atop a low rise, while the Confederate guns stood under slight cover on the far edge of the hill. As soon as Griffin's guns unlimbered and opened fire, the Union artillerymen recognized the great folly of their move forward. On Dogan Ridge they had been largely beyond the range of the smaller Confederate guns on Henry Hill, but now the Union advance made them an easy target for the Confederate guns. "We presented a better mark for them than they did for us," recalled Lieutenant Hazlett. The guns roared.[17]

Meanwhile, the Federal infantry support promised by Major Barry hurried into position. The 11th New York led the column, its advance impressive. "I was struck by the manner they marched forward, very handsomely in line of battle," Barry remembered. The spectacle gave Barry hope the regiment would do as well once the shooting started. The regiment, bedizened in blue uniforms with red fireman's shirts, took position on the slope immediately behind Ricketts's guns. Barry intended for the 14th Brooklyn to follow the 11th New York up Sudley Road, but before the men from Brooklyn crossed Young's Branch someone stopped them, and there the regiment remained for some time. This threw the Marine battalion (mostly fresh recruits lacking the aura of later-day marines) and the 1st Minnesota to the fore. The marines moved up the hill and sat down in column to the left of the Zouaves, while the 1st Minnesota took position considerably to the right of the 11th, bordering the woods on the south edge of the Henry farm. One Minnesotan conceded the men dodged noticeably as the Confederate shells screeched overhead. "It was a new and trying ordeal that strained the nerves and hurt our feelings," the man recalled, "but I am not aware that any other hurt was done."[18]

The 38th New York, commanded by future general John Henry Hobart Ward, also ascended Henry Hill, veering off to the left of the Henry house. The New Yorkers pushed well out into Mrs. Henry's fields, even before Griffin's guns arrived to their right-rear. In front was "an unseen enemy." The artillery on Jackson's line flailed the New Yorkers, "pouring out upon us their deadly shower of shell and canister."[19]

The short-range duel of artillery across Mrs. Henry's brush-strewn fields raged for probably twenty minutes. Every moment revealed something new about the experience of combat. One gunner came into battle convinced the horses of his battery "would be scared and give us trouble." Instead, he remembered, "the horses seemed to be perfectly indifferent to the danger and the only trouble was to keep them from getting tangled in harness in their effort to eat the scanty grass at their feet." The Confederate artillerymen labored in a contest rendered much more even by the suddenly reduced range between the combatants, allowing their 6- and 12-pounder smoothbore guns to do real damage. John Pelham, a West Point graduate from Alabama who commanded the Wise Artillery of Virginia, concluded after a walk over the battlefield a day later, "war is not glorious as novelists would have you believe." But while the aftermath of battle sickened him, Pelham claimed the experience of battle itself "delighted and fascinated me." He wrote on July 23, "I am now ashamed of the feelings I had in those hours of danger. The whistling of bullets and shells was music to me. . . . I feared not death in any form. . . . I gloried in it."[20]

Surely Pelham would not have reveled so joyously had the Union artillery fire been more accurate. Most Union shells whistled beyond the Confederate line, crashing through the pines or exploding harmlessly. But enough found their mark to render the experience a severe test of will—especially for the infantrymen behind the cannons, who could do nothing but huddle and cover their heads. "What love we manifested for the soil of Virginia that day," recalled one of them. Sgt. Charles Bell and Pvt. Benjamin Bradley were students from Lexington's Washington College, serving in the 4th Virginia. Bell and Bradley had been childhood playmates: they enrolled at Washington College and roomed together, enlisted in the army together, and now messed together. As they lay on the edge of Mrs. Henry's farm, a solid shot whistled in from the Union cannon across the field and killed them both.[21]

The nearness of the Union cannon and the constant crashing of shells rattled nearly everyone. One of the artillerymen remembered years later, "I do not recall the fact that I was frightened badly, but do recall the fact that I wished it was all over and I was well out of it." Jackson rode constantly along his line of infantry, telling his men again and again, "All's well, all's well." A man of the 5th Virginia recorded, "He seems to be very quiet, so we think that all is all right, and that this is like battles generally." Jackson directed anyone who could hear him to wait until the enemy closed to within 50 yards, and then "charge with the bayonet." For his part, Col. Arthur Cummings, who commanded the 33rd Virginia on the left of Jackson's line, doubted his inexperienced men could wait that long without breaking.[22]

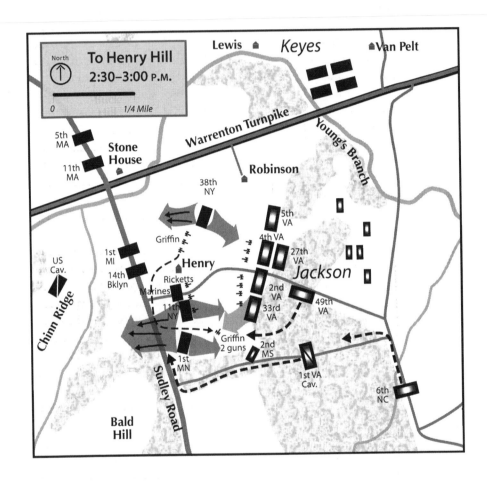

North

To Henry Hill
2:30–3:00 P.M.

0   1/4 Mile

Lewis   Keyes   Van Pelt

Warrenton Turnpike

Young's Branch

5th MA

Stone House

11th MA

38th NY

Robinson

Griffin

5th VA

4th VA

27th VA

US Cav.

1st MI

Henry

Jackson

14th Bklyn

Ricketts

Marines

2nd VA

49th VA

11th NY

33rd VA

Griffin 2 guns

2nd MS

1st MN

Chinn Ridge

Sudley Road

1st VA Cav.

6th NC

Bald Hill

Griffin's and Ricketts's Union guns had been on the hill for probably twenty minutes by now. The 11th New York (the Fire Zouaves) and the battalion of U.S. Marines waited behind Ricketts's battery as the 1st Minnesota marched up the hill. The 38th New York lay in the fields between the Henry and Robinson houses, off to Griffin's left-front—near enough to provide protection should the battery need it. Despite the proximity of the Confederate line of artillery, one great mystery remained for McDowell and his subordinates: What Confederates lay beyond? The question had immediate implications for the Union batteries, of course (as both Ricketts and Griffin had tried to point out), but the question also loomed large over Union prospects for the day. The question needed an answer, and when Union division commander Samuel Heintzelman (a wizened veteran— a "mass of wrinkles," wrote one man) rode onto the hill, he surveyed the ground and then gave orders to "feel the woods." The order transformed McDowell's idea for a limited movement of two batteries to Henry Hill into something vastly different: the placement of the batteries begot the effort by McDowell's subordinates to protect them, which in turn triggered an infantry advance that would spin the battle out of McDowell's control.

Just short of 3 P.M., the Union infantry on Henry Hill started to move.[23]

On the Confederate line, Cpl. Morton Brown stood at his gun in Pendleton's Rockbridge Artillery when he saw the Union movement. "I could see their long columns of infantry coming up in the rear of their artillery," moving obliquely off toward Jackson's left. "The United States flag—that once proud flag, now the hated badge of a self-imposed despotism[—]was borne in seeming triumph near the front." The Union infantry passed the batteries into the scrubby field beyond. "At once a shout of defiance rose [a]long our line," Brown wrote. His comrades urged him to aim his cannon at the flag, but instead Brown trained it on the ranks of soldiers marching near it. He ordered a load of canister. The blast whooshed through the brushy field and into the Union lines.[24]

Quite by happenstance, three Union regiments nearly joined together for the forward movement, something that would not happen again that afternoon. The 1st Minnesota—dressed in the most ubiquitous nonstandard apparel of the day, red shirts—marched obliquely toward the woods on the south edge of Henry Hill. The 11th New York—also in red shirts—moved a bit ahead and to the Minnesotans' left. The 38th New York, moving out from its position near Griffin's guns, marched on its own, to the left of the Fire Zouaves. This disconnected Union battle line edged forward. On the extreme left flank of the army, the men of the 33rd Virginia and their quiet, fretful colonel, Mexican war veteran Arthur C. Cummings, saw them approach. "Boys, they are coming," Cummings cautioned his men, "now wait until they get close before you fire."[25]

Heintzelman and his aide Col. William Averell rode in front of the Union line. From horseback, Averell spotted the distant line of battle first, not 100 yards off. "What troops are those in front of us?" he asked Heintzelman, then took out his binoculars for a closer look. Heintzelman described a line of men "drawn up at shoulder-arm, dressed in citizens clothes." He later explained, "It did not strike me at first who they were."

Uncertainty pulsed along the Union line. A German soldier in the 1st Minnesota had no doubt: "Dem is secessers," he yelled. He raised his gun and fired. The commander of the 1st, Willis Gorman, thought he saw a United States flag in front of the distant line. "No!" Gorman yelled. They are friends." For a few awkward moments the two lines glared at each other, while confused yells passed along the line and even between enemies. In front of the 1st Minnesota, an officer stepped out, approached Capt. Alexander Wilkin, and asked the identity of these troops. Captain Wilkin returned the question: Your regiment? The 2nd Mississippi, the stranger answered, and the Minnesotans promptly asked him to dismount. Wilkin dispatched the confused Confederate, Lt. Col. Bartley Barry Boone of the 2nd Mississippi, to the rear, a prisoner.[26]

In front of the 11th New York, Heintzelman deliberated the identity of the opposing line for only a moment. He turned to the Fire Zouaves and ordered them to charge. "That looks like it!" yelled a Virginian. The 33rd Virginia opened fire, though the first volley hardly impressed. Remembered a man of the 2nd Virginia: "I recollect that first volley and how unfavorably it affected me. It was apparently made [by the 33rd] with guns raised at an angle of forty-five degrees, and I was fully assured that their bullets would not hit the Yankees, unless they were nearer to heaven than they were generally located by our people."[27]

Smoke and bullets enveloped the Union line. Among the Minnesotans, confusion governed. An officer in the 11th New York yelled, "Down every one of you!" As one, the 11th New York and 1st Minnesota dove into the tall grass in time to miss the second Confederate volley. One Minnesotan asserted it was "the heaviest fire of musketry ever experienced by any regiment." The smoke "did not permit us to see anything clearly," remembered another man of the 1st Minnesota, "but bullets were hissing above our heads, and we could see red flashes through the smoke in front of us—at which we directed our fire." A Virginian admitted to a "most destructive fire" from the Union line, but Cummings's men did not run. Minnesotans and New Yorkers fell by the dozens.[28]

If the heavy Confederate volleys had discomfited the lines of Union infantry, they also caused havoc in Ricketts's battery, which continued firing about 100 yards behind the infantry. "Probably there never was such a destructive fire for a few minutes," recounted Averell. "It looked as if every horse and man of that battery just laid down and died right off." The Marine battalion, directly behind the guns, broke almost immediately, "struck," testified Averell, "with such astonishment, such consternation, that they could not do anything." Officers tried to hold them to their work, but the new recruits "gave way in disorder." The moment still stands as perhaps the most inglorious retreat in Marine Corps history, though many marines would find their way back into the battle later in the day.[29]

Off to the left, the 38th New York claimed to have moved with the Zouaves, "side-by-side," but clearly without much precision. Still, the battle exploded in front of them as well. "My men stuck like good fellows," wrote a captain of the 38th, "and if I do say it, was in the thickest and done some of the best fighting." Wrote Capt. Calvin DeWitt: "The balls whistled past my ears like hail, and a corporal of my company was shot. He was not two feet from me. A ball struck him in the throat and went straight through his neck." The man went down on his side; "O dear, I am shot!" he said. Staff officer Averell later praised the 38th, saying the regiment "held on very well—indeed splendidly."[30]

On the crest of the hill, the men of the 11th and 38th New York and 1st Minnesota fired perhaps four or five volleys each before they too, company by company and squad by squad, fell back. The 38th New York clung closely to Griffin's guns north of the Henry house, but farther to the right things went awry in a hurry. Officers rushed upon the 1st Minnesota and 11th New York, beseeching them to come back and fight. One of the most desperate was Ricketts, who rode up to the formerly vaunted Zouaves and yelled, "For God's sake boys, save my battery!"[31]

If Ricketts's battery were to be saved, someone other than the Fire Zouaves would have to do it. As the 11th New York and 1st Minnesota cascaded down the slope toward Sudley Road, new horrors emerged. J. E. B. Stuart's 150 Southern horsemen—patrolling Jackson's left flank—appeared in Sudley Road opposite the Federal right. In a scene repeated often this day, Stuart mistook the disorganized Union troops for Confederates. He rode to them and, as he later wrote, "exclaimed with all my might: 'Don't run boys; we are here.' They paid very little attention to this appeal." A nearby U.S. flag hinted at Stuart's error. He rushed back to his troopers and ordered them to charge.[32]

From just 70 yards away, the Confederate horsemen rode at the Yankees "like an arrow from a bow," said one Virginian. The screaming Confederates closed the distance in seconds. Men of the 11th tried to arrange themselves to fire; some knelt, while others stood. Stuart's men fired the first volley, but galloping horses made for erratic aim, and the bullets flew harmlessly over the Yankees' heads. The Federals immediately answered with a nasty volley. Each side claimed dreadful slaughter of the other. "Men and horses fell like ten-pins," claimed one New Yorker. "We shot the wretches down by scores," asserted a Confederate. In fact, the clash was more street-corner melee than military confrontation.[33]

The Confederates charged right through the Federals. One Southern horseman tried to leap his mount *over* the Union line; instead, the steed struck a Union soldier in the chest and sent him tumbling backward. "I leaned down in the saddle," the cavalryman wrote, "rammed the muzzle of [my] carbine into the stomach of my man and pulled the trigger. I could not help feeling a little sorry for the fellow as he lifted his handsome face to mine while he tried to get his bayonet up to meet me; but he was too slow, for the carbine blew a hole as big as my arm clear through him."[34]

"It was then about time to run," wrote one Northerner, and many did. Stuart tried to re-form his men for another attack, but the Fire Zouaves and Minnesotans sought cover in the woods west of Sudley Road, rendering another cavalry charge impossible. Well-satisfied nonetheless, Stuart drew his men back to once again cover Jackson's flank. Though his attack actually did little physical damage to the Federals (only a handful fell wounded or killed), the melee came at just the wrong time for the two Union regiments. Neither the 1st Minnesota nor the Fire Zouaves would fight again as a unit that day. In only twenty minutes of combat atop Henry Hill and in the melee in Sudley Road, the two regiments had each lost nearly forty killed. No other Union regiments would lose more.[35]

The nearly identical experiences of the 1st Minnesota and the 11th New York would lead to very different stories. The 1st Minnesota went on to become one of the legendary regiments in American military history, losing at Gettysburg a greater percentage of men killed or wounded than any other regiment of the war. The 11th New York—beset by dissension, bad leadership, unmet expectations, and poor discipline—simply faded to obscurity, to be disbanded within a year.

Elsewhere, officers of both armies rushed troops to the newly joined battle. By now, Johnston had been back at Portici for more than an hour. Information flowed in and out of the army's headquarters at dizzying speed. From Captain Alexander's signal station on Wilcoxen's Hill came warning of still more Federal troops at Sudley Ford (O. O. Howard's brigade). Not long after reporting that, Alexander wigwagged even more ominous news: a cloud of dust marked a column moving toward Manassas Junction from the northwest, heading toward the Confederate rear. Could it be Patterson's troops from the Shenandoah Valley?[36]

Events on Henry Hill pressed Johnston so hard that, for the moment, he ignored Alexander's warnings about approaching Yankees. If the Union army could not be stopped on Henry Hill, it mattered little if Patterson's entire army walked onto the field. (In fact, the mystery column was one of Johnston's own wagon trains, marching overland from Winchester). Johnston instead looked for additional troops to throw at the growing emergency on the Henry farm. He sent orders to brigade commanders Early, Holmes, and Bonham, hurrying them along. Johnston also rode to Philip St. George Cocke's brigade of Virginians, which defended Lewis and Balls Fords only a few hundred yards down the slope from Portici. Union skirmishers from Tyler's division still occupied the woods opposite Cocke's position; Cocke hesitated to withdraw in the face of them, but Johnston insisted. Urgency hung over the field. He ordered Cocke to move his troops to the battlefield with all possible haste. The undersized, undertrained 49th Virginia, commanded by ex-governor of Virginia William "Extra Billy" Smith, was the first of Cocke's regiments to move.[37]

Johnston soon returned to Portici to shuttle additional troops to Beauregard on Henry Hill. Between 2 and 3 P.M., he began a process that would continue until the battle's end. First, he dispatched Col. Charles Fisher's 6th North Carolina, fresh off the trains at Manassas Junction, to Beauregard. Johnston himself cobbled together what amounted to three companies from a variety of commands and hurried them off toward the battle as well, under the command of his own chief of ordnance, Col. Francis J. Thomas. This mini-battalion soon joined Billy Smith's 49th Virginia in its march toward Jackson's left flank.

Elsewhere, small bands of disorganized but determined veterans of the Matthews Hill fight also found their way back to the battlefield. Colonel Bartow prepared to lead his Georgians into the fight again. Other groups of Mississippians, Alabamians, and South Carolinians—men who had already given much to the fight on Matthews Hill—organized themselves into makeshift battalions behind Jackson's line.[38]

General Bee, too, worked to collect his scattered command, determined to return to the battle. In the process, he helped create a legend. Several hundred yards behind Jackson's line, Bee found a body of troops standing in wait. "What regiment is this?" he asked.

"Why General, don't you know your own men?" responded one of the captains. "This is what is left of the 4th Alabama."

"This is all of my brigade that I can find," said Bee with a hint of discouragement. "Will you follow me back to where the fighting is going on?"

"Yes, General, we will go wherever you lead, and do whatever you say."

Then Bee pointed off to his left, where Jackson's line stood in full combat with Union troops on Henry Hill. "Yonder stands Jackson like a stone wall; let's go to his assistance."

With that, the Alabamians headed back into the battle, Bee at their front.[39]

That afternoon, troops from both sides spilled onto Henry Hill like water from a garden hose, rushing along the narrow roads leading to it, and then released into combat, spreading across the plateau. After the repulse of the 1st Minnesota and the 11th New York, brigade commander Col. Orlando Willcox patched together a battalion of disorganized but willing Zouaves. He offered to push them to the woods on the right of Ricketts's battery—the woods that seemed to harbor so many of the riflemen that wrought havoc on the batterymen. "The movement was successful," Willcox later wrote. "About 20 of the enemy were killed & wounded, a few prisoners taken & the woods cleared." This seemingly small accomplishment would have large implications a few minutes later.[40]

Meanwhile the 14th Brooklyn rushed up Sudley Road, making its way through crowds of Zouaves "running humpbacked in disorderly retreat." The 38th New York also slid into position behind Griffin's battery north of the Henry house and lay down there to escape the enemy artillery fire. The 1st Michigan of Orlando Willcox's brigade and the 5th and 11th Massachusetts of William B. Franklin's brigade were also on the way. All the while, the Union artillery clung to the crest of Henry Hill, still swept by Confederate cannon fire.[41]

Griffin and Ricketts had warned against putting their guns in such a place, and their warnings now seemed increasingly accurate. In Ricketts's battery, dozens of horses lay dead or writhing, leaving the guns immovable except by hand. That meant one thing for Ricketts: the survival of his battery depended solely on Union victory. For him, there could be no retreat.

North of the Henry house, Griffin had escaped the ravages of Confederate musketry but suffered severely from accurate Confederate artillery fire. One of Griffin's brightest lieutenants, Charles Hazlett, suggested the battery withdraw. But Griffin would not yet give up the fight—he knew his withdrawal meant certain doom for Ricketts, just 200 yards to his right. Instead, the combative Captain Griffin offered a plan to neutralize the Confederate artillery. He told Hazlett to stay with three guns in his present position north of the Henry house while he, Griffin, took two 12-pounder howitzers beyond the right of Ricketts's line. If he could put a couple of his pieces on the flank of the Confederate line of artillery, he might be able to break it up with an enfilading fire. It was a risky, even desperate idea, but in the absence of Union infantry on Henry Hill, it might be the only chance the Yankees would have to hold the hilltop.

Griffin's men limbered the two pieces and moved down the hill to Sudley Road, where they turned to the left. Several hundred yards later they turned left again, rumbled up the slope to the right of Ricketts's battery, and went into position not far from the woods recently cleared by Colonel Willcox and his detachment of Zouaves (a deed that rendered this section of the field quiet enough that Griffin perceived it as safe). Quickly, the cannoneers readied the pieces for action. A ragged remnant of the 11th New York took position not far from the two guns, the only apparent support near enough to help Griffin should something go awry.[42]

Probably a thousand eyes watched Griffin's movement—at least its beginning and its end were visible to most of Jackson's line. Of all those eyes, none watched more intently than Col. Arthur Cummings of the 33rd Virginia. Jackson had warned Cummings to keep an eye out for Union artillery. That required the colonel to walk up the crest of the rise in front of him, and there he was when Griffin's two guns rumbled and jumped through Mrs. Henry's field to a small knoll no more than 200 yards from the Virginians' line. Cummings's men had stood well their first fire against the Fire Zouaves and 1st Minnesota, but their commander still harbored great doubt about their ability to fight. They were, he admitted, "undrilled" and "raw and undisciplined." In their ranks hovered an aura of confusion and uncertainty, the product of continued Union artillery fire and the intense infantry clash of twenty minutes ago. As Cummings watched Griffin's two guns approach, he doubted his men would stand in the face of artillery fire at so close a range. That left two choices: retreat or advance. Cummings rushed back to his regiment, determined to advance.[43]

As Cummings approached his regiment, the first of the latest wave of troops sent to the field by Johnston arrived: 450 men of the 49th Virginia and their commander, Col. William Smith. A former governor of Virginia and a veteran of Congress and business, Smith was, at sixty-three, the oldest and most famous citizen-soldier on the field that day. Unschooled in all things military, Smith might have been the closest thing to a populist commander the Civil War produced. He relied entirely on a practical understanding of men and practiced his military responsibility without pretension, even on occasion reading commands to his regiment right out of a drill book. On this warm Sunday, Smith brought both great patriotic intensity and an umbrella to the battlefield, the latter to shade himself in the hot sun. (Mid-battle, a nearby regimental commander sent orders to Smith to dispense with the umbrella, saying that he was "making himself a target for the whole Yankee army." Smith complied, though "under protest.") Just before 3 P.M., Smith reported to Beauregard near the Robinson house. Beauregard immediately ordered him toward the left of the 33rd Virginia to extend Jackson's flank.[44]

Smith's march took him behind the length of Jackson's line. As he neared his destination, a bullet struck his horse in the shoulder. Smith dismounted and led his battalion on foot. Sensing the moment, Smith stepped out in front of his battalion and made what one man called a "spirited speech, short and to the point." A few more yards, a few more maneuvers, and Smith's line neared the left flank of the 33rd Virginia. Directly in front were Union cannons, newly arrived. Smith admonished his men "to be cool and deliberate, and not to fire without an object under sight." He remembered later, "I am quite sure the enemy had not yet discovered us."[45]

That was only partly true. Griffin's batterymen—all of them Regular army— expertly unlimbered their two 12-pounder howitzers, sited the guns, and loosed two rounds that flew angularly along the Confederate line. Then Griffin saw it: the line of infantry approaching from his right-front, about 200 yards away—Smith's battalion. He watched as Colonel Smith stepped out in front of the infantrymen and made his speech. Griffin sensed an emergency and called for his guns to be loaded with canister. The team of cannoneers worked quickly. At each gun, one man carried a round forward from the limber and placed it in the barrel while another rammed it down. At the rear of the gun, a cannoneer pricked the powder bag through the vent, then placed the friction primer, which, when pulled, produced a spark that ignited the gun. Men manhandled the guns to the right to face toward the Confederates. The gunnery sergeants rushed forward to adjust the barrel's elevation to level, perhaps even slightly depressed. Everyone stepped back.

Then came a voice: "Captain, don't fire there."

Griffin turned to find Maj. William F. Barry riding toward him from Ricketts's guns. "Those are your battery supports," Barry said.

Griffin disagreed vehemently—the lives of his men might depend on the question. "They are Confederates; as certain as the world they are Confederates."

"I know they are your battery support," Barry reassured him, believing, apparently, that they were simply Willcox's men, turned around and reemerging from the woods.

Griffin rarely yielded an opinion, but he steadfastly abided military protocol, and Barry was a superior. Griffin "sprang" to his guns and ordered them not to fire. The cannoneers started the process of re-aiming the guns toward the Confederate artillery, wheeling their pieces left to do so. All the while, Griffin watched the distant line of infantrymen warily. He later recounted how their officer "faced them to the left and marched them about fifty yards to the woods, then faced them to the right again, and marched them about 40 yards toward us." Griffin had seen enough. He ordered his two guns limbered and taken off the field.

Before they could be moved, the Confederates leveled their muskets and fired a devastating volley. It was a catastrophic moment not often repeated in this war. Said Griffin, "That was the last of us."[46]

At the same time Smith's men fired their volley, Colonel Cummings ordered his wary, unsteady regiment to charge. "Yelling like savages," the men of the 33rd rushed up the slope. "No old regulars ever made a more gallant charge," wrote Cummings years later, "though not a very regular one." The Virginians lunged into Griffin's defenseless section, soon followed by the men of Smith's battalion. Dead horses and wounded men littered the ground. The surviving cannoneers fled, as did a few lingering Zouaves in the field beyond. The victorious Virginians milled about the guns. After a morning of reverses and a midday of just holding on, they had achieved the first affirmative Confederate success of the day.[47]

Years later, historians rightly pointed to the 33rd Virginia's capture of Griffin's two guns as the turning point of the battle. But to those caught in the cauldron of Henry Hill that afternoon, the staccato rhythm of events obscured the moment. Just ahead lay a procession of dramatic crises and glorious successes for both sides. For the Confederates, the capture of Griffin's guns represented a first and significant triumph, but like so many that followed that day, it would be short-lived.

Chapter Eight

MAELSTROM

The charge on Griffin's two guns and the exultation that followed disorganized the 33rd and 49th Virginia. Cummings and his officers tried to restore
order, and the 33rd, at least, managed to put together something of a front. Union
infantry soon appeared. Rising out of Sudley Road came the 14th Brooklyn, a
chasseur regiment dressed in red pants, trimmed jackets, and nifty red kepis. The
Yankees' line overlapped by far the Virginians' left, extending into the woods
bordering the southern edge of the field. As soon as the New Yorkers came
within 100 yards, they opened a jolting fire on the Virginians, raking their left
flank and "cutting us to pieces," said John Casler. Wrote another Virginian, "This
movement threw our regiment into utter confusion, and a 'free fight' ensued, in
which every man fought on his own hook, loading and firing at will." The Confederates gave way, leaving numbers of their comrades scattered around the
guns. The New Yorkers rushed forward and reclaimed Griffin's pieces. "The men
tried to drag them off," remembered Barry, "but [the guns] were too encumbered
with dead horses."[1]

Cummings's regiment fell back to its former position. Some of the men
rushed through the left of Col. James Allen's 2nd Virginia, throwing it into confusion as well. Meanwhile, the Brooklynites pushed on, maintaining a heavy fire.
Colonel Allen ordered his three left companies to draw back at an angle to meet
the enemy, but someone mistook the command as a general order for retreat.
Most of Allen's line joined the 33rd in a retrograde. Suddenly Jackson's left
seemed to be crumbling.[2]

Fortunately for Jackson, the smoke and intensity of the moment obscured the
Confederates' confusion from Federal eyes. The men from Brooklyn had no
idea they had brought Jackson's line to the brink of disaster. Instead, the 14th

Brooklyn concentrated on the Confederate batteries to its left-front. The New Yorkers raised a yell and streamed across the fields toward the Confederate guns. Jackson saw them coming. This was the moment he had counseled for all day. He went quickly to the 4th and 27th Virginia. "Reserve your fire until they come within 50 yards," he ordered, "then fire and give them the bayonet, and when you charge, yell like furies."[3]

The Federals closed. "Our boys were mowing them down in fine style," wrote one New Yorker, when suddenly Jackson's artillery and infantry opened fire, riddling the Union line with canister and bullets. A Yankee pessimist told his homefolk afterward, "I didn't go very far before I got just what I expected. . . . I was the second one that went down. . . . [A shell] knocked our pins from under as if they were made of straw." Between volleys, the New Yorkers re-formed and tried again, and again Jackson's men drove them back. A third time the Unionists dashed through the Confederate fire. This time, despite fearful casualties, they closed to within feet of the guns. But by then they could do no more. The New Yorkers' line wavered and broke; the red pants of their wounded and dead in the field marked their path, forward and back. One of the Brooklyn soldiers wrote his family the next day, "I have often read of battles but never thought I should see the horror of war. . . . I have seen enough."[4]

The attack and repulse of the 14th Brooklyn marked a dramatic pivot point for Thomas J. Jackson. The near advance of the Union infantry highlighted the vulnerability of the Confederate artillery that had been firing from the low rise in front of his infantry for nearly three hours. He ordered it off the field to safety.[5] Too, the Union infantry had crossed the 50-yard threshold set by Jackson earlier in the day. His regiments had repulsed the attack. Now they would charge with their bayonets. Jackson rode to Col. James Preston of the 4th Virginia. "Order the men to stand up," he snapped. Instantly, members of the 4th and the 27th Virginia (just behind the 4th), rose. "We'll charge them now and drive them to Washington!" Jackson yelled. The 4th and 27th moved to the left to clear their departing artillery (becoming considerably bunched up in the process), and then, screaming like "wild men," they marched straight for Ricketts's battery.[6]

Through the smoke, Ricketts's battered cannoneers spotted the advancing Rebels. Captain Ricketts lay amid the bloody wreckage of his battery, dangerously wounded in the thigh. Many of the battery's horses lay dead in their traces, rendering the guns immovable. His lieutenants tried to summon some Zouaves, still milling behind the guns, to come up and fight. They did not. "On came the enemy," wrote an officer of the battery, "pouring in their volleys of musketry." As the Virginians neared—their lines becoming bunched up along the way—the battery switched to canister, which tore huge, bloody gaps in the Confederates' line. Still they came. Without support, the cannoneers who could flee did so. Jackson's two regiments swept dramatically across the field and claimed the guns.[7]

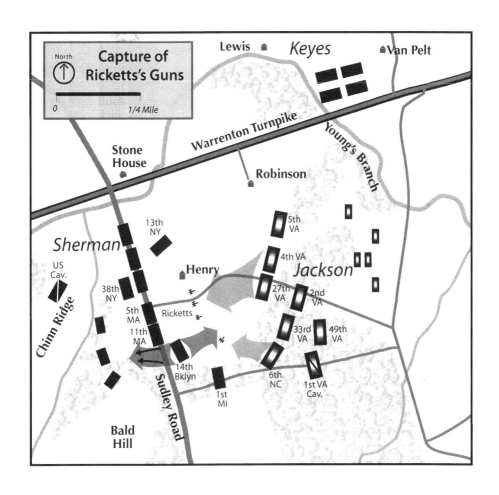

Capture of Ricketts's Guns

North

0   1/4 Mile

Lewis   *Keyes*   Van Pelt

Warrenton Turnpike

Young's Branch

Stone House

Robinson

13th NY

5th VA

Sherman

4th VA

US Cav.

Henry

Jackson

38th NY

27th VA

2nd VA

Chinn Ridge

5th MA

Ricketts

11th MA

33rd VA

49th VA

14th Bklyn

6th NC

1st VA Cav.

Sudley Road

1st MI

Bald Hill

Union lieutenant Doug Ramsay, seeing his peril, took cover behind a dis-abled limber as the Virginians swarmed into the battery. Pvt. C. A. Fonerden of the 27th Virginia lunged for Ramsay, trying to take him prisoner. Ramsay dodged and took off, attempting to make it to Sudley Road. Fonerden leveled his gun, but before he could fire, another Confederate lowered a musket over his shoulder and shot Ramsay from only a few feet away, killing him instantly.[8]

While the Virginians fought for Ricketts's guns, more Confederate regiments appeared on the field, most of them reinforcing and extending Jackson's left. Francis Bartow—more an orator than military man—led the remnants of the 7th Georgia into the maelstrom. Midway across the plateau, a Union bullet struck him in the breast, and he fell from his horse. His soldiers rushed to him. "They picked him up," one remembered. "With both hands clasped over his breast, he raised his head and with a God-like effort, his eye glittering in its last gleam with a blazing light, he said, with a last heroic flash of his lofty spirit, 'They have killed me, but, boys, never give up the field.'" It was perhaps the most famous dying utterance of the day.[9]

While Jackson's men rumbled across Henry Hill toward Ricketts's battery, other units captured (again) the section of Griffin's battery south of Ricketts's. Part of the 2nd Mississippi, which had fought that morning on Matthews Hill, pulled up alongside Extra Billy Smith's battalion. A short time later, probably coincidentally with Jackson's charge, the 6th North Carolina stumbled into posi-tion. Col. Charles Fisher, the novice commander of the regiment, discovered he had arrived at a propitious spot. Griffin's two abandoned guns stood just above him, up the slope, surrounded by only a handful of survivors from the 14th Brooklyn. Fisher's men opened fire; within minutes, all Union troops around the guns either fell or fled. Capt. Isaac Avery shouted to Fisher, "Colonel, don't you think we ought to charge?" Few achievements on the battlefield carried more prestige than the capture of enemy cannon (Fisher surely did not know these guns had already been captured once). "Yes Captain," Fisher replied. Then, turn-ing to his regiment, he yelled, "Charge!"

The blue-clad Carolinians rushed straight up the hill to Griffin's two how-itzers, encountering scarcely any resistance. Dead horses, artillerymen, and infantrymen lay scattered among the wounded. Without warning, Federals opened fire from the woods on the south edge of the field, raking the regiment. Nothing disrupts the battle lines of new troops faster than unseen enemies firing from an unexpected direction, and the 6th wavered. "We failed to keep a perfect alignment in distinct companies," understated one man. "They fired on us worse than ever," wrote another, while a third recorded that the fire came "from so many directions at the same time," the regiment could only fall back. Fisher tried to restart his regiment by dashing past Griffin's guns, bidding his regiment to fol-low him to Sudley Road. But after only a few steps, he fell dead, shot in the head. The fire from the woods continued, and the regiment's line degenerated into a ragged mass. "There was scarcely telling friends from foes," wrote one of Fisher's men. A rumor raced through the ranks that the 6th had fired on friends. In a scene repeated a dozen times that day, soldiers stopped firing and started yelling, urging those in the woods to stop shooting. But the Federal fusillade continued. Union bullets convinced the Carolinians of their mistake, but by then their lines had degenerated and the rookie troops could not hold Griffin's guns. The 6th North Carolina fell back. One man of the regiment summed up his experience that day: "Just before going into battle I put up the most earnest prayer that I ever did, and I know that it was answered, for the balls came by me as thick as hail stones and the bomb shells bursted all around me, and none but the hand of God could have saved me."[10]

The retreat of the 6th North Carolina could not obscure a hard Yankee fact: by 3:30 P.M., the dreamy victory that seemed like a mere formality two hours before had turned nightmarish. In just thirty minutes, the Confederates captured eight of the eleven pieces of artillery McDowell had ordered to Henry Hill. The remaining three—Griffin's guns north of the Henry house—had retreated. With the guns went any Union claim to the hill, save a toehold maintained on the southern edge by the 1st Minnesota and 14th Brooklyn.

McDowell now confronted the obverse of the question that haunted him earlier: *Was this defeat?* Perhaps more so than any commander in American history up to that time, McDowell's verdict of victory or defeat would be defined by public perception, not by objective results on the battlefield. Anything short of unambiguous victory would rattle the minds of the people and, perhaps, threaten the idea of the Union. Ricketts's entire battery and Griffin's section presently resided in Southern hands. No definition of Union victory could permit that to stand. McDowell and his subordinates needed to recapture those guns and drive the Confederates from Henry Hill.

In the middle of Mrs. Henry's fields, the 4th and 27th Virginia of Jackson's brigade formed a thin, ragged line around Ricketts's guns. Below the Virginians to the west, about 200 yards away, lay Sudley Road, whose deep cuts had become a covered passageway for Union troops ascending Henry Hill. Soldiers from several regiments now crowded the road, though no unit had a specific mandate to work directly with any other. Instead, to a degree that seems astonishing in retrospect, each regiment fought on its own. But each regiment also recognized the immediate objective: recapture the guns. The first Federal regiment to try was Col. Orlando Willcox's 1st Michigan. The Michiganders opened fire from the cover of fences along Sudley Road, but when they advanced, only half the regiment stepped forward. Confederates across the hilltop opened fire on the Michigan men, who charged close enough to the Confederates to lose their flag before falling back to the cover of the road.[11]

A hodgepodge battalion apparently from the 14th Brooklyn and the Fire Zouaves followed closely the efforts of the Michigan men. Jackson's Virginians once again mustered a deadly fire against the makeshift Union lines, and again an overmatched Federal force streamed back to the cover of Sudley Road. It was, said one Virginian, "a clear case, on their part, of self-imposed butchery."[12]

Ricketts's battery still stood in the middle of Widow Henry's farm, its dead and wounded batterymen scattered around, dozens of horses on the ground, and Jackson's 4th and 27th Virginia regiments clinging to the real estate around the guns. When organizing his army, McDowell had determined to assign batteries directly to his various brigades (a practice that would quickly cease after the battle). Ricketts's battery belonged to a brigade commanded by a brilliant Regular army officer, Col. William B. Franklin, first in the West Point Class of 1843. Earlier in the day, Franklin had been horrified to see Ricketts's guns ordered away from their relatively safe perch on Dogan Ridge to the perilous place on Henry Hill. Now, about 3:30 P.M., he sent two of his regiments, the 5th and 11th Massachusetts, toward Henry Hill with orders to "try to get back the guns." Using the cuts of Sudley Road as cover, the regiments arrived near Mrs. Henry's drive, where they beheld a discouraging sight, "enough to make a man grow mad," as a man of the 11th Massachusetts told his mother. "There was men laying dead and wounded and the artillery men had been killed and the horses were all dead piled together by the Cannon. The bullets were flying thick." And, he added, "the enemy wasn't more than a stones throw from us."[13]

To their right was more discouragement: the disorganized remnants of the 11th New York, 1st Minnesota, and now the 1st Michigan. And then came the rumble of hooves: a detachment of Federal cavalry thundering down the road from the south. "Get out of here or the Black Horse Cavalry will get you all," yelled one of the horsemen. Behind the cavalry came the bouncing retreat of Ricketts's caissons. The men of the two Massachusetts regiments scrambled up the bank of the road to let them pass. Scores of dazed or bloody Zouaves streamed by. "For a time fearful confusion prevailed," admitted a man of the 11th, but soon a few hardworking officers restored order to the regiments. Franklin ordered them to charge.[14]

The men of the 5th and 11th Massachusetts climbed up the road bank and aligned themselves along the edge. An officer stepped out in front, sword drawn, and yelled for the charge to begin. Almost immediately after emerging from the road, the 5th Massachusetts, on the left, received a "withering" fire from Confederates around the Henry house. The line fell into disorder. The 11th, on the right, did better and closed on Jackson's Virginians around Ricketts's battery. Several volleys drove the Confederates from the guns, and Franklin's men rushed among them, becoming their third possessor of the day. The infantrymen wanted to drag the pieces to safety, but they had gone only a few yards before officers yelled at them to get back into line. Every man would be needed to hold the guns.[15]

Every minute the fighting on Henry Hill raged meant more time for additional Confederate troops to arrive or for disorganized regiments to reorganize themselves. As the clock ticked toward 4 P.M., an impressive collection of Confederates approached the field: Early's brigade and two regiments of Bonham's brigade from the lower crossings; E. Kirby Smith's brigade, newly arrived on the trains from Piedmont Station and now pounding north toward the battlefield; and several Virginia regiments from Philip St. George Cocke's brigade, marching quickly toward the fighting from nearby Lewis Ford. Johnston would direct each of these units forward from Portici, and Beauregard would in turn direct them into the fighting on Henry Hill. Beauregard aspired to organize a decisive attack that would drive the Yankees off the plateau, but crisis after crisis intervened. As a result, before 4 P.M. Beauregard fought a battle that much resembled McDowell's, feeding regiments into battle one or two at a time without much plan.[16]

In addition to the fresh units arriving from elsewhere, Beauregard faced the task of rallying and posting units that had battled earlier in the day. While the experience of these units defies the efforts of historians to describe them—many went into battle in small groups aligned with other, fresher regiments—a few found their way back to the fighting intact. The 5th Virginia and Hampton's Legion had fought side by side against Keyes's attack about 2 P.M. Now, as the 4th and 27th Virginia yielded Ricketts's battery, Beauregard rode to the two regiments and commanded them to attack. To the Legion, he pointed out the Henry house and directed them to take it. To the 5th Virginia, he yelled, "Fight on brave Virginia boys," and led them forward personally. Both regiments rushed into the fight, spurred on by Beauregard's cry, "Give them the bayonet." The 5th Virginia moved on the left, closest to the contested battery. One man noticed "a great many little spots of dust rising before us," though it would be several moments before he realized the puffs marked the spots where Union bullets struck the ground. As the Virginians neared the Henry house, they spotted the line of Massachusetts men holding the guns. The soldiers of the 5th Virginia stopped and fired. The Massachusetts regiments at the battery broke. The Virginians shouted and charged into the battery, claiming it once again for the Confederates. "Every horse attached to the battery was either killed or disabled and not a man, except the dead and wounded, were left with the guns," recalled one man.[17]

Farther to the left, other troops joined in the fight, battling with remnants of the 1st Minnesota, 1st Michigan, 11th New York, and 14th Brooklyn. Fighting swirled around the eight captured cannon, a maelstrom of surging and retreating men, smoke, rattling muskets, and exploding shells. Regiments came onto the field one by one or in pieces and generally went into position as each particular colonel saw fit. Once in the fight, trim and polished ranks degenerated into seething mobs of frightened men who knew what they wanted to do but had little idea of how to go about doing it.

Pieces and parts of units found each other and formed momentary battalions, then often as quickly succumbed to the confusion on the field. Three companies of the 2nd Mississippi—the only regiment to be heavily involved in both the fighting on Matthews Hill and the battle in the Robinson yard earlier that after-noon—joined with a few companies of the 4th South Carolina. General Bee soon found them: "Men, there is a position here important to be held, move quickly up and support it." Bee led his 4th Alabama, the Mississippians, and the Carolinians up the rear slope of Henry Hill. Along the way, a battery of artillery withdrawing from Jackson's front dashed through the 4th Alabama, splitting it into two frag-ments. Bee found himself with the smaller part of the regiment, about 100 men. Soldiers from the 4th and 27th Virginia, both largely finished for the day, retreated across the front of Bee's improvised command. By now, artillery on both sides had either departed or been silenced, and the battle belonged to the infantry. As Bee's Confederate battle line approached to within 75 yards of the right gun of Ricketts's abandoned battery, Union troops in the timber opposite the Confederate left opened fire. Barnard Bee fell. He succumbed to his wound the next day, the highest-ranking officer to die in the battle.[18]

Meanwhile, the Hampton Legion and the 5th Virginia deployed along the fence lines and hedgerows surrounding the Henry house and among Ricketts's abandoned guns, now scattered in the field. Men broke from ranks to take cover behind outhouses, sheds, bushes, cannon, and caissons. The fight for Henry Hill rose to a crescendo. "The shouts of the combatants, the groans of the wounded and dying, and the explosion of shells made a complete pandemonium," recalled John Opie of the 5th Virginia. "The atmosphere was black with the smoke of the battle." Along the entire front, the Federals yielded and fell back to Sudley Road.[19]

Once again, the Confederates controlled (loosely, at least) all of Henry Hill short of Sudley Road. But few Southerners deluded themselves into thinking the battle won. The distant hills still bristled with Union artillery and infantry. And down in the valley near the Stone House, more Federals—thousands of them, it seemed—prepared to move into the fight.

Ominous though the Federal masses looked, Irvin McDowell knew what the Confederates could not: these troops represented his last hope for victory. He now reaped the consequences of his midday uncertainty. The Confederates had used the time to move a continuous flow of reinforcements to the field—enough, in fact, that eleven successive Union regiments had been unable to dislodge them. Of the 18,000 troops originally available to McDowell, probably 13,000 were now spent or in no position to assist in the fight for Henry Hill. Burnside's brigade rested on Matthews Hill (no one begrudged them that). Keyes's brigade remained secreted on the low ground east of the Robinson house, completely out of touch with McDowell. The 1st Minnesota, 11th New York, 14th Brooklyn, Marine battalion, and 1st Michigan had been roughly handled on the hill and now fought only as scattered remnants. The 5th and 11th Massachusetts had been driven back to Sudley Road with heavy losses. Of those units engaged on Henry Hill, only one would come back again: the 38th New York. Schenck's brigade, which McDowell had hoped would cross the Stone Bridge, had not moved. It passed the afternoon much as it had spent the morning: exchanging long-range artillery fire and light skirmishing with Confederates west of Bull Run (mostly Cocke's Virginians at Lewis Ford).

That left McDowell only two brigades—perhaps 5,000 men—with which to carry on the fight. Col. Oliver O. Howard's brigade brought up the rear of the Union flanking column and arrived on the field at about 2 P.M. after an especially tedious march of 10 miles under a warm midday sun. As they crossed Sudley Ford (on Bull Run) and Sudley Springs Ford (on Catharpin Run), Howard's New Englanders encountered the human wreckage of battle: "faces with bandages stained with blood; bodies pierced; many were walking or limping to the rear," Howard remembered.

McDowell gave small allowance for the fatigued condition of Howard's men and ordered them straightaway onto the battlefield. One of McDowell's staff officers directed Howard to move his brigade not to Henry Hill, but to Chinn Ridge, a long, angular piece of high ground 500 yards west of Mrs. Henry's farm. Conventional wisdom holds that McDowell intended Howard's movement to Chinn Ridge as a last-gasp attempt to drive the Confederates from Henry Hill by getting around their left flank. The geometry of the movement may have suggested such a thing, but the historical record reflects no such intent on McDowell's part. Howard's assignment was to "support a battery," though exactly which one is not clear. As the New Englanders marched to their assigned position, a wag offered them some advice: "You better hurry and get in if you want to have any fun."[20]

While Howard moved toward Chinn Ridge, McDowell had no choice but to continue the fight on Henry Hill, if for no other reason than to stave off complete disaster. The other—and last—brigade at his disposal was Sherman's brigade, well rested and 3,000 strong. After crossing Bull Run at Farm Ford at 11:30 A.M., Sherman's men had waited anxiously for a chance at the Rebels. At about 2:30 P.M., McDowell ordered Sherman to "join in pursuit of the enemy," but like those who had preceded him to Henry Hill, Sherman soon discovered that "pursuit" was fantasy. Sherman put the 13th New York in front and deployed the remaining regiments behind: from front to back, the 2nd Wisconsin, 79th New York ("The Highlanders"), and the 69th New York. The four regiments moved down the slope of Buck Hill, crossed the Warrenton Turnpike and Young's Branch, and filed into the deeply worn Sudley Road, now littered with the dead and wounded. "The poor fellows had crowded in, and crowded one upon another, filling the ditch in some places three or four deep," wrote a Wisconsin infantryman. "I will not sicken [you] with a description of this road."[21]

While most of the brigade took its position in the road, Sherman sent the 13th New York off to the left, up the slope toward the Henry house. The New Yorkers hurried to within 70 yards of the house, lay down behind a swell of ground, and opened fire. Before long came the seemingly inevitable cry, "You're firing on friends!" Indeed, at least two members of the 13th claimed they saw an American flag flying from the house. The New Yorkers' fire slackened and stopped. As had happened elsewhere, an unfamiliar officer wandered into the ranks of the 13th New York. "I asked him if he was a Union man," a Union lieutenant recorded. "No," said the Confederate officer, realizing his mistake, "I mistook you for a Baltimore regiment," and handed over his sword and revolver. The confusion in the ranks lasted only until a Palmetto flag appeared in front (surely that of the Hampton Legion), and the 13th New York shook under a heavy volley. The regiment returned the fire and waited anxiously for an order to charge that never came. The regiment spent the next half hour lying in the tall grass engaging Hampton's South Carolinians in a close-range firefight.[22]

It is a measure of the chaos of the day that Sherman, one of America's greatest military captains-to-be, sent his remaining three regiments into the battle not en masse, but one by one. Each used the cover of Sudley Road as its departure point, then surged up the slope toward the Henry house and Ricketts's battery. The 2nd Wisconsin moved first, magnificently and unfortunately clad in gray uniforms. The bedlam in the road, where unblooded units mingled with the remnants of their defeated predecessors, rendered all attempts at precision drill and movement impossible. The order to advance could not be heard, and instead filtered along the 2nd's line. "By sort of mutual consent," wrote Sgt. Nathaniel Rollins of the 2nd, "we rushed over the dead men, climbed up the bank, over the fence, and up the hill." As soon as the 2nd Wisconsin and their gray uniforms moved into the field below the Henry house, nearby Union soldiers mistook them for Confederates and opened fire. The men of the 2nd lay down to escape while officers rushed about, trying to stop the firing. After a few moments of deadly pandemonium—"hallooing all around us," wrote one man— the shooting from the rear stopped. The 2nd Wisconsin rose and started up the hill. The Confederates in front immediately opened fire. "The horrors of a battle field are supremely greater than my imagination had ever conceived," concluded J. C. Chandler of the regiment. A rough introduction to battle for the 2nd Wisconsin it was.[23]

The experience of the 2nd Wisconsin in these few minutes was a microcosm of the unusual experience of battle at Bull Run for men on both sides: horror intensified by confusion. As the Wisconsin men swept up the slope toward the Henry house, they stopped to fire on the Virginians and South Carolinians in front. More than one man concluded the Confederates occupied a literal fortress of earthworks around the house (they did not). Almost every first volley on Henry Hill that day triggered a common response: "You are shooting your friends! Stop, for God's sake! Spare your own brothers." Peering ahead through the smoke, some of the men saw what they perceived to be a U.S. flag around the Henry house. (The confusion would later inspire the Confederates to replace the First National flag—the Stars and Bars—with a more distinctive one less likely to be confused with the U.S. flag; thus was born the Confederate battle flag.) The musketry slackened, then exploded once more as the Confederates laced the Union line with bullets. By now, the 2nd Wisconsin had lost its organization; indeed, it was operating in two distinct wings, neither of which could drive the Confederates from the house or the nearby guns of Ricketts's battery. Finally, the colonel gave the order, "Fall back and reform." In shambles, the 2nd Wisconsin backed and stumbled down the slope toward Sudley Road. There, a new terror waited. Men of the 69th New York ("about which there has been so much gas," grumbled a man of the 2nd) mistook the gray-clad Northerners for Confederates again and fired a full volley into the regiment. The "friendly fire" thoroughly demoralized the "Badgermen." The 2nd tumbled into the chaos of Sudley Road, where the men mixed with the beaten remnants of other units.[24]

Around the Henry house and Ricketts's battery, the Hampton Legion and 5th Virginia took a moment to savor their small victory, then braced for another Federal attack. One Southern soldier carefully counted off his shots (seven) before a Union bullet found his thigh. Another man sat astride the barrel of one of Ricketts's guns, "yelling like a Comanche" in anticipation of a Union assault. Charles Wight of the 5th Virginia ran to take cover behind a caisson of Ricketts's battery. On the way, he stopped to fire; "as I did so I felt that something had happened," he remembered. "I could not tell what. I saw the sky, and thought there was something wrong. After a while I found myself lying on the ground on my back, and felt the blood streaming over my face." Around Wight the firing continued, though the Virginians could see nothing of the Union troops as long as they remained in Sudley Road. But they would not stay there long.[25]

The 79th New York ("The Highlanders") stood next in Sherman's bloody queue in Sudley Road. Most men in the regiment hailed from New York City, and many bore a Scottish lineage (a few had hoped to go into battle adorned in kilts, but practical realities overawed cultural enthusiasm). Col. James Cameron commanded the regiment; he was a Pennsylvanian whose qualifications for command amounted to some prior militia service, a Scottish surname, and some solid political connections: his brother was Secretary of War Simon Cameron. As the 2nd Wisconsin fell back into the road, Cameron stepped to the front of the 79th New York. "Come on my brave Highlanders," he yelled. Like the 2nd Wisconsin, the 79th pushed up the hill, making its way through the broken limbers and dismounted caissons of Ricketts's battery. Halfway up the slope, the New Yorkers suffered a Southern volley. "The first fire swept our ranks like a quick darting pestilence," remembered one man. "Rally, boys, rally!" shouted the officers. Rally they did, and a well-coordinated fusillade ripped the Rebels. For several minutes the two sides exchanged volleys. Colonel Cameron fell, mortally wounded.

Almost predictably, the cry of "Cease firing! You're shooting your own men," passed down the line. The New Yorkers flinched. Some lowered their guns, thinking the troops in front were Federals. Others yelled, "No they ain't. Don't you see they are firing at us?" Through the foul-smelling haze, someone spotted what appeared to be a U.S. flag. More men lowered their weapons. "Blaze away, boys! They're only trying to deceive us!" came a cry. "Cease firing, I tell you! They are our own men!" sounded a reply. The argument ended when the line in front fired another wicked volley, "against which we could only stagger," said one Highlander. A second Southern volley ripped the line. Like the 2nd Wisconsin, the Highlanders fell back to the road.[26]

Despite their success at holding their position, the South Carolinians and Virginians around the Henry house by now showed signs of wear. Both regiments had seen heavy fighting earlier in the day, and both were near exhaustion. But the Federals, protected by the road bank, made almost impossible targets and refused to yield. Hampton flirted with the idea of following up one of the Federal retreats with an attack of his own, but the energetic colonel fell not far from the Henry house, wounded in the leg. Command of the Legion fell to Capt. James Conner, who took a more cautious view—his men were too scattered and bloodied to risk an attack. The Hampton Legion would simply try to hold on.[27]

They would have to do so against yet another Union attack, this one more formidable than the two before. Col. J. Hobart Ward's 38th New York had taken part in the first infantry combat on Henry Hill, about an hour before. Now, Ward led his men, still largely intact, into Sudley Road to the right of Sherman's battered brigade. Ward's view of the field from the road would have daunted even veteran officers. Above him, 200 yards away, were the jumbled remnants of Ricketts's battery: caissons scattered in the field, horses lying everywhere, and the guns themselves now at odd angles and various positions. Ward's fear of the Confederates turning those guns on his regiment spurred him to action. He directed his men, along with some scattered detachments of the 14th Brooklyn, to open fire on the Confederates around the battery and the house.[28]

Shortly after, Ward received additional firepower. Rumbling up the road came a section of Reynolds's Rhode Island battery, led by Lt. J. Albert Monroe. The lieutenant boldly wheeled his two guns out of the road cut, unlimbered them not far from Sudley Road, and joined in the fire on the Confederates near the Henry house. At about the same time, Sherman put his last unscathed regiment, the 69th New York, onto the firing line. Rambunctious and habitually dissatisfied, the 69th went into battle with an attitude. Many in the regiment believed their enlistment had already expired and that they ought to be home rather than on Mrs. Henry's farm that day. They also had lost their lieutenant colonel in their first brush with the Confederates that morning. Some men in the 69th had stripped to shirtsleeves and even bare chests. "The difficulty," wrote an onlooker that day, "was to keep them quiet." As the 38th New York opened fire, so too did the 69th.[29]

The inaptly named Jonathan Coward of the 38th wrote, "It was raining bullets; two of them had the pleasure to strike me, but I had the pleasure to know that they were spent." He later tallied his day: "How many I shot I don't know. I am sure I killed one, for I picked him out from the rest and let him have it. I fired altogether 20 rounds." The combined fire of the 38th and 69th New York and Monroe's guns proved more than the men of Hampton's Legion and the 5th Virginia could bear. After probably twenty minutes of fighting, the Confederates yielded Mrs. Henry's house and, for the second time, Ricketts's guns.[30]

Seeing his advantage, Ward ordered his regiment forward. Joined by the Irish 69th on their left, the 38th New York rushed up the hill to the guns. Sherman went with them. A few days later, he reflected on that profound scene:

> Then for the first time I saw the Carnage of battle—men lying in every conceivable shape, and mangled in a horrible way—but this did not make a particle of impression on me—but horses running about riderless with blood streaming from their nostrils—lying on the ground hitched to guns, gnawing their sides in death—I sat on my horse on the ground where Ricketts Battery had been shattered to fragments, and saw the havoc done.[31]

The charge of the two New York regiments ejected Hampton's Legion and the 5th Virginia from around the Henry house and Ricketts's battery. With Jackson's artillery now withdrawn, and with any remaining Confederate infantry screened from view by the pines on the edge of the hill, Sherman and Ward set out to defend their hold on the battery. Ward ordered Ricketts's guns to be taken off the field. Officers detailed gangs to drag three of the pieces 200 yards back to Sudley Road.

While his infantrymen struggled to remove Ricketts's guns, Ward glanced to the right and saw Federal troops falling back from the woods on the south side of the field. These were Willcox's Michiganders (along with men from probably five other regiments) who, after their earlier attempt to recover Ricketts's guns, had moved into the woods. There they had been roughly handled—Willcox himself was wounded and captured—and now they sought safety in Sudley Road. Ward hurried his men in Willcox's direction to offer some help, but ran smack into a small force of pursuing Confederate cavalry and infantry. The New Yorkers engaged the Southerners "in a sharp and spirited skirmish" and drove them back. With that, once again all Confederates disappeared from the top of Henry Hill. "We appeared for a time to have complete possession of the field," wrote Lt. Col. Addison Farnsworth of the 38th. Was the battle won?[32]

"We were quite elated," remembered a man of the 69th New York, which, along with several members of the 11th New York Fire Zouaves, held the area around the Henry house. McDowell rode up to the regiment and congratulated Colonel Corcoran. Instead of congratulating the colonel, however, McDowell might have better spent his time trying to help him; the Union army would need far more than two regiments if they intended to hold Henry Hill. The problem was, McDowell had scarcely an organized regiment left on the field. He had thrown thirteen regiments into the fight on Henry Hill (more precisely, thirteen had found their way into the battle), and each of those, save the 38th and 69th New York, more resembled traumatized mobs than functional military organizations. West of Bull Run, only Howard's four regiments had not yet been in battle, and these McDowell had already sent toward Chinn Ridge. He had nothing left to commit to the fight for Henry Hill.[33]

McDowell's condition contrasted mightily with Johnston's and Beauregard's. The fight for Henry Hill had begun as a battle for time—time that would allow the Confederate commanders to move additional troops to the battlefield. Hampton, Jackson, Smith, Evans, Fisher, Bee, and Bartow had bought that time. True, at the moment the Federals held Ricketts's guns and a toehold on Henry Hill, but significant numbers of fresh Confederates had arrived at Portici or reported to Beauregard near Henry Hill, ready to enter the fight. Cocke's brigade arrived first, then Bonham's two regiments, the 2nd and 8th South Carolina, and Kemper's battery, which had hurried up from Mitchell's Ford. At about 4 P.M., when the fight for Henry Hill raged most fiercely, Arnold Elzey's brigade arrived, the most recent troops off the trains at Manassas Junction. Following Elzey marched Jubal Early. All told, between 3 and 4:30 that afternoon probably 7,000 fresh Confederate soldiers arrived at Johnston's headquarters. While McDowell's spigot of troops had run dry, the Confederates' was about to gush a flood. Johnston and Beauregard rushed the fresh regiments to the front.

The 8th and 18th Virginia of Cocke's brigade moved first, together only coincidentally. The 8th, commanded by Col. Eppa Hunton of Warrenton, bore northward and came up on the right of what had been Jackson's line, near the Robinson house. Col. Robert E. Withers's 18th moved toward the left of the line. As these Virginians neared Henry Hill, dozens of discouraged and wounded comrades streamed by, spreading tales of doom. Officers rode among these gloomsayers, trying to rally the healthy ones, and soon troops from a half-dozen states formed a ragged battalion and joined in the advance. Also turning about were the tired remnants of the Hampton Legion, which had done more fighting that day than any other Confederate regiment. Captain Conner formed his regiment on Withers's right. Before reaching Henry Hill, Withers saw Beauregard and approached him for orders. "Change your direction to the left oblique and charge across the Sudley Road," the general said. Orders flashed down the line of the 18th. "We dashed forward at the double-quick," wrote Withers.[34]

Without halting for speeches or realignment, the 8th and 18th Virginia swept across the top of Henry Hill. Their charge rocked the 38th New York near

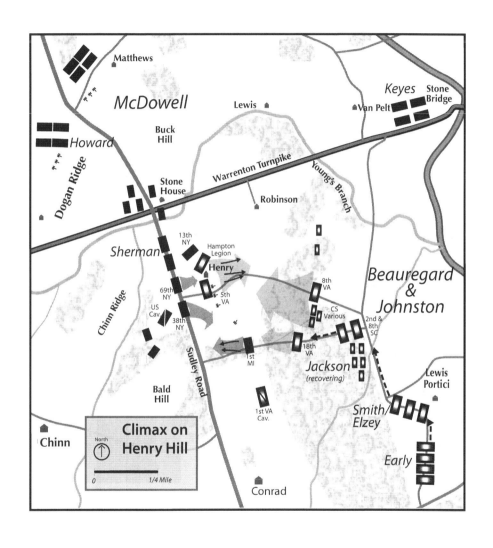

Matthews

McDowell

Keyes Stone Bridge

Lewis

Van Pelt

Howard

Buck Hill

Dogan Ridge

Warrenton Turnpike

Young's Branch

Stone House

Robinson

13th NY

Sherman

Hampton Legion

Henry

Beauregard & Johnston

69th NY

5th VA

8th VA

US Cav.

Chinn Ridge

38th NY

CS Various

2nd & 8th SC

18th VA

1st MI

Jackson (recovering)

Lewis Portici

Bald Hill

1st VA Cav.

Smith/ Elzey

Chinn

North

Climax on Henry Hill

0   1/4 Mile

Early

Conrad

Griffin's abandoned guns, and the surprised Federals hastily gave ground. Near the Henry house, the 8th Virginia smashed into the 69th New York. "We fought desperately, but we were cut down," a member of the 69th recalled. In the melee, the 69th lost its national colors, but Capt. John Wildey of the Fire Zouaves rushed forward and snatched it back, to the relief of the Irishmen. The 69th resisted briefly, then withdrew to Sudley Road.[35]

With the collapse of the 38th New York and 69th Virginia, only Sherman's 13th New York remained on Henry Hill. They had been about 100 yards north of Mrs. Henry's house for about an hour, hunkered down in the grass, keeping up a distant fire with their rifle-muskets (the only regiment of the brigade armed with rifles). The New Yorkers had suffered the same exasperating confusion about the identity of those opposite them and had accomplished little in their time on Henry Hill. Now, they too had no choice but to retreat. As the New Yorkers angled down the north slope of Henry Hill, they came under intensified Confederate fire. An exploding shell knocked one man 10 feet. "I thought I was dead," he wrote, "and shut my eyes—but finding myself still alive I got up and ran like thunder."[36]

The 8th and 18th Virginia surged past the Henry house and through the wreckage of Ricketts's battery to Sudley Road, over disabled caissons and limbers, dead horses, and the bodies of hundreds who had fought over the guns. The 13th, 38th, and 69th New York offered no resistance and fled down the hill toward the Stone House. The Virginians poured into the road, where the 8th Virginia found four guns of Ricketts's battery, hauled there by Union soldiers vainly trying to carry them off the field.[37]

Once more, after nearly two hours of the heaviest fighting any soldier could have imagined, the Confederates again held Henry Hill—every inch of it—along with eight pieces of Federal artillery and untold numbers of prisoners, including Captain Ricketts. Hundreds of dead and wounded littered the field. Fences knocked down, horses mutilated, and Mrs. Henry's battered frame dwelling at the vortex, its elderly occupant dying. Most Americans had expected a battle that Sunday. But few had expected this. July 21, 1861, was the deadliest day the nation had ever known.

Still, the battle raged on. Scattered pockets of Yankees continued to fight from the woods west of Sudley Road. Several Union batteries still fired from Matthews Hill and Dogan Ridge. And to the west, Oliver Otis Howard's four regiments of troops from northern New England trotted toward the slopes of Chinn Ridge. For the Confederates, those distant Yankees stood as their only barrier to complete, stunning victory.

Some of the defenses of Manassas Junction. This photograph was taken in March 1862, after the Federal occupation of the area. LIBRARY OF CONGRESS

Braddock Road in Centreville, looking northwest. A Union officer wrote of the village, "It looks for all the world as though it had done its business, whatever it was, if it ever had any, fully eighty years ago, and had since then bolted its doors, put out its fires, and gone to sleep." The winter following the battle, the population of Centreville exploded to more than 40,000 when it became the primary winter encampment for the Confederate army.
NATIONAL ARCHIVES

The Spindle (or Spinner) house rested along the Warrenton Turnpike near the turnoff used by the Union flanking column. During the retreat, Radford's battalion of Virginia cavalry attacked Union soldiers gathered around a well in the yard. Running through the foreground of the photo is the Warrenton Turnpike, its rocky, "macadamized" surface plainly visible. LIBRARY OF CONGRESS

Sudley Springs Ford over Catharpin Run, looking north. About 300 yards from Sudley Ford on Bull Run, the entire Union flanking column crossed Sudley Springs Ford on the morning of July 21. The four children in the image are almost certainly the Thornberry siblings. Laura, who would later write a memoir of the battle, is on the far left. LIBRARY OF CONGRESS

Ruins of the Stone Bridge, March 1862. This view is looking west. Van Pelt Hill in the distance is crowned by Abraham Van Pelt's frame house, used by Evans as his headquarters. The felled trees west of the bridge were cut down by Evans's men before the battle to clear their field of fire. The bridge was blown up under the supervision of Capt. Edward Porter Alexander when the Confederates abandoned the Manassas area that month. LIBRARY OF CONGRESS

The Edgar Matthews house on Matthews Hill, looking east. During the fighting, the Federals, according to a Georgia soldier, crowded into the yard: "They were in the shrubbery in the front yard, down through the horse lot, [and] behind the stables and barns and haystacks." Today the site of the Matthews house and much of Matthews Hill is shrouded in thick woods. LIBRARY OF CONGRESS

Panoramic view of the Stone House intersection, looking north toward Matthews Hill (1880s). The Manassas–Sudley Road runs through the foreground and snakes up the slopes of Buck Hill and Matthews Hill in the distance. The Stone House is visible in the right center of the photograph, with the Warrenton Turnpike running in front of it from right to left. The thicket so prominent in descriptions of the fighting on Matthews Hill is visible just above and to the right of the Stone House. U.S. ARMY MILITARY HISTORY INSTITUTE

VMI Cadet Charles R. Norris, acting captain, 27th Virginia Infantry. Just two months beyond his seventeenth birthday, Norris found himself in command of a company of the 27th Virginia. He died in the charge of the 4th and 27th Virginia on Ricketts's battery. His brother, a member of the Loudoun Artillery, found his body the next morning and carried it home to Leesburg, where Norris is buried. Cadet Norris's uniform jacket, bearing the scar of the wound that killed him, is on display at the Manassas National Battlefield Park Visitor Center.
MANASSAS BATTLEFIELD

Pvt. William Baker Ott, 4th Virginia Infantry. Killed in the fighting on Henry Hill.
MANASSAS BATTLEFIELD

Monument marking the spot where Col. Francis Bartow was killed. This monument, constructed in September 1861, was the first Civil War monument ever erected. When the Confederates abandoned the Manassas area in March 1862, they broke off the shaft and brought it with them. Its location, if it survived, is today unknown. Only the base of the monument remains on Henry Hill today. Visible on the left side of the engraving is the shot-torn Henry house, which would be dismantled by Confederate soldiers for construction materials during the winter of 1861. The Robinson house is visible to the right of the shaft. A WAR-TIME ENGRAVING

The Lewis house, Portici, General Johnston's headquarters during the fighting on Henry Hill and Chinn Ridge. The house burned in late 1862. U.S. ARMY MILITARY HISTORY INSTITUTE

Ruins of the Warrenton Turnpike Bridge over Cub Run, looking northwest. During the Union retreat, the suspension bridge that spanned Cub Run here became blocked, precipitating a wild scene of panic and confusion as soldiers, horses, cannons, and wagons plunged into the stream on either side. Like the Stone Bridge, the Cub Run Bridge was destroyed by the Confederates in March 1862, only weeks before this photograph was taken. LIBRARY OF CONGRESS

Union graves near Sudley Church. The church is visible atop the ridge in the background. Because Sudley Church was used extensively as a Union field hospital following the battle, the area around it was dotted with Union graves like these. Most Union dead were disinterred and reburied in a mass grave in Arlington Cemetery in 1866. The two boys in this photo are almost certainly Samuel and Joseph Thornberry, who lived across from Sudley Church and whose house was likewise appropriated as a Union field hospital. LIBRARY OF CONGRESS

Chapter Nine

DENOUEMENT

When, between 3 and 4 P.M. on July 21, Irvin McDowell ordered the brigade commanded by Col. Oliver Otis Howard to move to Chinn Ridge, Union victory still seemed at least a possibility. By the time Howard and his four regiments neared the base of the ridge not long after 4 P.M., McDowell surely realized that victory had slipped out of reach. By then, Howard's command represented the last undamaged Union regiments west of Bull Run, though the brigade had suffered severely in their midday march onto the field (part of it at a trot), and at least one of the regiments had seen nearly half its men drop by the roadside. Around them, hundreds if not thousands of men wandered aimlessly near the Stone House and dotted the slopes of Matthews Hill in search of their commands. Pieces of regiments that remained intact intermingled with others. The tidy brigades that had started the day had dissolved entirely. McDowell prepared for the worst. He sent orders to Col. Dixon S. Miles at Centreville to advance two brigades toward the Stone Bridge to cover a potential retreat, and also dispatched a message to Secretary Cameron in Washington: send all available troops in Washington to the front "without delay."[1]

More immediately, to quell the crisis on the slopes of Henry Hill, McDowell summoned Sykes's Regular battalion. Since their intervention on Matthews Hill that morning, the Regulars had been supporting Union batteries. Now mindful, as one man said, that "the safety of the army depended on the Regulars," they gathered their traps, formed into line, and headed toward the western shoulder of Henry Hill, just west of Sudley Road.[2]

Slightly ahead of the Regulars in their movement were the regiments of Howard's brigade. Their initial mandate to "support a battery" now morphed into a mission like that of the Regulars: to provide protection for the Union right

119

flank as the army's efforts to take Henry Hill dissolved into chaos. Howard's destination: Chinn Ridge, one of the generally north–south ridges that dominated the battlefield. Separated from Henry Hill by Sudley Road, 200 yards of undulating ground, and a bottomland cut by Chinn Branch, the ridgetop was largely clear and carefully managed, studded only by an occasional woodlot, numerous fence lines, and Benjamin Chinn's fine farm complex, Hazel Plain. Since the battle, some have surmised that Howard's orders envisioned a move down Chinn Ridge to work around the left flank of the Confederate position on Henry Hill—a final, climactic effort by McDowell to extract victory from disaster. In fact, Howard's orders were pedestrian: merely to support a battery. As his men moved toward the heights of the Chinn farm, Howard likely could not have known that his mission had become far more important than that, and far more dangerous, too.[3]

Howard received orders shortly after 3 P.M. Promptly, his brigade started forward from Matthews Hill, likely passing down the western slope of Dogan Ridge and across the Warrenton Turnpike. The situation in the Union rear resembled that behind the Confederate line, with wounded soldiers mingling with others plodding toward the rear. Caissons, cannon, disorganized regiments, and ambulances hindered Howard's progress. "I began to see sights that would wring tears almost from stones," wrote a Maine soldier. The wounded were horribly mangled, and the ambulances, recalled one man, looked like "meat cart[s], although they were much more bloody." Despite the dire situation on the firing line and the horrid scenes on Matthews Hill, some soldiers on Howard's route still basked in the mistaken presumption of victory that lingered after that morning's engagement. "Many told us that we must hasten if we wished to bear a part, for the enemy was running," recalled one of Howard's men.[4]

Along Young's Branch at the base of Chinn Ridge, Howard formed his brigade into two lines: the 2nd Vermont and 4th Maine in front, and the 3rd and 5th Maine behind. The brigade's march to the field in intense heat and humidity had decimated Howard's ranks, and as the four regiments stood waiting along Young's Branch, some companies had as few as eight men still standing (they generally started the day with about sixty). Howard watched his men closely. "Most were pale and thoughtful. Many looked up into my face and smiled," he wrote. As the New Englanders waited, a stray bullet struck a man of the 5th Maine in the forehead, killing him almost instantly. Frank Lemont of the 5th wrote of the moment: "He was standing about three feet from me, and I shall never forget the sound the bullet made as it struck him. He fell upon his back, threw up his arms, trembled slightly and was dead. He was the first man I saw killed that day." Lemont claimed that in the moment, the sight "did not unnerve me in the least." But, he conceded, "I did think of his mother."

After a few minutes' pause along Young's Branch, Howard ordered his two lead regiments up the slope of Chinn Ridge. "Boys, keep cool," cautioned an officer of the 2nd Vermont; "take good aim and mark your man."[5]

Howard's ascent of Chinn Ridge coincided with the arrival of massive Confederate reinforcements on Henry Hill, by far the largest influx of soldiers that day: the first two regiments of Milledge Bonham's brigade—the 2nd South Carolina, commanded by Col. Joseph Kershaw, and the 8th South Carolina, led by Col. E. B. C. Cash. As the men of these two regiments passed Portici and moved toward the fight (taking a more southerly course than had Jackson and most of the earlier reinforcements), they beheld a scene that challenged their will. Beaten, wounded, and discouraged men passed them constantly, spreading dire warnings of reverse and disaster. "No use to go on," yelled one of the discouraged ones, "our own men are firing on us." The Carolinians did their best to ignore these naysayers, while officers hurried their men forward through the rabble, yelling, "On, men, on! These fellows are whipped, and think that everybody else is."[6]

Kershaw led his regiment, with Cash on his left, through the woods on the south edge of Henry Hill, sweeping aside pockets of trapped Federal infantry as he advanced. Emerging from the woods into Mrs. Henry's fields, Kershaw and Cash found few organized Confederates—the 8th and 18th Virginia and the other units that had made the last charge across Henry Hill battled toward Sudley Road off to the right. As the Carolinians pushed through the woods, they suffered scattered musket fire and artillery shells screeching through the treetops. They neared Sudley Road, and the din rose, punctuated (as it so often was that day) by the cry, "Don't fire, for God's sake, don't fire, you are firing on friends." The men of the 2nd South Carolina lay down. Colonel Kershaw concluded the men in front were indeed Yankees: "Fire on men, fire on men, fire, fire." Union soldiers scrambled out of the cover of Sudley Road "in terror," as one man described it, while the Carolinians fired "with deadly aim."

Though raked by the fire of Union batteries on Matthews Hill and Dogan Ridge, Kershaw moved past Ricketts's and Griffin's captured guns and charged down the slope to the cover of Sudley Road. There his men fired into the woods and fields west of the road. "We shot them down like beasts of prey," a soldier reported to his homefolk. Soon, Delaware Kemper's Alexandria Artillery, which had been prominent at Mitchell's Ford on the eighteenth, joined Kershaw near Ricketts's captured guns. Together, the battery and the two infantry regiments—as well as the remnants of a half-dozen spent regiments holding the road north of Kershaw—opened fire on the Regulars and other scattered Union troops west of the road. For a time the firing grew fierce.[7]

Just behind Kershaw and Cash, a much larger Confederate force hustled toward the field: three regiments of Colonel Arnold Elzey's brigade (along with Robert Beckham's Culpeper Artillery) and all of Jubal Early's brigade. Few men in the Confederate army had a deeper record of professional military experience than Elzey, who graduated from West Point and then spent twenty-four years of service in Mexico and against Indians. On July 21, his three regiments were the last of Johnston's units off the trains at Manassas, arriving there about noon.

Brig. Gen. Edmund Kirby Smith rode with Elzey that afternoon, likely to the colonel's annoyance. At that moment, Smith's own brigade lounged 35 miles away at Piedmont Station, waiting for the train and destined to miss the battle. Smith concluded that if his brigade could not get to the battle, at least he could, and thus attached himself to Elzey's brigade. By virtue of superior rank, Smith assumed command, forcing Elzey back to command of his 1st Maryland Battalion.

After a 5-mile march, much of it at double-time, Elzey and Smith pulled their troops up the winding road leading to Portici. There, Johnston immediately ordered them toward the left of the Confederate battle line. Early's brigade, coming from McLean's Ford, followed closely. A civilian surgeon watched the continuous flow of Confederate troops that afternoon as they moved down the slope toward Holkum's Branch. He called it a "glorious picture" as the advancing columns rushed "to the field through the masses of wounded bodies which strewed the roadside. . . . I could see a regiment of infantry coming in at a trot, with their bright muskets glittering in the sun; then would come a battery of artillery, each gun-carriage crowded with men, and drawn by four horses in full gallop." The surgeon concluded, "The Alps themselves could not withstand such a rush."[8]

For a time, Elzey followed Kershaw's route, moving along a slightly worn path skirting the woods on Henry Hill's southern edge. Like Kershaw's men, Elzey's suffered the discouraged voices of those leaving the field: "All is lost, all is lost, go back, or you'll be cut to pieces." While some men wavered in the face of such gloom, Elzey did not: "Forward, forward my brave men! Pay no attention to those miserable cowards and skulkers." Where Kershaw had turned to the right onto Henry Hill, Elzey and Smith continued straight, intent on moving up on Kershaw's and Cash's left. In doing so, Elzey's men collided with a pocket of Union infantry Kershaw had failed to sweep away. As the Confederate column halted briefly, the handful of Federals fired a volley that seriously wounded Smith in the neck, knocking him from his horse.[9]

Elzey took time to see Smith off the field before resuming command of his brigade. He led his men through the woods on the south edge of Henry Hill, across Sudley Road to Cash's left, and onto Bald Hill, a circular open space on the plateau between Sudley Road and the bottom of Chinn Branch. There he formed his regiments into line of battle, facing northward, only to find that numbers of Federals hovered in the woods to his left. Elzey wheeled to his left and moved westward through the woods down the slope to Chinn Branch. In front of him now loomed Chinn Ridge. Keeping his foot soldiers under cover of the woods, Elzey ordered Lieutenant Beckham to take his battery farther to the left and position itself atop the ridge near the Chinn house.[10]

Following immediately in Elzey's dusty wake marched Early's brigade, which had had a tedious day bouncing between McLean's Ford and Blackburn's Ford. Beauregard's orders to march toward the firing gave Early and his men purpose, though their march was a highly irregular affair, afflicted by prodigious straggling, warm temperatures, and the ever-present lure of blackberries. Sometime after 3 P.M., Early followed Elzey's men up the slope to Johnston's headquarters at Portici. Johnston "expressed his gratification at our arrival," Early reported, and directed the colonel to attack the enemy's right with his three regiments. Early asked Johnston to show him the position he desired, but Johnston was too busy for such details. Instead, Johnston told him to move along the rear of the line and use the gunfire as a guide until he cleared the Confederate position. Then, if all went well, he should join Elzey in the attack against the Union flank. With this mandate, Early hurried toward the firing.[11]

As Elzey's and Early's men moved into position on the Confederate left—meaningfully extending the Confederate flank for the first time that day—the two South Carolina regiments of Cash and Kershaw battled from the cover of Sudley Road. Cash's 8th South Carolina stood in the woods, but Kershaw's right faced open ground, much of it covered with tenacious remnants of Union regiments and the more formidable lines of the U.S. Regular Battalion. For 200 yards in front of Kershaw's right that open ground rolled gently, then dropped abruptly to Chinn Branch. Beyond Chinn Branch, it rose sharply again to Chinn Ridge, the northern nose of which fairly dominated the Stone House intersection and much of the Confederate line in Sudley Road. Kershaw surely sensed the potential strength of a position on Chinn Ridge, and it could have been no surprise when a large body of Union troops appeared atop the ridge: Howard's New Englanders.

The 2nd Vermont and 4th Maine—the latter under the command of Col. Hiram Berry, the former mayor of Rockland who was destined to be a major general but met his end at Chancellorsville—crested the ridge, facing southeast. To their left, they saw both Kemper's battery on Henry Hill and the South Carolinians behind the fence bordering Sudley Road. Remembered one Vermonter, "Our boys drew up their guns, took deliberate aim at the fence, and then it would have done your soul good to see the devils jump." The Vermont soldiers surely overestimated the effect of their first volleys. Soon the Confederates responded, but at the range of 300 yards, the noise far outstripped the danger of the exchange. Only the shells from Kemper's battery did damage. The infantrymen generally discharged their guns in the direction that seemed most appropriate.[12]

Along the stream at the base of Chinn Ridge, Elzey also spotted the advancing ranks on the ridge above him, but was uncertain of their identity. "Get me a glass, get me a glass," he begged, but a staff officer had eyes acute enough. "The wind threw out the Stars and Stripes," the staff officer recorded a few days later; "the long line of light shivered along their ranks as they brought their guns to a ready preparation to fire." By now, Early's men had started to move into position on Elzey's left, extending his line up the slope to the Chinn house. Beckham's battery also found its place. Elzey rushed along his line: "Stars and Stripes! Stars and Stripes! Give it to them boys." The Marylanders unleashed a volley at

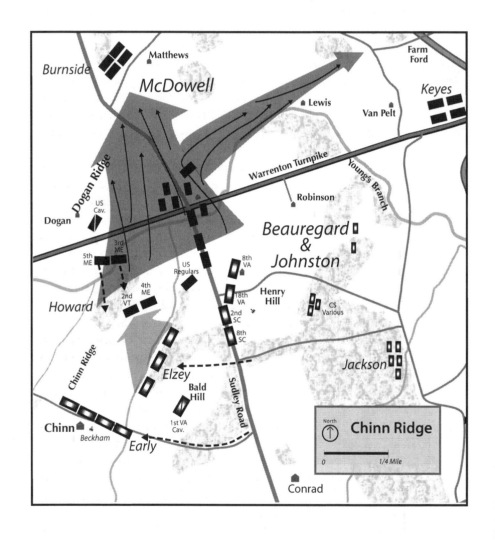

Burnside

Matthews

Farm
Ford

McDowell

Keyes

Lewis

Van Pelt

Dogan Ridge

Warrenton Turnpike

Young's Branch

US
Cav.

Robinson

Dogan

Beauregard
&
Johnston

3rd
ME

5th
ME

8th
VA

US
Regulars

4th
ME

18th
VA

Henry
Hill

2nd
VT

CS
Various

Howard

2nd
SC

Jackson

8th
SC

Chinn Ridge

Elzey

Bald
Hill

Sudley Road

Chinn

Beckham

Early

1st VA
Cav.

North

Chinn Ridge

0   1/4 Mile

Conrad

Howard's men above them, then cheered. Another volley; another cheer. Beckham's guns boomed into action near the Chinn house.[13]

Elzey's fire from a distance of 200 yards and Beckham's shells from 600 yards rattled Howard's line, though neither did much damage. "'Tis a miracle that so many of us came off safe," wrote one Union soldier. Still, the barrage had an effect, as Howard noted: "Every hostile battery shot produced confusion, and as a result our enemy could not be seen." Another man of the 2nd Vermont called it "a very uncomfortable position." He explained, "They were shooting at us with three batteries, and all the rifles and muskets in the Southern States—I thought." Still, the New Englanders held their places, firing back, though with little effect. After the 2nd Vermont and 4th Maine had fired perhaps twenty rounds per man, Howard rode back to the base of the ridge near the turnpike to bring up his second line, the 3rd and 5th Maine.[14]

To his chagrin, Howard found these regiments in disarray, the men rattled by waiting under fire. A cannon shot had struck and killed several men of the 5th. Following that, a body of Union cavalry galloped nearby. Some mistook them for Confederates—"Black Horse Cavalry!"—and a good part of the 5th regiment scattered. "It was a beautiful panic on a small scale," wrote one soldier, "in which shoulder-straps [officers] were conspicuous." Only Howard's arrival and some diligent work by lesser officers restored order in the 3rd Maine, but about half of the 5th had disappeared. The crisis atop the ridge allowed no time to chase fugitives now, and with Howard in the lead, the 3rd Maine and the remnants of the 5th Maine started up the hill to assist their comrades.[15]

Moving through the pine thicket behind the two regiments already engaged, the 3rd and 5th took their places on the firing line. The 3rd relieved the 2nd Vermont, which gratefully fell back to the thicket to act as reserve. The remnants of the 5th moved up on the right of the 4th Maine, extending the line still closer to the Chinn house and Beckham's battery. "Our men . . . marched up and fired, not an enemy in sight," a man of the 5th Maine remembered. The fire from Elzey's men in the streamside thickets below raked the ranks, and Howard's men fired blindly into the woods harboring Elzey's command, "though wholly ignorant of whether our efforts were any use or not," wrote the 5th Maine historian. One officer pulled out his revolver, with its effective range of 25 yards, and fired at Beckham's battery, fully 500 yards distant.[16]

For a few moments, everyone clung to his place in line. "Our men fought well and stood the fire like heroes," claimed a soldier of the 3rd Maine. But Howard soon ordered a wing of one regiment to retire and reposition itself. Someone misconstrued the order as a call for a general withdrawal. Though Howard's lines had in fact suffered relatively little damage, large portions of regiments fell back. A major of the 4th Maine asked Howard, "Did you order us to retreat?" Howard shook his head. Several subalterns tried to hold the disintegrating ranks in place, and some men did remain. But more did not, including

Col. Mark Dunnell of the 5th Maine, who at this critical moment became "exhausted by an attack of illness" (to use Howard's charitable words). Seeing the tide turn, Howard decided to swim with it. He ordered his brigade to fall back and re-form in the thicket to his rear.[17]

Elzey's men, in the Chinn Branch bottomland, rejoiced over Howard's disappearance behind the crest. With Early now in position on his left, Elzey ordered his brigade to charge on the New Englanders. The three regiments leaped from the timber bordering the stream with a shout and started up the ridge, "not in a very regular line but each one striving to be foremost," recalled a Marylander. The guns of Beckham's battery fired rhythmically by piece, "one, two, three, four . . . one, two, three, four."[18]

Crossing the field, Elzey's men discovered blackberry bushes heavy with their midsummer yield. The men had had little to eat that day, and the luscious fruit was too much to pass up. The charging battle line slowed, then came to a grinding halt and, wrote McHenry Howard of the 1st Maryland, "resolved itself into a crowd of blackberry pickers." Elzey's officers swore at and exhorted their men, and finally succeeded in getting the line moving again. "Still," wrote Howard, "whenever an unusually attractive bush was passed over, we reached down without stopping and stripped off berries, leaves and briers, which we crammed into our mouths; for days afterward I was occupied extracting the thorns from the palms of my hands."[19]

Elzey's line swept up Chinn Ridge to just below the crest, where wounded and dead marked Colonel Howard's former position. Leery of what lay beyond the ridgetop, Elzey sent an aide across, who saw nothing. Relieved, Elzey moved his command over the crest until it neared the pine thicket on the northernmost shoulder of the ridge. Howard's men had rallied there and now opened a sporadic fire on the Confederates. Elzey sent word back to Beckham to shell the thicket, and the combined fire of Elzey and Beckham pummeled the Federals. The 1st Maryland dashed into the thicket. "They fled like sheep," boasted one of the regiment's officers. "The last stand of Yankeedom at the battle of Manassas was taken."[20]

Up until now, Howard had managed to maintain a semblance of order in his regiments, but this renewed fire collapsed his line like a rickety camp stool. "It was no use," George Rollins of the 3rd Maine told his family. "All the other troops had left, and the rebels were coming upon us in overpowering numbers." Howard ordered yet another retreat, and this time there could be no containing the men. "Confusion, disorder seized us at once," admitted the 5th Maine historian. The fatigue that had gripped the men during the advance vanished. It was, wrote a man of the 5th Maine, "everyone for himself, and having a due regard for individuality, each gave special attention to the momentum of his legs." Defeat and disappointment had infected more than a dozen Union units that afternoon, but the New Englanders exhibited the first hints of panic.[21]

With the collapse of Howard's brigade, the only organized Federal troops remaining south of the Warrenton Turnpike were Maj. George Sykes's Regulars on the plateau at the southwest angle of the Stone House intersection. The Regulars fronted southeast, battling Kershaw and the other Confederates in Sudley Road. Howard's retreat exposed Sykes's flank and rear, and the major soon found Elzey's brigade—followed shortly by Early's and some of Stuart's commands—closing in on him from behind. The Regulars fired a few parting volleys, and then they too retreated, though with a good deal more decorum than Howard's men had demonstrated.[22]

Until this point in the battle, the tired or battered Union regiments north of the Warrenton Turnpike had maintained cohesion, if not organization, but with the retreat of Howard and the Regulars, that changed. "There were no fresh forces on the field to encourage or support them," recorded Chief of Staff Fry, and "the men seemed to be seized simultaneously by the conviction that it was no use to do anything more and they might as well start home." Governor Sprague gave the warning to the men of Burnside's 1st Rhode Island regiment: "Rhode Island, stand to your arms! Our troops are falling back on us!" From a cloud of dust in front thundered a half-dozen ammunition wagons, "driving furiously, followed by a confused crowd of soldiers of different regiments," remembered a Rhode Islander. At least one man in that crowd yelled, "Save yourselves, boys! We are whipped, and the enemy is close behind us!"[23]

As the rush of retreating soldiers increased, so too did the volume of Confederate artillery. "The scene was terrible," recalled a soldier of the 1st Rhode Island. Shells exploded, and "cavalry, infantry and artillery, in one confused mass hurried away as fast as possible." As men of the 1st Rhode Island grabbed their muskets, one gun accidentally discharged, wounding Jesse Comstock. Amid the swirl, he cried out, "Oh, dear, I'm shot. *Don't* leave me here!" His friends quickly bundled him into an ambulance. One of Comstock's friends remembered that before the ambulance started out, "a shell came tearing through the trees and landed directly on the ambulance, blowing at once to atoms one of our dearest companions." Comstock was, he wrote, "a fine fellow and a great friend of mine."[24]

McDowell and his staff, near the Matthews house, tried to rally the men, but to no avail. Fry remembered there was, however, no panic: "The men quietly walked off. . . . There was no special excitement, except that arising from the frantic efforts of the officers to stop [the] men, who paid little attention to what was said." To the Confederates, the spectacled thrilled. One of Elzey's men wrote that upon cresting Chinn Ridge, "we saw before us, and for a mile down to our right, no organized force, but one dense mass of fugitives."[25]

Rather than stop the retreat, McDowell gave orders to the Regulars and Capt. Richard Arnold's battery to cover it. With these units keeping up a bold front to discourage a too-vigorous Confederate pursuit, the Union army headed toward the crossings of Bull Run. Most followed the route that had carried them to the battlefield that morning. Heintzelman and Porter herded their divisions toward Sudley. Keyes and Sherman headed toward Farm Ford, their pace quickened by the ever-present fear of the Confederate cavalry. "Get into ranks here!" officers yelled. "If you straggle away the Cavalry will cut you down. Look out for the Black Horse Cavalry!" In some units organization collapsed, and officers simply gave up. O. O. Howard, his brigade badly scattered, passed the order, "To the old camp at Centreville. Rally at the Centreville camp." Behind them, on Henry Hill, Matthews Hill, and Chinn Ridge, the Federals left all their dead and wounded and eight pieces of captured artillery.[26]

To the Confederates, the sight of thousands of retreating Federals both thrilled and tempted. "They reminded me of nothing so much as a swarm of bees," one man wrote. On Henry Hill, amid the captured guns of Ricketts's battery, Capt. Henry Owen of the 18th Virginia Infantry fantasized about turning one of the guns on its former owners, but no one in his company knew how to fire a cannon. His disgust intensified when another company officer stepped forward with men who knew the drill. "Captain," Owen told him, "take charge of the gun and fire it. I don't know what to do with it." The other officer took over. Several shots from that gun as well as another that Kershaw's men had managed to turn and load drove the Federals out of sight.[27]

Into this triumphant scene Beauregard rode, waving his cap and yelling, "The day is ours! The day is ours!" The men cheered his every step. Across Henry Hill he galloped to Chinn Ridge, where he found Early's and Elzey's brigades. "Hail Elzey, thou Blucher of the day!" he proclaimed, shaking hands with nearly everyone within reach. This milieu mirrored that within the Federal lines on Matthews Hill that morning, when McDowell forsook immediate action to bask in the imagined glow of "victory." For Beauregard, though, there could be no doubt of victory. Only the magnitude of this stunning Confederate triumph remained a question.[28]

Chapter Ten

THE WAR
WATCHERS'
SURPRISE

As the Union army around Centreville stirred that July 21 morning, Washington, 25 miles to the east, rumbled with an excitement rarely matched in the capital's history. Throughout the city, newspapermen, politicians, and common civilians hunted up carriages for a trip to the front. It was Sunday, the week's only leisure day. Talk of battle hummed through salons and liveries, and many of the curious meant to see what they could of war. As the sun rose, clots of civilian wagons left the city heading westward, bound to witness what certainly would be unsparing, unequivocal victory over the rebellious Confederates.

A few civilians had already made the trip into the Virginia countryside, joining McDowell's army on the march to battle. These select few included some of America's luminaries: Congressman Elihu Washburne of Illinois (later Ulysses S. Grant's sponsor), Sen. Jim Lane of Kansas, future Speaker of the House Schuyler Colfax of Indiana, radical Sen. Henry Wilson of Massachusetts, and "Bluff Ben" Wade, future spiritual leader of the radical Committee on the Conduct of the War, plus a handful more. Despite their lofty positions and direct contact with McDowell and other generals, few of these civilians had any concept of the day's plan laid out by the army's commander. As the army started to march, the civilian luminaries, like the Confederates, had little idea what would happen next.

Throughout the morning and early afternoon, steady streams of hopeful spectators from Washington found their way to the Union army. They collected on the heights at Centreville, fully 5 miles from the battlefield. "They came in all manner of ways," wrote a Union officer, "some in stylish carriages, others in city hacks, and still others in buggies, on horseback, or even on foot. Apparently everything in the shape of vehicles in and around Washington had been pressed into service for the occasion."[1]

Shortly after 1 P.M. the most famous correspondent on the field, William H. Russell of the *London Times*, crested the Centreville ridge. "Stout of body, with a round chubby face flanked on either side with muttin [*sic*] chop whiskers," Russell was a bona-fide celebrity, perhaps the only veteran war correspondent on the field (he had covered the Crimean War). He immediately set out to record the day. The slopes were "covered with men, carts, and horses," Russell wrote, while spectators crowned the summit. To the west, a vast panorama lay before the audience: forest and field against the backdrop of the Bull Run Mountains, 15 miles distant. The civilian horde looked intently at the scene, but could divine little. Congressman Alfred Ely noted that the "thick woods hid from our view all the troops," though the smoke of the battle "was plainly seen, and the deep-throated roar of the artillery distinctly heard." Russell scanned the supposed battlefield intently with his glass, but he, too, was disappointed: "I failed to discover any traces of close encounter or very severe fighting."[2]

For most spectators at First Manassas, their experience was less a visual feast and more a forum for wanton speculation. Russell noted the spectators "were all excited"—especially one woman with an opera glass. She was "quite beside herself" when a louder than usual volley echoed from the distant battlefield. "That is splendid," she exclaimed. "Oh my! Is that not first-rate? I guess we will be in Richmond this time tomorrow."[3]

A handful of soldiers made their way among the spectators, offering commentary and interpretation of the unseen battle beyond Bull Run. At one point, the crowd stood rapt when an officer galloped up the Warrenton Turnpike from the direction of the battlefield (credentials enough, apparently, for the spectators to assume his word reliable). He waved his cap and conveyed stunning news: "We've whipped them at all points. We have taken their batteries. They are retreating as fast as they can, and we are after them."

The crowd atop the hill loosed a cheer that "rent the welkin," said Russell. Congressmen shook hands. "Bully for us! Bravo! Didn't I tell you so?" they exclaimed. To those safely perched on the heights of Centreville, it seemed the battle could not be going better.[4]

For curious reporters and congressmen—many determined to record rather than speculate on the proceedings—the view from Centreville offered little. Several ventured to get a closer look. Without much idea of how the battle would unfold, some headed in the wrong direction—toward the battlefield of July 18 at Blackburn's Ford, along Centreville–Manassas Road. That morning, on a ridge about a mile southeast of Centreville, Capt. John Tidball had positioned his battery, part of the force calculated to keep the Confederates' attention away from the Union flanking column to the north. Tidball watched with some amusement as civilians thronged to his position, hoping to see or learn something momentous.

"All manner of people were represented in this crowd," he wrote, "from [the] most grave and noble senators to hotel waiters." (Tidball noted tellingly, however, that "I saw none of the other sex there, except a few huxter women who had driven out in carts loaded with pies and other edibles.") They pulled up with their carriages, strewing their vehicles on the roadsides. Once the shoulders filled, the drivers pulled into the fields behind the battery, hitching their horses to bushes. All of them made a beeline to Tidball's battery. "I was plied with questions innumerably," sighed the captain.

John Tidball spent as much time providing commentary as commanding his battery that day. But, situated as he was on a secondary front far from the fighting, he could do nothing to satisfy his visitors. "Most of the sightseers were evidently disappointed at what they saw, or rather did not see," recorded Tidball. "They no doubt expected to see a battle as represented in the pictures."

The most distinguished of Tidball's visitors were the troika of Senators Henry Wilson, Ben Wade, and "Old Jim" Lane. Tidball recorded that all three were "full of the 'On to Richmond' fever," impatient to see more of the battle than Tidball's overlook offered. Mexican War veteran Senator Lane was particularly intent, declaring "he must have a hand in it [the battle] himself." When someone pointed out he lacked a gun, Lane retorted, "I can easily find a musket on the field." Lane led the trio, on foot, across the fields toward the Warrenton Turnpike. There, it seemed, a close encounter with battle (a victorious one, of course) was more likely.[5]

Wilson, Wade, and Lane would indeed find a better vantage point—the best available to any of the Manassas spectators, and indeed available only to a select few. The senators' cross-country trek would bring them to the Warrenton Turnpike, about a mile east of the Stone Bridge (more famous by the minute) over Bull Run, where Tyler's division churned in place that morning.

There, a ridge overlooking the bridge and stream afforded the best view to be had of the battlefield, short of being in the midst of it. Beyond the bridge, rising and falling crescendos of musketry and artillery fire rolled across the landscape. White smoke rose over the distant battlefield; occasionally, a skittering line of battle could be seen between the white billows as the Union battle lines on Matthews Hill eventually pushed southward. During the day, only a small knot of civilians had managed to get to this place: a half-dozen reporters, the aspiring New Jersey politico John Taylor, and the prominent Ohio judge Daniel McCook (scion of perhaps the Civil War's most militaristic family; sixteen of his kin would serve) and one of his sons.

As word of the Union's morning successes filtered back to Centreville, more civilians, like the senatorial triumvirate of Lane, Wade, and Wilson, trickled onto the ridge. Those who got to the overlook (today a huge quarry, hundreds of feet deep) were generally the well-connected and the literate: a half-dozen senators, a dozen representatives, and sundry other scribes and voyeurs, probably not more than fifty in all. Though these lucky few were but a fraction of the probably 500 civilians who ventured forth that Sunday to watch the battle, these were the men who would write of their experiences, and in doing so would convey as typical a harrowing experience that properly belonged only to a few.

Most of these civilians arrived at the overlook fired by good news and optimism. Judge McCook had been there all morning with his son Edwin, his carriage parked only a few hundred yards behind the battle line of the 2nd Ohio, in which another of his sons, Charles, toiled as an officer. While the intensity of events beyond the stream rose during the day, the mood at McCook's outpost relaxed, so much so that he invited Charles to leave his regiment and lunch with him. Congressman Elihu Washburne arrived at the overlook to the announcement from a staff officer that the "day was ours and that the enemy were on the retreat." The civilians—politicians included—cheered.[6]

By 4 P.M., the politicians had lost most of their inhibitions about involving themselves with military affairs. Washburne took it upon himself to reconnoiter for Col. Robert C. Schenck's Ohio brigade at the bridge. He spotted the enemy, then beseeched Schenck to take a look himself. Schenck did and ordered a few cannon to fire across Bull Run. When the return fire "whistled over our heads pretty sharply," Washburne decided to retire to high ground.[7]

New York Herald reporter Henry Villard was a rare civilian who maneuvered his way across Bull Run that day, with Keyes's brigade. Villard came under fire during Keyes's early assault on Henry Hill, then held close to Keyes's regiments as they huddled along Young's Branch for the two hours after the assault. From there, Villard could see nothing of the battle, but the surging and receding sounds of the fighting hinted at much. After 4 P.M., the firing on Henry Hill faded away. "Ominous fears came over us," Villard remembered. Soon word came of the Union reverse. General Tyler ordered Keyes's men to head for the Stone Bridge. Villard rode ahead of them "as fast as the ground permitted."

At the Stone Bridge—still in Union hands—Villard urgently asked for directions to McDowell's headquarters. No one could tell him, and he watched in horror as the tide of blue-clad refugees grew until the Warrenton Turnpike "swarmed with fugitives." At the bridge, Villard spotted a familiar staff officer and repeated his query for McDowell. "You won't find him," came the shocking response. "All is chaos in front. The battle is lost. Our troops are giving way and falling back without orders. Get back to Centreville."[8]

Not far from Villard, New York congressman Alfred Ely had "strolled down the road" for a better look at the battle, unaware it had gone awry. After several hundred yards, as Ely stood in the road, a bullet struck the ground near him. The congressman dodged out of the road and found refuge with some others behind a tree, frozen, as he admitted, "from fear of being shot if I moved." How long he remained there, he was unable to say, but it must have been nearly an hour—long enough for the situation around him to change dramatically.[9]

Slowly but steadily, defeat rippled through Union regiments. "It was not in the power of human exertion to restrain them [or] to form them," one of McDowell's staff officers wrote in a letter. Only one battalion, Sykes's Regulars, retained much in the way of order, gaining fame that day not by their fighting, but by their refusal to panic. First on the western shoulder of Henry Hill, then on Matthews Hill, the Regulars faced the looming Confederates, each time attracting fire from Southern batteries (which one man said were "particularly attentive" to the Regulars). But the efforts of the Regulars could not diminish the reality of the moment. The Confederates who now controlled Henry Hill, Sudley Road, and Chinn Ridge beheld a panorama few of them would have dared to predict at the day's beginning: the Union army reduced to a swarm, surging back toward the crossings of Bull Run.[10]

The Confederates had put the Yankees to flight, but could Beauregard and Johnston do the Federal army even more damage—perhaps destroy it altogether? Certainly they had the weapons to do so. Elzey's brigade was winded after its attack on Howard, but still stood intact on the northern shoulder of Chinn Ridge. So too did Beckham's battery, Stuart's cavalry battalion, and Early's brigade, which joined Elzey in the latter stages of his attack against Howard. The 19th Virginia of Cocke's brigade soon joined Early and Elzey, while on Henry Hill Beauregard had Kershaw's 2nd South Carolina, Cash's 8th South Carolina, the 8th and 18th Virginia, and the newly arrived 28th Virginia. With these regiments were pieces of a half-dozen other units, battered from earlier fighting but still more than willing to join the battle. All told, the Confederates could muster probably 7,000 troops on or near Henry Hill.

In the days, months, and years to follow, that moment on July 21, 1861, seemed pregnant with possibilities for the Confederates. Certainly Beauregard recognized this at the time, but he also quickly recognized the obstacles. Most important of all was the speed of the Union retreat. It was no panic yet, but certainly the Union fugitives proceeded purposefully toward and across Bull Run (most of them leaving by the same route they had come). The need to act instantly and without plan forced Beauregard to repeat what he had done all afternoon: throw the nearest troops forward, without much design.

Beauregard ordered Col. Robert T. Preston's 28th Virginia to move first. The regiment, which had earlier claimed the honor of capturing the wounded Federal colonel Orlando Willcox in the woods south of Henry Hill, stormed down the north slope of the hill and across the turnpike to the Stone House, where it found many wounded and dead and thirty-six men who had sought safety behind the massive stone walls. The 28th surged onward, up the slopes of Matthews Hill, following the footsteps of much of the Union army toward Sudley Ford. But the Virginians found only more wounded—hundreds dotted the fields—and disappointment: the Union army had retreated out of sight.[11]

After a short rest, Early's brigade likewise set out in pursuit, following the route of those Union troops heading toward Farm Ford, above the Stone Bridge. Past the John Dogan and Matthews houses to Pittsylvania Early's men rushed.

There they too lost the trail. "Nothing could be seen of the enemy," wrote Early, "and his troops had scattered so much in the retreat that it was impossible for me to tell what route he had taken." Early advanced his brigade to Poplar Ford on Bull Run, and there he halted.[12]

Beauregard needed cavalry to run down the Union army, just as Joachim Murat had famously led Napoleon's cavalry in pursuit of the Prussians after the Battle of Auerstedt in 1806. But Beauregard, like McDowell, had little of that arm, and what he did have he had dispersed in small clots of a few companies all along his front. Johnston had organized his cavalry differently, putting twelve companies under the command of Stuart. But Stuart, too, had split his force, and now the largest part of the 1st Virginia, perhaps 150 strong, stood with Early and Elzey on Chinn Ridge. Though Stuart's men had already done much, they set out rapidly after the Union troops streaming northward across Matthews Hill and along the road to Sudley. A soldier from Maine who saw them coming admitted to a sensation of fear—the first of the day: "The idea of going as far I had been that day and getting out so far and so well, and then having my head cut off was anything but pleasant."[13]

Stuart and his men soon swooped down on the Federal rearguard. The Regulars and Arnold's battery made a brief stand. The Regulars formed a "hollow square" as defense against Stuart, an old Napoleonic tactic that would, after this battle, quickly vanish from the armies' tactical repertoire. But on this day, the maneuver impressed enough observers to be memorable. More importantly, it dissuaded Stuart from a too-vigorous chase. While the cavalrymen failed to do real damage to the Yankees, they did manage to corral dozens of Union stragglers—so many that the Union prisoners managed to do what the Federal army could not: slow Stuart down. Stuart shuttled them to the rear as fast as he could, but each group of captives needed escorts, and the colonel soon found his command whittled to almost nothing as squad after squad headed rearward with prisoners. Still, a few horsemen continued the pursuit northward toward Sudley.[14]

Meanwhile, McDowell's retreating regiments re-crossed Bull Run, most units repeating in reverse that morning's 10-mile flank march. Near Sudley Ford, several local women had taken refuge during the day at the home of Robert Carter Weir, not far from Sudley Mill. Throughout the day, the women had suffered the boasts of Union stragglers, convinced Union victory loomed. As the clocks ticked toward 5 P.M., a "lively little widow" in the group looked up and saw "dark-looking objects" running across a distant field. "What does that mean?" she wondered. It took only seconds for her Union audience to recognize Federal troops in retreat, with some of Stuart's cavalrymen not far beyond. The blue-clad visitors to the Weir house concluded, as one of the gleeful women put it, that they "had better be going." The widow broke into a triumphant song, "beating time with her hands to a quick step for them."[15]

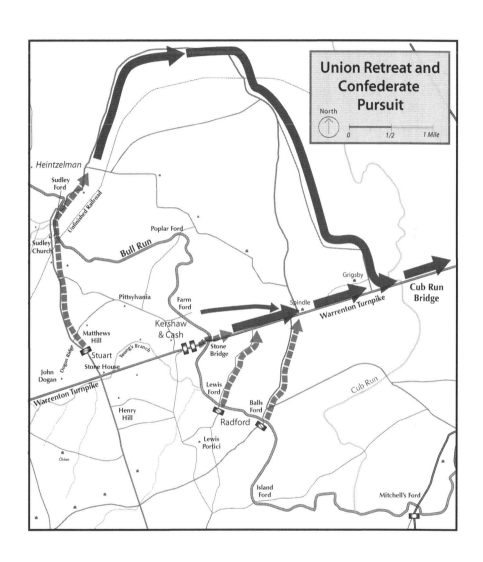

Union Retreat and Confederate Pursuit

North

0   1/2   1 Mile

Heintzelman

Sudley Ford

Unfinished Railroad

Poplar Ford

Sudley Church

Bull Run

Pittsylvania

Farm Ford

Grigsby

Cub Run Bridge

Spindle

Warrenton Turnpike

Kershaw & Cash

Matthews Hill

Young's Branch

Stone Bridge

Dogan Ridge

Stuart

Stone House

Cub Run

John Dogan

Lewis Ford

Balls Ford

Warrenton Turnpike

Henry Hill

Radford

Lewis Portici

Chinn

Island Ford

Mitchell's Ford

Across Bull Run at Sudley Ford, Governor Sprague of Rhode Island confronted Union fugitives, but in vain. "The panic had gone too far," a Massachusetts man wrote days later, "and the only thing left for the men was to fly for their lives." The prospect of marching back to Centreville at first seemed preposterous to this Massachusetts soldier, but, he admitted, "finding no other course open I joined the mob and made my way."[16]

The Union march from the field proceeded, not surprisingly, faster than the morning's march to it. In the morning, the management of troops at the junction of the Warrenton Turnpike and the road to Sudley Ford had carefully avoided tangles. But during the Union retreat, that crossroads became a bottleneck as men rushing south from Sudley merged with Union troops heading east from the Stone Bridge and Farm Ford.

This bottleneck would become Beauregard's great opportunity. If he could get a sizable force in motion across the Stone Bridge, he might disrupt the Federal retreat along the turnpike—the only reasonable avenue of escape. Beauregard directed three regiments and one battery to undertake the job. Robert Withers's 18th Virginia moved first, but the fear of encountering Hains's massive cannon at the Stone Bridge inspired Withers to cross at Lewis Ford, below the bridge. That cast the two South Carolina regiments under Kershaw (the 2nd) and Cash (the 8th) as the snapping jaws of the Confederate pursuit. Robert Beckham's battery from Culpeper, Virginia, followed. The Confederates rushed eastward on the Warrenton Turnpike and across the bridge. Kershaw stopped there, eyeing with some concern a considerable Federal force deployed on the heights above him. Rather than attack, he sent an aide to inform Beauregard that the stream was crossed, that the enemy was in front, and that he awaited orders.[17]

Near Portici, Gen. Theophilus Holmes arrived with his brigade of infantry and a company of cavalry from Albemarle County under Maj. John Scott. Scott rode expectantly to Holmes for orders. "Go on, sir," Holmes said, as though the next phase of battle were universally understood. "And away we did go," wrote one of the cavalrymen, "without knowing . . . exactly where we were going to or what we were going after." The horsemen cared little about that. "We were all too high strung," the cavalryman recorded, "and there was only a general impression that it was a sort of fox chase on a very expanded scale." Scott's men soon caught up to Kershaw's regiment east of the Stone Bridge.[18]

Beauregard had managed the pursuit by units once engaged on Henry Hill, but Johnston, too, looked for a way to get at the retreating Yankees. From his headquarters at Portici, Johnston had far less with which to work—virtually all the troops in sight had moved northward to support the combat on Henry Hill. He had nearby only a makeshift battalion of six companies of cavalry under Col. R. C. W. Radford and another smaller battalion commanded by Col. Thomas T. Munford. These he ordered across Bull Run at Lewis Ford. The road from Lewis Ford intersected the Warrenton Turnpike on the high ground fully a mile east of the Stone Bridge, not far from Mrs. Spindle's house. A swift movement might strike and break apart the retreating Union column. Within minutes, nearly a thousand mounted troopers galloped across Bull Run at Lewis Ford, toward the Warrenton Turnpike. The geometry of the Confederates' movement looked promising, if only they moved quickly enough.[19]

On the ridge overlooking Bull Run and the Stone Bridge, where the gaggle of well-connected civilians had gathered, those who remained sensed the predicted triumph across Bull Run had unraveled. Soon, Confederate cavalry charged up the hill from the left, from the direction of Lewis Ford. Their sudden appearance startled soldier and civilian alike. Judge Daniel McCook had spent the day watching over his son Charles's regiment, the 2nd Ohio, and occasionally providing Private McCook with private refreshments. Now he watched in horror as Confederate cavalry bore down on his son. Charles McCook fled along a fence line, with a Confederate officer on horseback chasing him. "Charles kept him most manfully at bay with his bayonet," wrote Judge McCook a few days later. The Confederate demanded Charles McCook's surrender. "No, never; no never to a rebel," young Charles declared. The horseman circled around McCook and shot him in the back. Someone in turn shot the Confederate officer. Judge McCook gathered up the mangled body of his wounded son and, laying him on a makeshift bed in his carriage, started a mournful ride back toward Centreville. Charles would die within hours; Judge Daniel McCook became perhaps the only parent to witness his son's death on this or any other battlefield of the war.[20]

Radford's cavalry likewise threatened hundreds of Union soldiers gathered around the well of the Spindle house, yards farther east on the Warrenton Turnpike. The horsemen struck just as two guns of Romeyn B. Ayres's battery pulled up and unlimbered in the yard. The sudden movement roused Union lieutenant Peter Hains, the commander of the 30-pounder Parrott rifle the Confederates liked to call "Long Tom," as he waited his turn at the well. "Fall in here!" Lieutenant Hains yelled. "Fall in, men! Rally about me, quick—that's rebel cavalry!" Few of the tired soldiers paid any attention to the twenty-one-year-old officer, and only three heeded his order. "Fire, for God's sake, fire—that's Virginia cavalry!" Hains screamed. The four-man line managed only two shots. Meanwhile Ayres's two guns loosed two rounds of canister. The thunderous boom did little to dissuade the Confederates, but it did jolt to action the Federals in Mrs. Spindle's yard. Some men (including civilians) pulled out their weapons and fired. Others insisted the horsemen were friendly. Still more simply ran. And then Radford's cavalry charged.[21]

Any appearance of Confederate horsemen that day prompted cries of "Black Horse Cavalry" from Union soldiers. The specter of the "Black Horse" and "masked batteries" lived vividly in the mind of vulnerable Yankees, though in fact few Union soldiers experienced either. Still, the charge of Radford's troopers was frightening enough. Ayres's battery fired another volley that briefly stayed the onrush, but soon Radford's horsemen laid claim to dozens of prisoners, several wagons and ambulances, and the biggest prize of all: several guns of Carlisle's battery, which had been abandoned along the road.

As the horsemen hacked their way along the turnpike, they came upon a heavy Federal line secreted along the roadside. A few volleys brought the Confederates to a halt. Radford decided to wait for artillery support before pushing farther. While waiting, he undoubtedly derived great pleasure from the sight of hundreds of frightened Federals hurrying toward the bridge over Cub Run. A northern congressman amid the mayhem admitted, "Everybody seemed to have gone crazy."[22]

While Radford and his troopers swiped at the flank of the Federal column, Kershaw, Cash, and Kemper awaited orders near the Stone Bridge. Before long—after Radford's charge—a staff officer appeared, authorizing Kershaw to pursue the enemy "with a view to cut them off," Kershaw recalled. Withers's 18th Virginia regiment took over as security at the bridge, while the Carolinians and Kemper's battery started down the turnpike toward the east.

As the 8th South Carolina crossed the low ground east of Stone Bridge, two officers spotted a small man huddled behind a tree. They asked his identity.

"Alfred Ely," the man replied.

"What state are you from?"

"From the State of New York," Ely answered.

"Are you connected with the government?" prodded the soldiers.

"A Representative in Congress," answered Ely (stupidly).

One of the officers grabbed Ely by the arm, stripped him of a pistol, and proclaimed him a prisoner. The two officers hustled Ely to their commander, Col. E. B. C. Cash of the 8th South Carolina. When they announced the identity of their prisoner, Cash—a cantankerous old farmer who would kill a man in a duel in 1880—pointed his pistol at Ely's head. "God damn your white-livered soul!" screeched Cash. "I'll blow your brains out on the spot!"

Ely ducked behind the officers, and the junior officers interceded: "Colonel, Colonel, you must not shoot that pistol, he is our prisoner."

"He's a member of Congress, God damn him," thundered the colonel. "Came out here to see the fun! Came to see us whipped and killed! God damn him! If it was not for such as he there would be no war. . . . God damn him. I'll show him." Again Cash tried to get an angle on Ely to kill him, and again the congressman— "evidently scared almost into a fit"—dodged away. The signalman Capt. Porter Alexander watched all this and finally intervened, invoking Beauregard's name. "You must not shoot a prisoner. Never shoot an unarmed man," Alexander said. Cash finally put away his pistol and quelled his pique. The South Carolinians hustled Ely to the rear. He would spend the next six months in a Richmond prison, a political prize tormented all the while by his captors. Once released, Ely would write a best-selling book about his ordeal.[23]

Meanwhile, Kershaw's and Cash's infantry and Kemper's artillery resumed their advance eastward on the Warrenton Turnpike, up the ridge to the plateau between Bull Run and Cub Run. With Radford's battalion stilled by Union resistance, any chance of cutting off the Union retreat was now gone. Kershaw could only hope to harass the rearguard and exacerbate the chaos among the retreating Yankees.

Mounting the ridge, Kershaw's men beheld a scene that almost defied description. Not far in front of them, the Union troops who had retreated along the road from Sudley Ford merged onto the Warrenton Turnpike, mixing with men heading eastward from the Stone Bridge and Farm Ford. The result was a tangle of traffic likely unmatched in American history up to that time. Men, ambulances, limbers, caissons, quartermaster wagons, and even a few civilian conveyances jammed the Warrenton Turnpike. Thousands of soldiers, with perhaps eighty civilian spectators mixed in, spilled off the road into the fields, hastening toward the bridge over Cub Run. Debris covered the roadsides, including buggies cut loose from horses, accoutrements, clothing, musical instruments, muskets, and provisions—anything that might slow an urgent man. "The officers of the army and the civilian spectators brought with them every conceivable comfort and delicacy," recalled one of the first Confederates to reach the booty. One pursuing cavalryman remembered passing tables set up along the roadside, and horsemen regularly jumped from their mounts to scoop up goodies. "I fancied some white sugar," the cavalryman wrote, and filled his tin cup with it. By day's end, the sugar had all been jostled away, save a few grains. Another Confederate looter proclaimed, "Their viands fell into the possession of those who, to say the least, were in a condition to do them more than justice."[24]

Ignoring the temptations around him, Kershaw saw the potential this seething mass of retreating Yankees held as a target for artillery. The topography rolled, but the road was arrow-straight, offering a narrow but certain field of fire 2 miles deep. Kershaw deployed skirmishers and ordered Captain Kemper to place two guns of his Alexandria Artillery south of the turnpike.

With Kemper that day rode one of the most famous civilians the war had yet produced: sixty-seven-year old planter Edmund Ruffin. With his long white mane and scowling, Yankee-hating visage, Ruffin had managed to put himself in the middle of things at Fort Sumter in April, and he did the same again. Kemper offered him the chance to fire the first shot at the retreating Yankee horde. Soon an explosive round of spherical case shot whistled the 1,000 yards toward the rickety bridge over Cub Run, where hundreds of men and dozens of wagons and cannon sought to squeeze across. Kemper's fire turned a disorderly retreat into an abject rout.[25]

Ruffin's first shot exploded directly over the crowded span, the blast causing a wagon on the bridge to career and flip. "It was the first time that day that I had seen anything to startle me," remembered a Rhode Island artilleryman standing on the bridge. "Before the third shell struck near us, every man as far as the eye could reach seemed to be running for [his] very life."[26]

With the bridge blocked, men and animals poured into the adjacent fields and woods and splashed into the waist-deep stream, flailing over each other to get across. One man explained to his family what was probably the feeling of many at the time: "I thought to myself Ames you have got to get across that brook or have your throat cut." Another recalled, "I do not think a man of us really expected to escape." Teamsters cut loose their teams and some ambulance drivers emptied their wagons of wounded to improve their speed.[27]

While men and individual horses might get across Cub Run anywhere (though not without difficulty because of its steep banks), anything with wheels had nowhere to go. Teamsters struggled with wagons and artillerymen with cannon, and Kemper's shells prevented anyone from thinking long about trying to clear the bridge of wreckage. One of Burnside's men observed, "Baggage wagons were piled one upon another, the guns crowded together, and men lay all around, some dead, others wounded and dying."[28]

London Times correspondent William H. Russell arrived at Cub Run just in time to see the disaster unfold. His account would do more to shape the public—and historical—perception of the Union defeat than anyone else's, and his was not a flattering narrative. "The scene on the [Warrenton] road had now assumed an aspect which has not a parallel in any description I have ever read. Infantry soldiers on mules and draught horses. . . . Negro servants on their masters' wagons; ambulances crowded with unwounded soldiers; wagons swarming with men who threw out the contents in the road to make room, grinding through a shouting, screaming mass of men on foot, who were literally yelling with rage," he wrote. Union men—civilians or soldiers—had no option "but to go with the current one could not stem."[29]

The tangled mass at the bridge made an easy mark for Kemper's guns. Indeed, many felt the continued Confederate attack to be nothing short of cruel. "I leaped over the fence," wrote a man of Burnside's brigade, "when I heard a loud crash and looking back I beheld the upper half of a soldier's body flying up the hill. He had almost been cut in twain by a solid ball. At this almost barbarous cruelty—that is, firing upon an almost unarmed and entirely unopposing force, a cry of mortal terror arose among the flying soldiers."[30]

Congressman Elihu Washburne had started away in his buggy before the panic spread and managed to cross Cub Run, only to come across a wounded soldier. The congressman nobly gave up his seat to the man and began walking. In moments, "I beheld a perfect avalanche pouring down the road immediately behind me," he later wrote. "*It was the retreat of the army* . . . a perfect panic had seized every body. The soldiers threw away their guns and their blankets. . . . Officers, I blush to say, were running with their men." He conceded, "Never before had I such feelings."

New congressman Albert Gallatin Riddle of Ohio constantly "implored, beseeched, and denounced" the fleeing troops for what he saw as a "dastardly, needless flight." At least twice during his trip back to Centreville, hangers-on brought Riddle's buggy to a standstill by their sheer weight. "We ordered them off sometimes in very peremptory terms," Riddle wrote, conceding his own language in doing so "could be easily reprehended."[31]

Washburne hitched a ride with an acquaintance, but then concluded he might do something about the panic. He stopped the carriage and tried to rally the men, but, as he later wrote, "we might as well have attempted to stop the current of the Mississippi with a straw."

Other politicians also sought to reverse the rout along the road to Centreville and Fairfax; indeed, one newspaperman claimed that only civilians—no soldiers— attempted to rally anyone that day. Beyond Centreville, Riddle jumped out of his buggy to join Senators Benjamin Wade and Zachariah Chandler and others in confronting the crush of panicked soldiers. Riddle recalled that eight members of Congress spread themselves across the road and "forbade any man to pass," using "some strong language to bring them to their senses." Wade stood in the middle "with his hat on the back of his head and his rifle in his hand, and said he would shoot the first man who attempted to run any further." Chandler brandished a big navy revolver; his face "was pale and his eyes were bloodshot." He called the soldiers "fools and cowards," and declared they would go farther only over his dead body. It's unlikely any of the soldiers knew the identity of their beseechers, but some stopped nonetheless. The pause of a few, however, did nothing to slow the tide of the many.[32]

New Jersey grocer and aspiring politician John Taylor stood agape at the spectacle, "dazed and confounded," he admitted. On either side of the road, crowds of soldiers surged toward Centreville. The men had discarded so much that Taylor was certain he "could almost have walked from the field to Centreville on bags of oats, bales of hay, and boxes of ammunition." But, Taylor wrote, the most startling aspect of the retreat was its hurry. "Every one seemed after the honor of being the first man to enter Washington," he wrote. Soldiers dashed at wagons to cut loose the horses and, "with two on a horse, gallop off toward home." Lamented Taylor, "Every sentiment of shame, and all sense of manhood was absent for the moment."[33]

The panic at the bridge over Cub Run persisted for perhaps a half hour. By 6:30 P.M., presumably all of the Federals who would cross the stream had gotten over. Among the last to reach Cub Run was Lt. Peter Hains and his beloved 30-pounder Parrott gun, which his ten-horse team managed to haul through the run. But the hill east of the stream proved insurmountable, steep and hopelessly obstructed with discarded debris. "My wheelers strained the utmost," Hains explained. "The men lashed the sweating, panting animals again and again. But the great gun refused to move up the incline." There it remained, tangled with tons of debris and refuse, destined to fall into the hands of the Confederates—perhaps the greatest trophy of the battle.[34]

Around Centreville, McDowell's reserves took steps to cover the retreat of the army, despite the impaired condition of their commander, Dixon Miles, who had been unwell and received a prescription for liquor from his doctor. That medicinal prescription turned into something else entirely, and by early evening Miles stumbled about, clearly inebriated. (A court of inquiry later confirmed his drunken state, but concluded that a court-martial would not serve "the interests of the service.") Nonetheless, Miles did manage to cordon off Centreville against a potential Confederate advance. Col. Louis Blenker moved his brigade west of the village to the ridge overlooking Rocky Run, where his regiments watched carefully as retreating fugitives streamed past them. Colonels Israel Richardson and Thomas Davies moved their brigades back from near Mitchell's Ford, though Richardson suffered the misfortune of leaving behind his sword and (worse!) his omnipresent wife's horse and sidesaddle. Richardson asked permission to send a flag of truce into Confederate lines to seek the return of the items, but no one seemed inclined to permit such a thing amid a national emergency. Richardson instead requisitioned his surgeon's horse for his wife's use, sending her off toward Alexandria with her own cavalry escort. The surgeon later reasoned, "I considered it a privilege to render any service to either the male or female commander of our brigade."[35]

As the sun inched toward the distant Bull Run Mountains, Confederate signal officer Porter Alexander rode back through the pursuing Confederates to the Stone Bridge. There he encountered Capt. Sam Ferguson, a staff officer from Beauregard on a mission, looking glum. "Hello, Sam, what's the matter?" asked Alexander.

"I'm going to bring everything back," Ferguson announced, "to our side of [Bull Run]." A rumor of a Union advance against the Confederate right near Union Mills had made the rounds, Ferguson explained, the product of "some fool." Now Beauregard wanted everyone back.[36]

Still, Kemper, Kershaw, and Cash could rejoice at the havoc they had created. That morning, such a stampede seemed unthinkable. The Confederates had won a victory and inflicted humiliation. "The setting sun saw the grand army of the north flying for dear life," proclaimed a South Carolinian. Not a few observed with evident pleasure that, though it took the Union army nearly four days to get from Washington to Bull Run, it would likely require less than twelve hours for it to retrace its steps.[37]

As the panicked mob moved toward and beyond Centreville, it transformed into a discouraged flood, protected by a strong line of infantry and artillery just west of the crossroads. Artillery captain John Tidball had by now moved his battery to the Warrenton Turnpike and watched as the bedraggled crowd flowed by. Tidball recognized the Senatorial troika of Lane, Wilson, and Wade. Lane came by first, mounted on a "flea-bitten gray horse with a rusty harness on" and wielding a musket he had picked up on the field. Not far behind Lane trundled Senator Wilson, "hot and red in the face from exertion . . . in his shirtsleeves, carrying his coat on his arm." When he reached Tidball, Wilson—who would later briefly command the 22nd Massachusetts ("Henry Wilson's Regiment")—swabbed the sweat from his brow and growled, "Cowards! Why don't they turn and beat back the scoundrels?"

And finally up the hill toiled Bluff Ben Wade, future chair of the Joint Committee on the Conduct of the War, without the strength to do anything but drag his coat on the ground behind him. Wrote Tidball, "As he approached me I thought I had never beheld so sorrowful a countenance." Wade's normally long face seemed "still more lengthened by the weight of his heavy under-jaws . . . so heavy it seemed to overtax his exhausted strength to keep his mouth shut."

The scenes seem comical in remembrance, but the presence of some of the most powerful men in the nation accorded the disastrous retreat even more significance. Newspapermen, congressmen, and captains of industry found themselves not just witness to disaster, but part of it. Their powerful pens and public utterances would shape perception of the battle. More importantly, their experiences at Bull Run would inspire a years-long suspicion of the army and its leaders—a suspicion that found voice in Congressional efforts to oversee the war effort.[38]

As the Union army trudged into and through Centreville that evening, soldiers and civilians alike reckoned with a historic day. The panic in the ranks subsided beyond Centreville, and indeed several regiments got a couple hours' sleep in Centreville before the last troops departed about 10 P.M. The adjutant of the 16th New York sat on the grass with his chaplain and colonel. "Rumor after rumor" came to them from the passing crowd, each seeming to confirm the latest and worst news: the army's retreat had been intercepted; the Confederates held Alexandria; large Confederate forces already stood on the verge of the capital. The three sat there, the adjutant wrote, "with the solemn conviction that we had each of us seen the sun shine for the last time."[39]

Rumors swirled and subsided (the Confederates would not again cross Bull Run), then yielded altogether to the largest question of all: Did this humiliation mean the end of the war, the end of the Union? Thousands of soldiers contemplated that question as they marched through the night in untidy, quiet columns, eventually through a steady drizzle of rain. The wounded limped along. A few carried injured friends. "We stumbled along through the hours of darkness, gradually becoming scattered," recorded a man of the 1st Rhode Island. Surveying the scene, another Rhode Islander expressed simply the feeling of the entire Federal army that night: "I think I never felt so badly in my life."[40]

Chapter Eleven

WRECKAGE

No one doubted that whatever battle raged near Manassas that July would have immense political and social implications—and it did. But few could possibly have foreseen the physical and emotional imprint of battle on the land and on those who experienced it. The aftermath of battle revealed a simmering mix of chaos, horror, and jubilation.

At the bridge over Cub Run, about fifty men of the Albemarle Light Horse— riding with Kershaw—poked through the tangled spoils of the Union retreat. One of the horsemen counted sixteen abandoned Yankee cannon, caissons and wagons of all sorts (some with horses still attached), and a "little two-horse carriage . . . elegantly fixed up, with oil cloth coats, bottles of cologne, [and] a fine guitar." Another carriage of "a more substantial character" produced hermetically sealed meats, vegetable soup, and "oh! a box of elegant liquor"—whiskey, brandy, champagne, and other wines. The soldier conceded, "We could not help feel some respect for this fellow [the former owner]. He was certainly a fine judge of spirits, and treated us in style. We actually drank to his health and reformation." For the next several hours, Confederates worked through the jumble of abandoned vehicles and guns. By 1 A.M., the best of everything, including all the cannon, was on the road to Manassas Junction.[1]

Around Confederate headquarters at Portici, dusk shone on a chaotic, jubilant, and even uncertain scene. The Union collapse had provoked a furious though unorganized pursuit across Bull Run, one that created panic in Yankee columns. Beauregard desperately wished for something more, but rumor defeated him once again. The false word of a Union crossing at McLean's Ford prompted Beauregard, as Capt. Sam Ferguson had noted, to halt the pursuit on the Warrenton Turnpike and rush at least two brigades (Ewell's and Holmes's) to meet the emergency. Beauregard himself thundered ahead of the infantry, but when he arrived at the ford, he realized the mistake: the force crossing was not

145

Federal, but rather D. R. Jones's brigade returning from its demonstration against the Union rearguard on the Manassas–Centreville Road.[2]

Though Johnston and Beauregard lamented the false report and their not-unreasonable reaction to it (the episode ended any pursuit of the Yankees), the victory seemed complete enough. President Davis, a West Point graduate and former secretary of war who would much rather have been leading soldiers on a battlefield than presiding over a government, arrived on the battlefield late in the afternoon. At first, he heard only doom as the wounded and disheartened passed him, heading rearward. He rode toward Henry Hill and down the slope toward Holkum's Branch, where the Confederates had placed their largest field hospital and where fought-out soldiers lingered by the hundreds. Jackson's surgeon, Hunter McGuire, remembered that Davis "looked around at this great crowd of soldiers. His face was deadly pale and his eyes flashing." The president rose in his stirrups. "I am President Davis; all of you who are able follow me back to the field." General Jackson was nearby, getting his wounded finger treated. When told of Davis's presence, Jackson stood up, took off his cap, saluted, and announced, "We have whipped them; they ran like dogs. Give me ten thousand men and I will take Washington city to-morrow [sic]."[3]

Thus corrected (and surely relieved), Davis rode back to Johnston at Portici. The two spoke briefly before Davis turned his attention to the hundreds of Confederates in the fields around him. Lifting his hat, he called for cheers, which soon resounded across the fields as each unit in turn took to jubilant yelling. Within minutes, the cheering spread as far as Longstreet's brigade at Blackburn's Ford, 4 miles away. "As the noise of battle died away," wrote one of Longstreet's men, "from away up the run we heard shouts and cheers, at first scarcely audible, then louder and louder . . . rolling down the valley of Bull Run in seeming waves of mingled voices. . . . Messengers mounted on fleet-footed steeds . . . hurried down the lines along the run shouting, 'Victory! Victory! Victory; complete victory!'" Another of Longstreet's soldiers remembered, "Such excitement ensued which beggars description, a scene which in all of my soldier's experiences, before, or after, I never seen the like [sic]. The enthusiasm passed all bounds, it approached madness. . . . Every man of the thousands assembled threw their caps in the air, officers and all. We cheered everybody from Beauregard down to the captains and lieutenants."[4]

At Portici, soldiers of all stripes crowded around their president. A cavalry unit organized an impromptu review. The jubilant horsemen circled Davis and draped him in their Confederate flags, nearly pulling him from his horse in the process. The president made halfhearted efforts to protect himself, but in the end yielded to his enthusiastic volunteers. This army had made history that day.[5]

The question remained: Should the army make more history the following day? What next? If Hunter McGuire can be believed, Jackson emphatically answered "Yes," and promised to take Washington with just 10,000 soldiers.

Beauregard later claimed that he, too, urged a vigorous assault on the Union army and its capital. Indeed, he saw the possibilities in grand terms: the fruits of victory at Manassas should have included nothing short of the scattering of all Union forces south of Baltimore and east of the Alleghenies, the liberation of Maryland, and the capture of Washington, D.C. Jackson's outburst, surely, reflected the excitement of the moment rather than careful consideration of the circumstances. As for Beauregard's assertions, four years of efforts by armies far larger and better organized than his never came close to achieving any of those objectives. Johnston was closer to being correct than either of them when he asserted, "The Confederate army was more disorganized by victory than that of the United States by defeat." There would be no pursuit after the victory at Man-assas.[6] Instead, there would be the inevitable reckoning with the horror and legacy of one of America's most historic days.

That Sunday evening, a mile beyond Confederate headquarters at Portici, the battlefield heaved and twitched under the weight of carnage. Hundreds of wounded men lay on the field, some of them struggling or signaling for help. Around them, hundreds more lay frozen in death.

The sheer number of dead—nearly 900—on the Matthews, Henry, Robinson, and Chinn farms was shocking: July 21, 1861, was the deadliest day in America's short history. The night of the battle, a group of Georgians searched for the body of Col. Francis Bartow. They moved from corpse to corpse, and in the process suffered a stark lesson in the destructive power of bullets and artillery. On one corpse: "the lower part of his face has been carried away." Over there, "the bloody track" left by a dying man vainly trying to reach water. At another place, only a leg. Just beyond, a body without its head. And here, "the scattered fragments of a body." Along the line of Ricketts's guns, "five horses in a heap" marked the location of a limber or caisson. Not far away was "another heap of as many more." Dozens of similar descriptions appeared in letters and newspapers across the South, conveying to sitting rooms everywhere the harsh reality of death on a battlefield, and perhaps the loss of a loved one.[7]

For dozens of Confederate soldiers, their recompense for glorious victory was the gory task of burying the dead on a rainy Monday. They buried Confederates first, interring most by the end of the day; a brown mound of dirt marked each grave. A visitor the next day noted that some clearly had been interred by caring friends: a few graves had tidy enclosures built around them, while others had evergreen boughs laid upon them. Headboards and even footboards, carved or painted, marked some with the names of the fallen. Occasionally, a board nailed to a tree indicated the nearby graves of those from a common regiment or company.[8] Someone with a sense of history also troubled himself to mark the places where men of rank had fallen—perhaps Bee, Bartow, Fisher, Jordan, and others—by driving inscribed posts into the ground. At least some of these rudimentary monuments, likely the first commemorative devices placed on any battlefield of the war, yielded to more durable successors and remain marked on the field today.[9]

If the 900 dead was a stunning figure, the more than 2,600 wounded at Manassas presented a challenge by the immense care they required. Indeed, few aspects of the battle illustrated more vividly the nascent condition of the armies and their unpreparedness for war than did their improvised management of men often mangled in ways few physicians had ever seen.

The wounded appeared almost immediately after the opening volleys, stumbling or dragging themselves rearward, sometimes on the arm of a willing stranger or friend, looking for safety and care. Behind the lines, clots of medical men waited, equipment at the ready. The first cases to appear received the sort of close, careful attention the doctors might have given a neighbor girl's broken ankle in their hometown. But as the number of wounded quickly grew, the examinations became more hurried, even cursory. It soon became obvious to all these medical men of the armies just how unprepared they were for the dreadful day ahead.[10]

Early in the fighting on Matthews Hill, Union surgeons set up at a house just behind the firing line—probably the abandoned Carter mansion, Pittsylvania. The scenes there shocked *New York Tribune* reporter William Croffut, who had accompanied McDowell's flanking column. "Such a scene of death and desolation!" Croffut wrote. Wounded, the dying, and even the dead filled the house and yard—a "frightful misery." He joined other civilians and common soldiers in washing and binding wounds. Someone hung a white flag from the house, though the protection was largely imagined. Shells exploded nearby and "flew over and around, with their prolonged 'whish!'" Croffut imagined the artillery fire to be purposeful (it was not) and attributed it to "the heartless and diabolical foe."[11]

A few hundred yards away, the surgeons of the 7th and 8th Georgia established an aid station in a stand of trees just beyond the reach of bullets. An observer recorded, "I saw legs and feet taken off, arms and hands amputated, deep wounds probed, and ghastly gashes sewed up rapidly and set skillfully."[12]

If indeed the Georgians performed amputations at such a place, theirs was an uncommon practice. Among the first lessons learned that day was that medical care simply could not be rendered under fire, except for emergency efforts to staunch hemorrhaging. As the bullets flew, the surgeons moved their aid stations steadily backward. And as the day progressed, both sides realized the need for two tiers of care: one near the front, where wounded could be stabilized and transported, and another in formal field hospitals to the rear, well out of harm's way. But while the seeds of a system of care emerged, July 21, 1861, was in fact a day of medical improvisation and chaos.[13]

About fifty surgeons and assistant surgeons accompanied the Union army onto the fields west of Bull Run that day. Only a handful had experience in war. Likely just a few had treated gunshot wounds before. They collectively did no advanced planning for the coming battle. Each surgeon's responsibility extended only to his regiment; some of them rigidly abided by this, refusing care to men of other units. Worse, McDowell's directive that the army should travel light meant the twenty wagons filled with medical stores had been left behind in Alexandria. Medical personnel appeared on the field with whatever supplies they could stuff into haversacks, regimental wagons, and ambulances (typically one per regiment, their operators usually untrained). One of the army's assistant surgeons—"as green as the grass around me as to my duties on the field"—later claimed that he "never received a single order from either colonel or other officer, medical inspector, the surgeon of my regiment, or anyone else" all day.[14]

The expectations of McDowell's titular medical director that day, Dr. William S. King, likely reflected those of his colleagues: he later wrote that he anticipated a "brisk skirmish" only. King seemed most intent on keeping a list of the killed and wounded. "I thought it would be a small task," he explained, and when the shooting started on Matthews Hill he stood behind the line, notebook in hand, literally counting the men as they fell. When he reached 100, he concluded that the day might go differently than he had planned. He ordered his assistant, Southern-born Dr. David L. Magruder, to find some buildings that might be turned into a hospital. Magruder quickly rode back to Sudley Church. This building, surrounded by a grove of shade trees, would be the Union army's major field hospital—the war's first major experiment in field medical care.[15]

Magruder sent out ambulances and orderlies with orders to transport the wounded to Sudley. He then directed the sanctuary to be cleared—pews removed, blankets laid out, buckets filled, and instruments and dressings "placed in convenient places for use." He improvised an operating table from two boards laid on two boxes and placed it just in front of the pulpit. Within minutes, the wounded started arriving. By afternoon, surgeons had also appropriated the home and wheelwright shop of John Thornberry and his family, across Sudley Road.[16]

Some men walked. A few appeared on stretchers carried by friends. Ambulances transported most others. The chaplain of the 1st Minnesota, Edward Neill, directed the regiment's ambulance. Receiving word of some wounded, the ambulance driver pulled into the yard of a house. Wounded men lay all around, Neill remembered. "All were eager to be placed in the ambulance, but I was obliged to tell them it was reserved for the wounded of the Minnesota Regiment." After a little searching, Neill found four men of his regiment and soon hauled them back to Sudley. The men left behind faced a long wait, for the Union army had no system for transporting wounded to the rear.[17]

Reporter William Croffut of the *New York Tribune* set aside his pencil to assist with carrying the wounded to Sudley. The church "was a sickening spectacle," he reported. "The pulpit had the appearance of a drug store," and the floor was so thickly covered with wounded "that it was difficult to get across by stepping carefully." From the gallery peered dozens of men less seriously wounded. "For hours we made the rapid trips between the battlefield and the hospital," wrote Croffut, "and still the carnage went on." By late afternoon, nearly 300 Union wounded filled Sudley Church and Thornberry's house and shop. (Among them were Col. John Slocum and Maj. Sullivan Ballou of the 2nd Rhode Island; both would die there in the coming days.) About ten surgeons cared for this multitude of suffering. The Union army detailed no one to tend to the physical details of hospital work: moving wounded, carrying water, and preparing food.[18]

The Confederates experienced many of the same challenges and shortcomings as did the Federals, though the Confederates at least had access to their medical wagons and stores. They, too, found themselves stepping their aid stations back from the firing line and established a dominant hospital to receive the wounded. The Confederate hospital appropriated not buildings but rather farm fields astride Holkum's Branch, along the road leading from Portici to the Henry farm. The advantages of this site for surgeons and patients were obvious: it was safely beyond Union bullets and shells, it had access to good water, and it was easily found along the most direct route off the battlefield. Porter Alexander described the site as "a beautiful grassy meadow [with] shade trees on [the] edges." By day's end, as many as 800 men sought treatment here. Porter also estimated that by then 100 men lay dead.[19]

But the location had a major disadvantage to the Confederates: virtually every soldier who entered the fighting on Henry Hill that afternoon had to pass through this landscape of suffering—an unhappy experience for soldiers entering battle for the first time. One of Stuart's cavalrymen recalled the chaos: "The prayers, the curses, the screams, the blood, the flies, the sickening stench of this horrible little valley were too much for the stomachs of the men, and all along the column, leaning over the pommels of their saddles, they could be seen in the ecstasies of protest."[20]

The experiences of Union and Confederate wounded—virtually identical for much of the day—diverged with the Union collapse on Henry Hill. Dr. William Keen came to Bull Run as the assistant surgeon of the 5th Massachusetts, entirely bereft of military experience. He worked the yard outside Sudley Church late that afternoon. As he applied a splint and an 8-yard bandage to a man with a broken humerus, he suddenly heard, from the direction of the battlefield, the rising clamor of running men, about 100 in full sprint from the battlefield: "The rebs are after us!" Keen recalled, "It did not take more than one positive assertion of this kind to convince the man whose arm I was bandaging that it was time for him to leave." The wounded soldier jumped up and ran for the distant woods; as he did, his unfinished bandage unwound. "I last saw him disappearing in the distance, with this fluttering bobtail flying all abroad."[21]

The rush of retreating soldiers presented the Union surgeons at Sudley and elsewhere on the field with a dilemma no one had considered in advance: Stay or go? Dr. Luther Bell of the 11th Massachusetts boldly declared his intention to stay, but when someone warned, "the enemy are just upon us, in hot blood. It is not

likely they will spare us," Bell reconsidered his choice. He had just placed a tourni-
quet on a soldier's leg before amputating it and was about to make the first inci-
sion. "I thought an hour in a moment," he wrote a few days later, then exclaimed,
"Let us go!" He grabbed his coat and sash and rushed out, leaving the soldier on
the amputating table. He abandoned his horse in the panic at Cub Run and later
paid ten dollars for a ride into Arlington on a "wretched old lager-beer wagon."[22]

As the flood of retreating troops accelerated, Dr. Charles Gray of the U.S.
Cavalry Battalion found his commander, Maj. Innis Palmer, in the mass. "He
seemed in an awful state of mortification," Gray wrote in his diary. "When I
asked for orders, he 'wept' in reply." Gray opted to leave Sudley, at least until he
met a group of surgeons at Sudley Ford, watering their horses. The group agreed
that some of the medical officers should return to Sudley and give themselves up
as prisoners. Dr. David Magruder, who had established the hospital at the
church, offered that he ought not to be one of them, fearing his Southern origins
would bring him vengeance from the Confederates. Gray and several others
agreed to go back.

Gray arrived before the Confederates and found a scene that seemed to capture the doleful mood of the day. Occasional shells screeched overhead, while in
the grove around the church milled innumerable Union soldiers, "mostly
unwounded & many without arms." They could be made to do nothing, Gray
recorded, "but loitered along or sat down as though the war—or this part in it at
least—was over. They did not seem frightened, but stupid, tired, & indifferent."

With Confederate shells flying uncomfortably close, Gray found a white
cloth of some sort and hung it from a branch beside the road, vainly signifying a
hospital. Shortly, Stuart's cavalry thundered up the road, driving prisoners before
them. Gray and everyone else also became prisoners.[23]

Sgt. Urban Woodbury of the 2nd Vermont lay in Thornberry's wheelwright
shop when the Confederates appeared. He had just awakened from his dose of
anesthetic, still groggy, with his amputated arm sitting on a low bench beside
him, when yelling from outside stirred him. A Confederate cavalry major burst in
and proclaimed the wounded Yankees prisoners. The Vermont soldier had come
to the field confident of victory, sure that the war would end and the Union
would be preserved. Now, the realization that the army was routed and he was a
prisoner and "maimed for life" put him, he wrote, "in an unhappy state of mind
from which I did not entirely recover until I left Dixie" months later.[24]

Confederates would eventually come to see the great value in allowing Union
surgeons to remain behind to care for their own wounded. At later battles, Confederates readily paroled both Union surgeons and their wounded charges, and
Northern surgeons willingly remained, relieving the Confederates of caring for
thousands of enemy wounded. But on this day, every Yankee seemed a prize, and
Union surgeons had to argue loudly against being carried away from the men they
had given themselves up to care for. They succeeded only for twenty-four hours.

Late on the afternoon of July 22, Confederate officers ordered all the Union surgeons away from Sudley and other Union field hospitals to Manassas for transport to Richmond as prisoners. Beauregard later declared the act a mistake made by overzealous subordinates. The Confederates did parole some Union surgeons and return them to the hospitals, but the decision left many Union wounded neglected until they, too, could be transported to prisons in Richmond.[25]

Some of the hospitals for Union wounded at Manassas and Centreville remained—in constantly deteriorating condition—for nearly two weeks. After the close of battle on July 21, Johnston and Beauregard swiftly left Portici, which became a hospital for both Union and Confederate soldiers. Union officers Orlando Willcox and James B. Ricketts received care there; indeed, because of its famous patients, the house became something of an attraction. After several days, Ricketts's wife, Fanny, arrived, a determined woman who had come to care for her husband and would stay with him even after his evacuation to prison in Richmond. The reality of a field hospital ripened by time overawed anyone's efforts at relief. "The piazzas were strewn with amputated limbs for several days, dead bodies were lying under the trees in the yard," Colonel Willcox later remembered. "The stench of the sloughing wounds in the house & from the dead horses in the yard & men on the battle field was loathsome." The colonel called his time at Portici "melancholy days."[26]

While more than a few Southerners viewed the dire condition of the hospitals holding Union wounded as testament to the inferiority of their Yankee enemies, the Confederate army's experience with wounded Union prisoners after First Manassas at least proved instructive. Never again in Virginia would the Confederates seek to hold wounded soldiers as prisoners.[27]

In contrast to their Yankee enemies, the Confederate wounded received constant care and quick transport, since the Confederates had all of their wagons and ambulances on the field. It is likely they evacuated the wounded from the great hospital at Holkum's Branch in a day or two, carrying them off to Manassas Junction. Newspapers recorded the spread of hospitals along the major rail lines farther south. At Culpeper Courthouse, Orange Courthouse, Charlottesville, and Louisa Courthouse, families opened their homes to the wounded. Churches and public buildings were transformed into hospital wards. Charlottesville took in 1,200 sick and wounded, mostly in the lecture halls and dormitories at the University of Virginia. Professors and women alike rushed to provide care. At least one woman came from as far away as Alabama to help. "Throughout the broad limits of our beloved country, every heart is beating with sympathy for our sick and wounded soldiery," concluded the *Richmond Dispatch*. Relatively few Confederate wounded found their way to Richmond itself, but a substantial number ended up at St. Paul's Episcopal Church in Haymarket, an 8-mile wagon ride west of the battlefield. Today, along a grassy walkway in front of the church, lie more than eighty Confederate dead from the war's first battle.[28]

Chapter Twelve

TALLYING FAILURE
AND VIRTUE

In the days and weeks following the battle, clergymen took to their pulpits and newspapermen to their presses to both shape and reflect the minds of their nation, region, or state. In the North, few observers denied the magnitude of defeat. Instead, editors of Union newspapers cast about for those responsible— Patterson (a favorite), Scott, McDowell, Lincoln, and even the cabinet. Reporters, politicians, soldiers, and civilians all speculated on the reasons for failure, ranging from the North's overconfidence to the poor quality of officers (another favorite target) to the wretched food provided to soldiers, and even the failure of the soldiers themselves. The chaplain of the House of Representatives blamed failure on McDowell's decision to fight on the Sabbath—a decision made partly, the chaplain said, to allow civilians to witness the battle: "Had the Sabbath been observed, had citizens been at church, and had the soldiers . . . been permitted to rest and eat, and assemble to sing and pray, and hear the words of life from their chaplains, no doubt the results might have been different."[1]

Many Americans embraced (and still do) the shibboleth that civilian war-watchers had somehow caused the panic, a perception largely shaped by the writings of *London Times* correspondent William Russell, who spent the day with civilians and wrote vividly of the panic that swept by them. A Syracuse newspaper explained it all: the civilians "were the first to fly" and "spread confusion as they advanced, and filled with consternation many a man who would have remained firm as granite but for that society."[2]

A few commentators blamed the press for its pre-battle clamoring and rosy predictions that cast ultimate defeat in even darker shades. Democrat Thurlow Weed, the powerful editor of the *Albany Evening Journal*, perhaps summed it up best: "The major blunder includes all the minor ones."[3]

153

Of course, glib generalities like that never satisfy the body politic, or at least the politicians they elect. This war would see dozens of major battles. No other ended with such decisive, disastrous results for one side than did Bull Run: pure, unadulterated humiliation. The question was: How could such a magnificent, finely equipped army be so thoroughly thrashed? In the days and weeks after the battle, the nation's second-guessers and accusers mobilized to answer that question.

Many contemporary commentators (and McDowell himself) pointed to the obvious ingredients for failure: untrained Union troops and inexperienced leaders asked to fight on the offensive before they were ready to do so. The Confederates, however, suffered many of the same obstacles; indeed, the Confederates fought the last hour of the battle entirely on the offensive, and successfully. The argument in defense of Union failure implies that defeat was a foregone conclusion, that the Union high command could not have overcome these obstacles. More than a century of study tells us otherwise. The Federals, who surpassed their foes in terms of weaponry, had ample opportunity to win the battle and succeed in the campaign.

Several circumstances contributed to Union defeat. The first, and most easily recognized, was Robert Patterson's inability to do his job in the Shenandoah Valley. By allowing Johnston's army, which he outnumbered by more than three to two, to slip away to Manassas, Patterson guaranteed that the strength of the Union and Confederate armies at Manassas would be roughly equal. While it was true that McDowell expected to confront about 35,000 Confederates along Bull Run and could have defeated them in any event, Patterson's failure robbed the Union army of a significant advantage.

More than that, the arrival of Johnston's 11,000 men gave the Confederates a mobile reserve that Beauregard alone sorely lacked, a decisive factor in the battle. Johnston's men allowed the Confederates to first confront the Union flanking effort and eventually transition the battle from defense to offense without stripping entirely their defensive positions at the key lower crossings of Bull Run. Johnston's newly arrived men did more fighting on July 21 than did Beauregard's. (Johnston's units lost 1,343 killed and wounded; Beauregard's lost 614). Despite Patterson's being 60 miles away and only days from retirement, few individuals had a greater impact on the outcome of the battle than did he.

Though Patterson allowed Johnston to escape, McDowell gave Johnston's troops the time to become a decisive factor in the campaign. Most of Johnston's army arrived on July 19 and 20—the same two days McDowell's army lingered in Centreville while engineer Barnard searched for crossings of Bull Run above the Confederate left. We do not know what conditions McDowell set upon Barnard to guide his reconnaissance, but we do know the outcome: the Union army traded knowledge and time for security, and it proved a bad transaction. Barnard's unwillingness to reveal his search in any form—no probing by cavalry, no testing of any crossing, no mapping of roads—not only meant the search required extra time, but also left McDowell and his commanders only slightly better informed about the upstream fords and the roads leading to them than they had been days before. Johnston put the two days consumed by this peek-and-duck operation to good use, and the uncertainty of the route to Sudley and Poplar Fords delayed the Union column on July 21.

Another contributor to McDowell's defeat was the poorly planned and executed early morning march of July 21. Two days of waiting provided plenty of time to inspect and shore up the wooden bridge over Cub Run, but no one did. Instead, the bridge creaked and groaned under the heavy loads and had to be buttressed during the march that Sunday morning, costing the army precious time. Asking a still-green army to march at 2:30 A.M. also ensured both sloth and confusion. In the darkness, every shadow became a hostile picket, every noise a gunshot. Tyler's column lurched along slowly and clogged the Warrenton Turnpike for almost three hours.

That, of course, delayed the rest of McDowell's column and highlighted McDowell's most important error that morning: moving his diversionary force, Tyler's division, before moving his main striking column, Hunter's and Heintzelman's divisions. Tyler's column had by far the easiest march—only 2 miles over an excellent road—while the flanking column needed to cover four times that distance over roads uncertain. Had McDowell allowed Hunter's and Heintzelman's divisions to move out on their flank march first, Tyler most certainly could have reached his position in front of the Stone Bridge by the appointed time. As it was, Tyler delayed the flanking column long enough to make a critical difference. Rather than cross Sudley Ford at 7 A.M.—when Evans was still unaware of the Federal flanking movement, and Bee and Jackson were still in their camps near Mitchell's Ford—Hunter's division crossed between 9 and 9:30 A.M. By then, Evans had shifted position to meet him, and Bee and Jackson were on their way to help. The hours lost were critical to the Union army.

It's common and easy to point to yet another reason for Union failure, perhaps the most obvious and dramatic of all: the two-hour delay that followed McDowell's "victory" on Matthews Hill. If only McDowell had not proclaimed victory and then basked in it, if only he had determinedly pushed his troops forward, he would easily have seized Henry Hill, dislodged the left of the Confederate line entirely, and changed the axis, tenor, and trajectory of the battle entirely. Instead, McDowell waffled, and the Confederates put those hours to good use. The Hampton Legion delayed and harassed while Jackson arrived to establish a new line on the rear slope of the hill. A steady stream of other troops followed. By the time McDowell finally moved, he did so with little resolve and without any clear sense of what he might encounter on Henry Hill. The Federal army commander spent precious lives and energy that afternoon trying to claim a position that only hours before was his for the taking.

All of these things are true, but they fall short of adequately explaining the circumstances that begot the delay and mark this battle as unique in the war: Irvin McDowell simply did not know what victory would look like on July 21, 1861, and neither did most of men on the field, be they privates or generals, Union or Confederate. McDowell clearly hoped that brilliant maneuver and massive show of force might be enough. His orders called for the flank march and an advance to the Warrenton Turnpike, clearing the crossings of Bull Run as he moved. He did not use the word "attack" or "assault" (though given the closeness of the armies, he clearly recognized there would be fighting). Instead, his plan amounted to the bold step forward of a playground bully, chest out, hands clenched, visage threatening, hoping the frightening combination might be enough to make his opponents cower. McDowell's morning encounter with Evans, Bee, and Bartow required a good deal more than glowering, but by midday the Union army was nearly in the place and circumstance McDowell hoped it would be. To all appearances, the Federals had that morning cowed the Confederates. When McDowell and his staff rode down the line proclaiming "Victory! Victory!" they meant it.

The two hours that followed forced McDowell to reconsider. Stubborn resistance from some of Bee's men on the slopes of Matthews Hill and the Hampton Legion along the Warrenton Turnpike bought the Confederates time and alerted McDowell to a new reality. The appearance of cannon on the rear slope of Henry Hill and the fierce resistance Keyes encountered in his assault on the northern shoulder of Henry Hill demonstrated beyond all doubt that the "Victory! Victory!" presumed by McDowell that morning was not yet nigh.

The two hours between noon and 2 P.M. were no lull. They were a revelation—the first real recognition that the war would require more than bluster and posturing. Still, when McDowell finally did push on to Henry Hill, he did so not with a prizefighter's crisp punch, but with an underdog's timid pawing. He conceived not an attack, but yet another step forward, chest out. This time, the Confederates punched back. Hard.

At the beginning of the battle for Henry Hill, the troops available to McDowell outnumbered the Confederates on the hill three to one. In the tumultuous fighting that followed, fifteen Union regiments ascended Henry Hill, but only once did more than two of those regiments go into the fight together. Most went up singly, and with bad results. Why? Certainly McDowell underestimated the task confronting him on Henry Hill—the Confederates had carefully concealed their infantry on the rear slope. But more importantly, McDowell's own inexperience and inadequate staff made it impossible for him to coordinate the movements of 15,000 men on the battlefield, even though most stood within his view. While McDowell (unlike the Confederates) organized his army at the division level (multiple brigades placed under a single commander), once on the field, no division acted as a cohesive unit—and indeed few brigades did either. The large-unit tactics that later became a staple of every battle would in part emerge from Bull Run, a reaction to one of the battle's most obvious characteristics. Inexperience and incompetence among McDowell's junior officers only made matters worse. Even Sherman, a future American military hero, sent his four regiments into battle not together, but in succession, one deadly advance at a time.

Months later, Congress would create the Joint Committee on the Conduct of the War, chaired by Sen. Benjamin Wade of Ohio, a witness to the disaster at Bull Run. (His senate cohort on the committee was Zachariah Chandler of Michigan, who also stood watching the battle that day.) Sen. Henry Wilson, who like Wade found himself swept up in the retreat, chaired the Senate Committee on Military Affairs. Together, Wade's and Wilson's committees would forge as hostile a political environment as any U.S. army has ever suffered, calling officers of the Army of the Potomac to account for both their performances and their politics. (The politics of officers mattered far more as the war transformed from a purely military exercise to a war that assailed not just armies, but also slavery and the Confederate economy.) That key members of these committees bore personal witness to Bull Run helped to foster a culture of suspicion and a tradition of second-guessing that would define the Union war effort for years to come.

In anything political or military, the greatest fruit of success is not joy, but the absence of scrutiny. While Union observers debated and dissected July 21, 1861, Confederates reveled in victory and celebrated new heroes.

During the battle, the Confederates suffered many of the same handicaps that hobbled McDowell, yet they won. Beauregard, naturally, attributed the Confederate victory to only one noble and dramatic factor: "the Federal troops came as invaders, and the Southern troops stood as defenders of their homes." Beauregard loved platitudes and bold language, often at the expense of thoughtful reflection. What had allowed the Confederates to turn certain defeat into stunning victory?[4]

First and foremost, the Confederates exploited virtually every extra hour granted them by the Federals to their advantage. From small-unit commanders like Evans and Wade Hampton to army commander Johnston, the Confederates consistently converted time gained into more men and stronger positions. Once McDowell moved against Henry Hill, the Confederates met the Union soldiers on something close to equal terms, and as the fighting continued, the pendulum swung decisively in the Southerners' favor. Like the Federals, the Confederates rarely moved more than two regiments into the fight for Henry Hill simultaneously. But those single and twin regiments not only drove away Union regiments—for which McDowell increasingly had no replacements—but also bought the Confederates still more time. More time meant more troops arriving from the right of the line or from Manassas Junction: Smith, Fisher, Hunton, Withers, Kershaw, Cash, and finally Elzey and Early. When at 4 P.M. McDowell had no regiments left to put into the battle on Henry Hill, the Confederates had more than at any other time, and in the right places. The fight for Henry Hill amounted to a battle of attrition: Who would be standing to deliver the final punch? It was likely the only such battle in the eastern theater that the Confederates won during the war.

From the Confederate victory emerged the requisite heroes. Foremost were Johnston and Beauregard. Their joint arrival on the field after the debacle on Matthews Hill did much to rally the Confederates. Their improvised system of shared command worked nearly flawlessly: Johnston shuttled troops forward from Portici, and Beauregard placed them on the field. (For his more visible role, Beauregard received the more credit for victory; one soldier in the 5th Virginia wrote of him, "I believe him to be the greatest general in the army.") Egos and ungraceful wrangling in the months to come would later obscure the rather remarkable partnership they established when the Confederacy needed it most.[5]

In most battles of the war, a subordinate commander emerged for exalted public notice. For the Confederates, First Manassas produced several notables. No subordinate commander on either side did more to shape the battle by his own actions than did Nathan Evans, who acted decisively under difficult circumstances. His career would blossom briefly, then perish largely at the hands of alcohol.

No regiment on the battlefield rendered more important service than did Wade Hampton's legion. The fighting of the South Carolinians in the Warrenton Turnpike and around the Robinson house forced on McDowell a major reconsideration of the day. Likely no other regiment on the field received more acclaim afterward than did Hampton's, abetted greatly by Charleston's hyperactive press.

Arnold Elzey received the loudest public praise that day when Beauregard lauded him with European flair. But Elzey's star would brighten quickly and fade as fast—he would never again be in such a place at such a time with such results as he was on Chinn Ridge that Sunday afternoon. Bee and Bartow also received deserved acclaim, though often wrapped in eulogy.

Thomas J. Jackson's name would not shine as brightly as others right after the battle, but his would shine longer than anyone else's over time. On July 21, he selected and maintained the position that would become the heart of the Confederate line on Henry Hill. And then he set the conditions for engagement, telling his regimental commanders to permit the Yankees to close, then strike back. On Jackson's left, Arthur Cummings and his 33rd Virginia abided by the orders precisely. Jackson himself ordered the counterattack of the 4th and 27th Virginia that captured Ricketts's guns. Those who have accorded Jackson credit for Confederate victory at Manassas go too far, but he and his brigade played a key role over a three-hour period. Bee's famous utterances—likely misquoted as they were—accorded Jackson a catchy public identity that subsequent service only enhanced. Within days of the battle, the nickname "Stonewall" appeared in Southern newspapers, and in a year he would be a legend.[6]

Chapter Thirteen

AWAKENING

The hours and days after battle are like that awful instant after a car crash, while the sound still echoes, the glass skitters across the pavement, and the steam boils forth. Everyone stops, looks, and wonders; the pit of every stomach knows something awful has happened. But no one knows yet how bad it is, what it means, or what comes next.

From the first fire on Matthews Hill, the effect of battle reverberated outward—across the landscape, across the nation—forcing on a frenzied people an awakening. Just beyond the edge of the battlefield, local residents bore witness to what they all knew was a historic day. Marianne Compton, who lived a mile west of Henry Hill, recalled the sounds of the cannon—"Then it was new to us, and we listened with bated breath"—and the musketry—"a continuous rattle, less terrifying, but more suggestive of sharp fighting." Her father, Alexander Sr., was the pastor at Sudley Church, but on this day lay seriously ill in bed. The Reverend Compton called July 21 "the most awful day of my life." The family huddled and worried for their son and sibling Alex, a member of the 8th Virginia. He charged across Henry Hill at the close of the fighting, dressed in a new gray uniform with green trim, made for him by his mother and sisters. Every hour or so a messenger arrived at the Compton house with word from the battlefield, most of it "anything but cheery." The reverend prayed fervently for day's end. Word finally came that Alex had survived, though six in his company did not.[1]

Six-year-old Laura Thornberry, her siblings, and her mother had fled their house across from Sudley Church on the battle's eve. They, too, had a loved one in the battle just down the road. Wheelwright John Thornberry, thirty-six, served in Extra Billy Smith's 49th Virginia. The family watched snippets of the battle from the hillside on Laura's uncle's farm, about a mile west of Sudley. Years later, when she recalled the day for her grandchildren, Laura wrote of seeing "the firing of muskets and cannons, and falling men." She remembered army wagons filled with bodies "piled high as anyone would pile up wood." And she remembered the story her uncle, William Wilkins, told her. The night of the battle, Wilkins heard a cry of distress from the nearby woods. He searched and found a "young soldier boy about seventeen years old." Wilkins asked him what he wanted. "I want my mother," the young man said. Wilkins filled the soldier's canteen from a nearby spring and told him he would come by to see him first thing in the morning. The soldier said, "No, I will be gone before tomorrow." When Wilkins returned the next morning, he found the soldier dead.

That gloomy, rainy Monday morning, Laura's mother, Martha, returned to their home, one of three buildings that composed the great Union hospital at Sudley. She found a bedroom spattered with blood, the carpets and furniture gone. Soldiers had tossed china, utensils, flat irons, "and everything you can imagine" into a well behind the house. "Everything was broken," Laura remembered, "and no prospects of replacing any of it." At some point, news arrived that John Thornberry was wounded, seriously enough to keep him out of the service for the rest of the war. He was the only soldier from the Sudley neighborhood to be wounded in the battle that raged literally in their yards and woodlots.[2]

While the Comptons, Thornberrys, Dogans, and a dozen other local families agonized in anonymity, Mrs. Judith Carter Henry died in the glare of the public eye. Her house stood at the center of the battlefield, torn, as one visitor wrote, "all to a fiddle." Months earlier, Mrs. Henry's son Hugh had advised his sister, Ellen, that their mother's "entire helplessness" would render them safe if the armies came around. In fact, the immobility of an eighty-five-year-old bedridden woman proved her doom. Ellen and their slave, Lucy (hired from the Comptons), tried to move Mrs. Henry away as the shooting started, but simply could not. The entirely helpless Widow Henry—who had survived infirmity beyond her neighbors' expectations—suffered mortal wounds when a shell from Ricketts's battery exploded in her house. Born in the year of her nation's birth, 1776, she died in the year of its dissolution, one of the first martyrs for the Southern cause.[3]

Mrs. Henry's death fueled a postbattle propaganda machine as both sides tried to paint the other as barbaric practitioners of atrocities—accusations intended solely to confirm the virtue of one side and to inflame the populace to a more intense support of the war. In fact, propagandists on neither side had much with which to work. Beyond Mrs. Henry's death, the Confederates made great to-do of a supposed load of 30,000 handcuffs (the number varied by the teller) captured in the detritus of Union retreat. The widely publicized supposed Yankee plan was to handcuff together thousands of captured Confederate soldiers and place them in front of advancing Union lines during the final assault on Richmond as a vast, moving human shield. A minister in Macon, Georgia, declared, "Nothing that has yet been done by the North has so deeply moved my indignation."[4]

The revelation about handcuffs and the Union army's dastardly intent for them "must move the South to the most united, determined and heroic resistance that the world has ever seen." In the days following the battle, the story of "Lincoln's handcuffs" became ubiquitous (in Macon, E. J. Johnston & Co. even displayed a pair of the supposed handcuffs in their storefront). When Union prisoners denied any such diabolical plans, at least one editorialist accepted their argument and instead posited that the cuffs were intended for mutinous Union soldiers and that "old Scott found the fear of handcuffs necessary to stimulate his heroes."

Like most legends, this one included a small kernel of truth. The governor of Maine refused to appoint a captain of the men's choosing in a 5th Maine Infantry company in Howard's brigade, and state authorities feared a mutiny. Col. Mark Dunnell of the 5th brought a store of about sixty handcuffs in case of trouble, and these fell into Confederate hands during the retreat. In just a day or two, they morphed into an imagined 30,000, and a legend was born.[5] No matter its telling, the story of the Union handcuffs and claims of other atrocities spoke powerfully to what Confederates wanted to hear. Their enemies were, as one man put it, "despicable and degraded men," and righteous necessity demanded their defeat.[6]

Windswept by defeat, Union soldiers, newspapers, and government officials also manufactured a colorful tableau of Southern atrocities intended to diminish the virtue, if not the magnitude, of the Confederate victory. Union soldiers happily shared stories of Confederates bayoneting or cutting the throats of the wounded or firing into hospitals. The following spring, the Joint Committee on the Conduct of the War held hearings on the question of "Rebel barbarities." The litany of supposed Confederate atrocities did little to arouse the Northern public (the intended purpose of the Committee), largely because few notable outrages actually took place. The committee documented some disrespectful burials and the desecration of the grave of Maj. Sullivan Ballou, but little else of credibility. Indeed, in the swirl of emotion and letter writing that followed the battle, many Union soldiers pointedly denied the savagery of their enemies.[7]

After the battle, observers across the North noted a sudden and almost universal gravity in the people. "Men no longer speak lightly of the present war, or of the manner of conducting it, or of the time or conditions of its termination," wrote the editor of the *Albany Argus*. Rather than treat the coming of battle like sport, citizens in the aftermath of Bull Run confronted stark questions: What is to become of the country? Where is this all to end? Have we been mistaken in our estimate of this whole subject? Is not the war likely to linger for years?[8]

Just as Pearl Harbor mobilized a later generation, the battle at Bull Run awakened the North to the idea that this would be a longer and more difficult war than most had imagined. Many foresaw in the aftermath of Bull Run the need for a supreme effort by the nation. In the army, most soldiers kept good heart, though all wished to see changes. A constant drumbeat from them underscored two requirements going forward: patience and better leaders. "Give us men or true principles and sound judgment for leaders, and we will be ready to obey every command," declared a man from the battered 27th New York.

The battle also compelled a newfound respect for Southern armies, one that would persist until Appomattox. A New York officer wrote just days after the battle, "And here let me tell you, the South has been tremendously underrated by us Northerners; that they have a *splendid* army, of enormous strength . . . and what is still more, they will fight *for* the South, all the stories to the contrary notwithstanding."[9]

For others, the disastrous battle prompted deep reflection on the value of the Union and all that the war threatened. The *Oneida Weekly Herald* in Utica asserted, "The Rebellion is not an uprising on the mistaken plea of self-defense, but a deliberate conspiracy to ruin." A Boston journal noted that the rebellion brought the Union "from a state of unexampled prosperity, not easily acquired," to the "verge of anarchy" where "men find themselves wanderers in dark and unknown regions." The journal concluded, "No surer remedy exists against such an evil than" success in war. Again and again, editors and preachers saw the defeat as a cleansing stimulant to a somnambulant people. "Better die, all of us, than live to look on a nation disgraced and ruined," a Massachusetts clergyman declared. *The New York Times* predicted Bull Run would "unquestionably prove a great national blessing. . . . It is only [a] mortifying experience, which will, we believe, secure us from its repetition." In Washington, D.C., the *Star* foreshadowed, "Though [the defeat] may delay the final triumph of the Union . . . it will but insure it in the end."[10]

While a handful of newspapers like the *New York Daily News* agitated for immediate peace, those voices did not find expression among those in the government who decided what came next. On Monday, July 22, Congress authorized a call for 500,000 volunteers to serve for three years. The next day, President Lincoln privately outlined nine steps for emboldening the Union war effort. On July 26, he appointed Gen. George B. McClellan as McDowell's replacement in command of the largest army on the continent. Bull Run produced no wavering in the determination of Congress and the president to wage this war to its end. And the dramatic measures that followed the battle signaled loudly to the Confederates that the Northerners would not yield easily the cause of Union.[11]

In drawing rooms across the South, joyous news of the army's victory mixed awkwardly with the fear or pain of personal loss. In Charleston, Confederate soldiers fired a twenty-one-gun celebratory salute from Forts Sumter and Moultrie at the same time workers draped City Hall in the black crepe of mourning. In Fredericksburg, schoolteacher Jane Beale waited for word of her two sons in Longstreet's brigade. She wrote in her diary of the "deep but sad enthusiasm" that accompanied news of the battle. Her sons survived unscathed. In Richmond, Varina Davis carried the news of Col. Francis Bartow's death to his wife, Louisa. When Mrs. Davis entered her room, Louisa rose, then sank back on the bed at the sight of the woman's pale look. "As soon as I saw Mrs. Davis's face, I could not say one word," Louisa later explained. "I knew it all in an instant. I knew it before I wrapped the shawl about my head." In towns across the South and North, doleful news crushed and reordered households.[12]

On July 26, Charleston shut down for a display of grief not seen since the death of John C. Calhoun in 1850. Stores closed and "thousands upon thousands, with grave faces," assembled for the funeral of three heroes: Barnard Bee and Francis Bartow, both shot down on Henry Hill, and Lt. Col. Benjamin Johnson of the Hampton Legion, killed along the Warrenton Turnpike. From the train, a procession carried the bodies to city hall, where the coffins lay on biers in the shadow of a statue of Calhoun, his finger pointing to a scroll: "Truth, Justice and the Constitution." The *Charleston Mercury* reported, "For three hours not a sound was heard in that chamber of death save the measured tread of the sentries and the frequent sobbing of those whose grief could not be controlled."[13]

In Lexington, Virginia, Miss Virginia Bedinger suffered three days knowing that her brother's unit, the Rockbridge Artillery, had been "cut to pieces," but having heard nothing of his individual fate. "You may imagine my suspense and anxiety," she told her mother, until finally she learned of his safety. "My heart overflowed with love and thanksgiving," she wrote, but remembered, "there are many mourning hearts in our country." She then described the deaths of five family friends at Manassas: "We think of all the sad & stricken hearts throughout the land."[14]

To the editor of the *Richmond Whig*, intense public mourning interfered with what should have been a national celebration of affirming victory. He took to the pages of his paper to urge Southerners to dispense with "the usual emblems of external mourning." He cited the practical expense of mourning attire, which "many families who have lost a dear relative cannot well afford," since the demands of the moment had made it more expensive than ever. In his oft-copied editorial, he also suggested that mourning conveyed "a distressing and gloomy aspect . . . to our streets and our churches" at a time that should be reserved for rejoicing a "victory almost unparalleled." Indeed, he wrote, the victory at Manassas rendered mourning almost unnecessary: "The gloom is brightened by the glory of triumph in the discharge of the holiest obligation of duty."[15]

While for Northerners the defeat at Bull Run threatened the cherished notion of the Union, for Southerners the victory affirmed a new identity—the Confederacy, an entity fully formed just two months before. The victory at Manassas accorded a nascent nation instant heritage, much as Lexington and Concord had for the colonists in 1775. Before the battle at Manassas, the Confederacy still seemed a mere possibility. But the victory unleashed a flood of patriotic fervor that turned even formerly reluctant secessionists into ardent Southern patriots and nationalists. A soldier from Georgia cheered the captures, the loot, and, he wrote, "above all the moral effect; it was a great and brilliant victory." After the battle, Virginia Soutter Knox of Fredericksburg referred repeatedly to "our beloved Southern Confederacy" in letters to her soldier-sons. Lt. Frank Paxton of Lexington, who fought with Jackson and the 4th Virginia at Manassas, wrote his wife two days after the battle, "We spent Sunday last in the sacred work of achieving our nationality and independence. The work was nobly done." Paxton's enthusiasm in his letter's climactic line overawed his marital tact: "It was the happiest day of my life, our wedding day not excepted."[16]

Though in the days following the battle a few exuberant Southerners believed the war to be finished with the victory at Manassas, the vast majority made no such misjudgment. The greatest change was that most Southerners now believed the South strong enough to bear what might lie ahead and to ultimately succeed. "I have no fears now for the final result of the contest," wrote Asher Harman, an officer in the 5th Virginia. "Are we not fighting for all we hold dear on earth?"[17]

Every battle of the Civil War, every congressional act, every presidential order, revealed something new about a war that constantly evolved over four years. No battle of the war revealed so much so quickly as did Bull Run. Most obviously, the battle exposed the naivety of the idea that a few hours of combat on Mrs. Henry's farm on a July afternoon could possibly resolve eighty-five years of disagreement over the issues that lay at the very core of the nation's identity and existence. As the next four years would demonstrate, the war would be an immense, surging tide, and no individual battle resolved anything by itself (though soldiers never lost hope that each one would and that it might be the last).

Instead, the clash along Bull Run ushered in a new phase of discourse in the North, one that vigorously debated the method and purpose of the war. Should Southern civilians be treated as future countrymen or as enemies? Should the property of Southern civilians be respected, even protected? And what of slavery? Should (or could) the war be the means by which slavery in American perished? Was the war, as a Boston editorialist put it, the means to "clear away the moral and mental rubbish that is so apt to accumulate in prolonged periods of national peace"?[18]

Before Bull Run, these were the whispered questions of solons and caucuses. After Bull Run, as the nation faced a longer, more challenging war, these issues bubbled forth in the press, in churches, and on street corners across the North. With every month, the volume of debate rose until, in 1862–64, political fissures deep and wide threatened the viability of the Lincoln administration and the Union war effort. Days after Bull Run, abolitionist senator Charles Sumner declared it both the worst and best event in the nation's history. The worst part was the "calamity and shame" of defeat. The best part was that the result of the battle—the extension of the war—"made the extinction of slavery inevitable." Bull Run spawned a debate about the nature of war that prior to the battle most Northerners would have thought unnecessary and unwanted, and one that would govern politics in the North until war's end.[19]

The battle of July 21, 1861, known as Bull Run in the North and Manassas in the South, unveiled the horrific possibilities of America's Civil War. On this, both sides agreed. "Its effect will be to enrage the Yankees, mortify their pride and incite revenge," wrote Confederate chaplain Robert Lewis Dabney. A correspondent for the *New York Times* rightly foresaw "miles of rich harvests consumed" and "thousands of innocent families . . . ruined." Another Confederate, Maj. Samuel Melton of Bonham's staff, squashed his homefolk's hopes for a quick war: "I have no idea that they intend to give up the fight," he predicted. "On the contrary, five men will rise up where one has been killed, and in my opinion, the war will have to be continued to the bloody end."[20]

Precisely how bloody the path to that end would be, no rational man could then say.

FIRST MANASSAS: JULY 21, 1861

UNION FORCES—BRIG. GEN. IRVIN MCDOWELL
First Division—Brig. Gen. Daniel Tyler
  1st Brigade—Col. Erasmus D. Keyes
    2nd Maine Infantry, Col. C. D. Jameson
    1st Connecticut Infantry, Lt. Col. Speidel
    2nd Connecticut Infantry, Col. A. H. Terry
    3rd Connecticut Infantry, Col. J. L. Chatfield

  2nd Brigade—Brig. Gen. Robert C. Schenck
    2nd New York Infantry, Col. G. W. B. Tompkins
    1st Ohio Infantry, Col. A. McD. McCook
    2nd Ohio Infantry, Lt. Col. R. Mason
    Company E, 2nd U.S. Artillery (7 guns), Capt. J. H. Carlisle

  3rd Brigade—Col. William. T. Sherman
    13th New York Infantry, Col. I. F. Quinby
    69th New York Infantry, Col. M. Corcoran (W&C); Capt. J. Kelly
    79th New York Infantry, Col. J. Cameron (K)
    2nd Wisconsin Infantry, Lt. Col. H. W. Peck
    Company E, 3rd U.S. Artillery (6 guns), Capt. R. B. Ayres

  4th Brigade—Col. Israel B. Richardson
    1st Massachusetts Infantry, Col. R. Cowdin
    12th New York Infantry, Col. E. L. Walrath
    2nd Michigan Infantry, Maj. A. W. Williams
    3rd Michigan Infantry, Col. D. McConnell?; Lt. Col. Stevens
    Company G, 1st U.S. Artillery (2 guns), Lt. J. Edwards
    Company M, 2nd U.S. Artillery (4 guns), Capt. H. J. Hunt

Second Division—Col. David Hunter (W); Col. Andrew Porter
  1st Brigade—Col. Andrew Porter
    8th New York (Militia), Col. G. Lyons
    14th New York Infantry, Col. A. M. Wood (W); Lt. Col. E. B. Fowler
    27th New York Infantry, Col. H. W. Slocum (W); Maj. J. J. Bartlett
    U.S. Infantry Battalion (8 cos.), Maj. G. Sykes

U.S. Marine Corps Battalion, Maj. J. G. Reynolds
U.S. Cavalry Battalion (7 cos.), Maj. I. N. Palmer
Company D, 5th U.S. Artillery (6 guns), Capt. C. Griffin

2nd Brigade—Col. Ambrose E. Burnside
2nd New Hampshire Infantry, Col. G. Marston (W); Lt. Col. F. S. Fiske
1st Rhode Island Infantry, Maj. J. P. Balch
*2nd Rhode Island Infantry, Col. J. S. Slocum (K); Lt. Col. F. Wheaton
**71st New York Infantry, Col. H. P. Martin

Third Division—Col. Samuel P. Heintzelman (W)
1st Brigade—Col. William B. Franklin
5th Massachusetts Infantry, Col. S. C. Lawrence (W)
11th Massachusetts Infantry, Col. G. Clark
1st Minnesota Infantry, Col. W. A. Gorman
Company I, 1st U.S. Artillery (6 guns), Capt. J. B. Ricketts (W&C)

2nd Brigade—Col. Orlando B. Willcox (W&C); Col. J. H. Hobart Ward
11th New York Infantry (Fire Zouaves), Col. W. C. Farnham (W)
38th New York Infantry, Col. Ward; Lt. Col. A. Farnsworth
1st Michigan Infantry, Maj. A. F. Bidwell
4th Michigan Infantry, Col. D. A. Woodbury
Company D, 2nd U.S. Artillery (4 guns), Capt. R. Arnold

3rd Brigade—Col. Oliver O. Howard
3rd Maine Infantry, Maj. H. G. Staples
4th Maine Infantry, Col. H. G. Berry
5th Maine Infantry, Col. M. H. Dunnell
2nd Vermont infantry, Col. H. Whiting

Fourth Division—Brig. Gen. Theodore Runyon
Militia
1st New Jersey Infantry, Col. A. J. Johnson
3rd New Jersey Infantry, Col. H. M. Baker
3rd New Jersey Infantry, Col. W. Napton
4th New Jersey Infantry, Col. M. Miller

Volunteers
1st New Jersey Infantry, Col. W. R. Montgomery
2nd New Jersey Infantry, Col. G. W. McLean
3rd New Jersey Infantry, Col. G. W. McLean
41st New York Infantry, Col. L. Von Gilsa

Fifth Division—Col. Dixon S. Miles
1st Brigade—Col. Louis Blenker
8th New York Infantry, Lt. Col. J. Stahel
29th New York Infantry, Col. A. von Steinwehr
39th New York Infantry (Garibaldi Guards) Col. F. G. D'Utassy
27th Pennsylvania Infantry, Col. M. Einstein
Company A, 2nd U.S. Artillery (4 guns), Capt. J. C. Tidball
Brookwood's New York Battery (6 guns), Capt. C. Brookwood

2nd Brigade—Col. Thomas A. Davies
   16th New York Infantry, Lt. Col. S. Marsh
   18th New York Infantry, Col. W. A. Jackson
   31st New York Infantry, Col. C. E. Pratt
   32nd New York Infantry, Col. R. Matheson
   Company G, 2nd U.S. Artillery (4 guns), Lt. O. D. Greene

*The regiment had a company of artillery (Reynolds's) armed with six 13-pounder James rifles.
**The regiment had a section of 12-pounder Dahlgren boat howitzers.

Confederate Order of Battle

FIRST MANASSAS: JULY 21, 1861

ARMY OF THE POTOMAC—BRIG. GEN. P. G. T. BEAUREGARD
1st Brigade—Brig. Gen. Milledge L. Bonham
    11th North Carolina Infantry, Col. W. W. Kirkland
    2nd South Carolina Infantry, Col. J. B. Kershaw
    3rd South Carolina Infantry, Col. J. H. Williams
    7th South Carolina Infantry, Col. T. G. Bacon
    8th South Carolina Infantry, Col. E. G. R. Cash
    30th Virginia Cavalry, Col. R. C. W. Radford
    Alexandria Light Artillery (4 guns), Capt. D. Kemper
    8th Louisiana Infantry, Col. H. B. Kelly
    1st Company, Richmond Howitzers (4 guns), Capt. J. C. Shields

2nd Brigade—Brig. Gen. Richard S. Ewell
    5th Alabama Infantry, Col. R. E. Rodes
    6th Alabama Infantry, Col. J. J. Seibels
    6th Louisiana Infantry, Col. J. G. Seymour
    Washington Artillery (4 guns), T. L. Rosser
    Cavalry Battalion, Lt. Col. Jenifer

3rd Brigade—Brig. Gen. David R. Jones
    17th Mississippi Infantry, Col. W. S. Featherson
    18th Mississippi Infantry, Col. E. B. Burt
    5th South Carolina Infantry, Col. M. Jenkins
    Flood's Company, 30th Virginia Cavalry, Capt. J. W. Flood
    Washington Artillery (2 guns), Capt. M. B. Miller

4th Brigade—Brig. Gen. James Longstreet
    5th North Carolina Infantry, Lt. Col. Jones
    1st Virginia Infantry, Maj. F. G. Skinner
    11th Virginia Infantry, Col. S. Garland
    17th Virginia Infantry, Col. M. D. Corse
    Washington Artillery (2 guns), Lt. J. J. Garnett
    Company E, 30th Virginia Cavalry, Capt. E. Whitehead

5th Brigade—Col. P. St. George Cocke
  8th Virginia Infantry, Col. E. Hunton
  18th Virginia Infantry, Col. R. E. Withers
  19th Virginia Infantry, Lt. Col. J. B. Strange
  28th Virginia Infantry, Col. R. T. Preston
  49th Virginia Infantry (battalion), Col. W. Smith
  Loudoun Artillery (4 guns), Capt. A. L. Rogers
  Lynchburg Artillery (4 guns), Capt. H. G. Latham

6th Brigade—Col. Jubal A. Early
  7th Louisiana Infantry, Col. H. T. Hays
  13th Mississippi Infantry, Col. W. Barksdale
  7th Virginia Infantry, Col. J. L. Kemper
  Washington Artillery (5 guns), Lt. C. W. Squires; J. B. Richardson; J. B. Whittington

7th Brigade—Col. Nathan G. Evans
  1st Special Louisiana Infantry Battalion, Maj. C. R. Wheat (W)
  4th South Carolina Infantry, Col. J. B. E. Sloan
  Alexander's Troop, 30th Virginia Cavalry, Capt. J. D. Alexander
  Terry's Troop, 30th Virginia Cavalry, Capt. W. R. Terry

Reserve Brigade—Brig. Gen. Theophilus H. Holmes
  1st Arkansas Infantry, Col. J. F. Fagan
  2nd Tennessee Infantry, Col. W. Bate
  Purcell Artillery (6 guns), Capt. L. Walker
  Hampton's South Carolina Legion (6 companies), Col. W. Hampton (W); Capt. J. Conner
  Camp Pickens Battery (15 guns), Capt. Sterrett

ARMY OF THE SHENANDOAH—GEN. JOSEPH E. JOHNSTON
1st Brigade—Brig. Gen. Thomas J. Jackson
  2nd Virginia Infantry, Col. J. W. Allen
  4th Virginia Infantry, Col. J. F. Preston
  5th Virginia Infantry, Col. K. Harper
  27th Virginia Infantry, Lt. Col. J. Echols
  33rd Virginia Infantry (8 companies), Col. A. C. Cummings
  Rockbridge Virginia Artillery (4 guns)

2nd Brigade—Col. Francis Bartow (K)
  7th Georgia Infantry, Col. L. J. Gartrell
  8th Georgia Infantry, Lt. Col. W. M. Gardner
  Wise Artillery (Alburtis's Battery) (4 guns), Capt. E. G. Alburtis

3rd Brigade—Brig. Gen. Barnard E. Bee (K)
  4th Alabama Infantry, Col. Jones (K); Col. S. R. Gist
  2nd Mississippi Infantry, Col. W. C. Falkner
  11th Mississippi Infantry (Companies A & F), Lt. Col. P. F. Liddell
  6th North Carolina Infantry, Col. C. F. Fisher (K)
  Staunton Artillery (4 guns), Capt. J. Imboden

4th Brigade—Brig. Gen. Edmund Kirby Smith (W); Col. Arnold Elzey
  1st Maryland Infantry Battalion, Lt. Col. G. H. Steuart
  3rd Tennessee Infantry, Col. J. C. Vaughn
  10th Virginia Infantry, Col. S. B. Gibbons
  Culpeper Artillery (4 guns), Lt. R. F. Beckham

Not Brigaded
  1st Virginia Cavalry, Col. J. E. B. Stuart
  Thomas Artillery (Stanard's Battery) (4 guns), Capt. P. B. Stanard

Notes

CHAPTER 1: The Certainty of Triumph

1. E. R. Conner III, Mary H. Ferguson, Elizabeth Johnson, *History in a Horseshoe Curve: The Story of Sudley Methodist Church and Its Community* (Hagerstown, MD, 1982), 70; Hugh Henry to Ellen, May 30, 1861, Henry Family Papers, Manassas National Battlefield Park Library. For Mrs. Henry's tenuous hold on life, see Rev. Alexander Compton to Mrs. Davis, July 30, 1861, James S. Schoff Collection, Clements Library, University of Michigan. Basic information about residents is generally derived from the census of 1860.
2. Samuel Wickliffe Melton to his wife, June 2, 1861, Samuel Wickliffe Melton Papers, South Caroliniana Library, University of South Carolina.
3. William King ("Choctaw") to his wife, July 21, 1861, King Family Papers, Alderman Library, University of Virginia. See also King's letter of June 26 for documentation of the armaments in the Confederate defenses at Manassas Junction.
4. E. Porter Alexander described his network of signals in a letter to his wife, July 10, 1861, E. Porter Alexander Papers, Southern Historical Collection, University of North Carolina, Chapel Hill.
5. "L. W. S." letters to *Charleston Mercury*, June 24, 1861.
6. Henry Calvin Conner to Ellen, June 30, 1861, Henry C. Conner Papers, University of South Carolina.
7. *Charleston Mercury*, June 24, 1861.
8. Beauregard in W. P. Snow, *Southern Generals* (n.p., 1865), 214.
9. *Battlefields of the South: Bull Run to Fredericksburgh, With Sketches of Confederate Commanders, and Gossip of the Camps*, by an English Combatant (New York, 1864), 32.
10. Gary W. Gallagher, ed., *Fighting for the Confederacy* (Chapel Hill, 1989), 48–49. E. P. Alexander described Johnston as "more the soldier in looks, carriage & manner than any of our other generals. . . . His whole aspect was to me military discipline idealized & personified."
11. Martin Crawford, ed., *William Howard Russell's Civil War: Private Diary and Letters, 1861–1862* (Athens, GA: 1992), 82; McDowell's testimony in *Report of the Joint Committee on the Conduct of the War, In Three Parts* (Washington, 1863), 35–36 (hereinafter *CCW*).
12. *CCW*, 38.
13. McDowell to E. D. Townsend, June 1861, United States War Department, *War of the Rebellion: A Compilation of the Official Records of the Union and Confederate Armies*, 128 vols. (Washington, 1881–1902), 719–21 (hereinafter *O.R.*). McDowell outlined his plan in an undated June 1861 letter to Townsend, Scott's assistant adjutant general.

14. Peter C. Hains, "The First Gun at Bull Run," *Cosmopolitan* magazine 51 (1911), 389.
15. Ai Baker Thompson to his father, July 15, 1861, Ai Baker Thompson Letters, Manassas NBP Library.
16. Letter of Charles Dow in George Otis, *The Second Wisconsin Infantry*, Alan D. Gaff, ed. (Dayton, 1984), 133.
17. Sullivan Ballou to his wife, July 14, 1861, Civil War Letters Collection, Chicago Historical Society.
18. Jack C. Mason, *Until Antietam: The Life and Letters of Major General Israel B. Richardson, U.S. Army* (Carbondale, IL, 2009), 85, 87.
19. *CCW*, 39.
20. Gaillard Hunt, *Israel, Elihu, and Cadwallader Washburn: A Chapter in American Biography* (New York, 1925), 196–97.
21. Ibid., 197; letter from a member of the 2nd Rhode Island, *Providence Evening Press*, July 22, 1861; Martin D. Haynes, *A History of the Second Regiment, New Hampshire Volunteer Infantry, in the War of the Rebellion* (Lakeport, NH, 1896), 21.
22. *Rochester Union and Advertiser*, July 24, 1861.
23. William Todd, *The Seventy-Ninth Highlanders New York Volunteers in the War of the Rebellion* (Albany, 1866), 21.
24. *CCW*, 39.
25. *O.R.* 2:312; Barnard, "McDowell's Advance to Bull Run," in Robert Johnson and Clarence Buel, eds., *Battles and Leaders of the Civil War* (New York, 1887) 1:178.
26. *O.R.* 2:307.
27. See unpublished order, dated July 11, 1861, in the James L. Kemper Papers, University of Virginia.
28. *Charleston Mercury*, July 23, 1989; *O.R.* 2:450.
29. *O.R.* 2:440, 478.
30. Ibid., 447–48.

CHAPTER 2: First Blood

1. *O.R.* 2:306, 312.
2. Thomas F. Meagher, *The Last Days of the 69th in Virginia* (New York, 1861), 10–11.
3. Daniel Tyler, *A Memorial Volume Containing His Autobiography and War Record* (New Haven, 1883), 49, 54.
4. *CCW*, 199.
5. Ibid.; *O.R* 2:311.
6. *O.R.* 2:450, 452, 454.
7. Ibid., 442.
8. Regarding the specific deployment of the 1st and 17th, both Alexander Hunter, MS "Four Years in the Ranks," 35, Virginia Historical Society, and an unidentified correspondent of the 1st Virginia, *Savannah Republican*, July 26, 1861, are at variance with Charles T. Loehr, *War History of the Old First Virginia* (repr., Dayton, 1970), 9–10. Hunter maintains, probably correctly, that the ford proper was defended by Company A of the 17th and Company H of the 1st. See also Loehr, *First Virginia*, 9–10; *O.R.* 2:461.
9. *O.R.* 2:440–41. McLean's house no longer stands, though a modern structure now occupies the historic foundation. The foundation of the barn is still visible just south of Route 28.
10. P. G. T. Beauregard, "The First Battle of Bull Run," in Johnson and Buel, *Battles and Leaders* 1:200–201.
11. Ibid., 311, 313; *CCW*, 19–20, 199.

12. Tyler maintained that the Confederate battery Ayres fired upon was on the opposite side of Bull Run, but the Confederate descriptions make it clear that Kemper's guns were the target.
13. W. H. Morgan, *Personal Reminiscences of the War of 1861–65* (Lynchburg, 1911), 53–54.
14. John G. Barnard, *The C.S.A. and the Battle of Bull Run* (New York, 1862), 48–49; *O.R.*, 2:311–13.
15. *O.R.* 2:330; Barnard, *Battle of Bull Run*, 48.
16. Hunter, MS "Four Years in the Ranks," 35, VHS; Frank Potts, MS Diary, July 18, 1861, 31, VHS; Morgan, *Personal Reminiscences*, 54.
17. Letter of Capt. William Day, *Portsmouth [NH] Journal of Literature and Politics* August 3, 1861; E. A. Johnson, ed., *The Hero of Medfield: Containing the Journals and letters of Amos Alonzo Kingsbury* (Boston, 1862), 41.
18. Hunter, MS "Four Years in the Ranks," 35–36; Thomas W. Cutrer, ed., *Longstreet's Aide: The Civil War Letters of Major Thomas J. Goree* (Charlottesville, 1995), 26–27.
19. Warren H. Cudworth, *History of the First Regiment [Massachusetts] Infantry* (Boston, 1866), 43; Letter of J. W. Day, *Portsmouth [NH] Journal of Literature and Politics*, August 10, 1861.
20. Letter of Col. Ezra Walrath, *Washington Star*, July 29, 1861; Letter of Capt. A. I. Root, *The Daily Republican Advocate* [Batavia, NY], July 27, 1861.
21. Potts, Diary, July 18, 1861, 36.; *CCW*, 199; Cudworth, *First Massachusetts*, 45.
22. *O.R* 2:311.
23. Potts, Diary, July 18, 1861, 33; *O.R.* 2:462, 464.
24. Colonel Wells to John A. Andrew, July 20[?], 1861, John A. Andrew Papers, Massachusetts Historical Society; Letter of William R. Wells, July 23, 1861, William R. Wells Papers, Southern Historical Collection, University of North Carolina.
25. Letter of Col. Ezra Walrath, *Washington Star*, July 29, 1861.
26. Potts, Diary, July 18, 1861, 34.
27. Hunter, MS "Four Years in the Ranks," 36; Charles M. Blackford, *Annals of the Lynchburg Home Guard* (Lynchburg, 1891), 56; Patrick O'Rorke to his brother, Thomas, July 28, 1861, published digitally at https://bullrunnings.wordpress.com /2008/05/11/838; John Lipscomb Johnson, *Autobiographical Notes* (n.p., 1958), 136.
28. Hunter, MS "Four Years in the Ranks," 36.
29. Letter of Colonel Walrath, *Washington Star*, July 29, 1861; "Letter from Col. Walrath," *Syracuse Daily Courier and Union*, July 31, 1862; *CCW*, 20; Patrick O'Rorke to his brother, Thomas, July 28, 1861, published digitally at https://bullrunnings.word press.com/2008/05/11/838.
30. Letter of J. V. R., *Detroit Free Press*, July 30, 1861; Daniel G. Crotty, *Four Years Campaigning in the Army of the Potomac* (Grand Rapids, 1874), 22; Letter of Charles Jackson, *Chelsea Telegraph and Pioneer*, July 27, 1861.
31. *CCW*, 199–200.
32. Morgan, *Personal Reminiscences*, 57.
33. Hunter, MS "Four Years in the Ranks," 39–40; Letter of Charles A. Jackson, *Chelsea Telegraph and Pioneer*, July 27, 1861.
34. Hunter, MS "Four Years in the Ranks," 41.
35. William T. Sherman, *Memoirs of General William T. Sherman* (New York, 1886), 1:209.
36. Todd, *Seventy-Ninth Highlanders*, 25.
37. *CCW*, 200.
38. *Savannah Republican*, July 26, 1861; Cutrer, *The Civil War Letters of Major Thomas J. Goree*, 22–23, 25–27.

CHAPTER 3: Planning a "Waterloo"

1. *CCW*, 39.
2. Tyler, *Memorial Volume*, 54; James B. Fry, *McDowell and Tyler in the Campaign of Bull Run, 1861* (New York, 1884), 14. Fry's entire booklet addresses Tyler's performance during the campaign, with special emphasis on his actions on July 18.
3. For the contention between Walrath and Richardson, see the statement of an unidentified member of the U.S. Sanitary Commission, no date, Franklin B. Hough Papers, New York State Library.
4. *O.R.* 2:307; *CCW*, 39.
5. *O.R.* 2:330.
6. Beauregard, "The First Battle of Bull Run," 203.
7. Joseph E. Johnston, "Responsibilities of the First Bull Run," in Johnson and Buel, *Battles and Leaders*, 1:250.
8. Jubal A. Early, *Autobiographical Sketch and Narrative of the War Between the States* (Philadelphia, 1912), 11.
9. *O.R.* 2:307; Barnard, *Battle of Bull Run*, 50.
10. Barnard, *Battle of Bull Run*, 49–50; *O.R.* 2:330–31.
11. *CCW*, 39; *O.R.* 2:307.
12. Robert G. Carter, *Four Brothers in Blue* (Washington, 1913), 12; William Westervelt, *Lights and Shadows of Army Life: As Seen By a Private Soldier* (Marlboro, NY, 1886), 3.
13. *O.R.* 2:308, 745; James E. Smith, *A Famous Battery and its Campaigns, 1861–64* (Washington, 1892), 20.
14. *O.R.* 2:326–27.
15. For McDowell's detailed plans for campaign, see his letters to E. D. Townsend, June 24, 1861, and undated (June 1861), in *O.R.* 2:718–25.
16. *O.R.* 2:168.
17. *O.R.* 2:309; *CCW*, 48, 168, 172, 207; Tyler, *Autobiography*, 56–57. For a reconsideration of McDowell's planning and the assessment of Patterson's role in McDowell's defeat, see the analysis of Harry Smeltzer, keeper of Bull Runnings, an excellent digital archive and blog devoted to the First Battle of Manassas, https://bullrunnings.wordpress.com.
18. Letter of William C. Heriot, *Charleston Courier*, August 7, 1861; "From a Member of the Washington Light Infantry," *Charleston Courier*, August 5, 1861.
19. Johnston, "Responsibilities of the First Bull Run," 246.
20. *O.R.* 2:486–87.
21. Ibid., 479–80.
22. Johnston, "Responsibilities of the First Bull Run," 246.
23. The best descriptions of the July 20 conference at McDowell's headquarters are in Edward K. Eckert and Nicholas J. Amato, eds., *Ten Years in the Saddle: The Memoir of William Woods Averell* (San Rafael, 1983), 293; O. O. Howard, *Autobiography of Oliver Otis Howard* (New York, 1908) 1:152.
24. *O.R.* 2:326–27.
25. Hunt, *Washburn: An American Biography*, 199.
26. John Taylor, "The Story of a Battle" (recited before the Young Men's Catholic Club, Trenton, NJ, December 11, 1893), 5–6.
27. Ai Baker Thompson to his father, July 20, 1861, Ai Baker Thompson Letters, Manassas NBP Library.
28. Letter from the adjutant of the 18th New York, *Albany Evening Journal*, July 29, 1861.

29. Muriel Phillips Joslyn, *Charlotte's Boys: The Civil War Letters of the Branch Family of Savannah* (Berryville, VA, 1996), 43; Berrien M. Zettler, *War Stories and School-Day Incidents for the Children* (New York, 1912), 61.
30. Nannie Neville Leachman Carroll, *Folly Castle Folks*, published by the Hugh S. Watson, Jr., Genealogical Society of Tidewater, Virginia, 1976. Copy on file at Manassas NBP Library; Alexander Compton to Mrs. Davis, July 30, 1861, Schoff Collection, UM; Laura Thornberry Fletcher, "A few memories of the 'War Between the States' by an eye witness, for my grandson, Westwood Hugh Fletcher," unpublished TS, copy on file at Manassas NBP Library.

CHAPTER 4: "You Are Turned"
1. The Warrenton Turnpike Company had become insolvent several years before, and the road's macadamized surface had since fallen into some disrepair, though it was still highly serviceable.
2. Thomas M. Aldrich, *The History of Battery A, First Regiment Rhode Island Light Artillery* (Providence, 1904), 18; August Woodbury, *A Narrative of the Campaign of the First Rhode Island Regiment in the Spring and Summer of 1861* (Providence, 1862), 89; *CCW*, 201.
3. For reference to the road west of Cub Run, see Andrew Porter's testimony, *CCW*, 212, and Daniel P. Woodbury's report, *O.R.* 2:333. Woodbury claimed the road left the turnpike "about one-third of a mile west of Cub Run."
4. Woodbury, *First Rhode Island*, 90; Letter of Ambrose Burnside published in the *Providence Manufacturers and Farmers Journal*, April 26, 1869.
5. M. A. DeWolfe Howe, ed., *Home Letters of General Sherman* (New York, 1909), 205.
6. *O.R.* 1:485, 558–59, 560, 563.
7. Hains, "First Gun," 390.
8. Ibid., 291; Edmund D. Stedman, *The Battle of Bull Run* (New York, 1861), 20. The time of the first shot is given variously. Tyler put it at 6:30 A.M., Lt. Edward B. Hill of Carlisle's battery at 5 A.M., and Evans at 5:15 A.M. Many other witnesses put it sometime in between these extremes. The delay in the march and the preparations that took place before the first shot was fired suggest something toward the later time is correct. Hains, "First Gun," 291; Alan D. Gaff, *If This is War* (Dayton, 1991), 186–87.
9. Hains, "First Gun," 291; *O.R.* 2:348, 358, 500.
10. *O.R.* 2:559, 560; J. W. Reid, *History of the Fourth Regiment of South Carolina Volunteers* (repr. Dayton, 1975), 24.
11. B. B. Breazeale, "Co. J, 4th South Carolina Infantry at the First Battle of Manassas," TS Manassas NBP Library.
12. "Letter from the Battleground of Bull's Run," *The British Colonist*, August 10, 1861.
13. *O.R.* 2:374.
14. Ibid., 487.
15. Johnston, "The First Battle of Bull Run," 205.
16. John Imboden, "Incidents of the First Bull Run," in Johnson and Buell, *Battles and Leaders* 1:231.
17. Johnston, "The First Battle of Bull Run," 205; P. G. T. Beauregard, "The First Battle of Bull Run," 207.
18. *O.R.* 2:543; Hunter, MS "Four Years in the Ranks," 44–45.
19. *O.R.* 2:537.
20. George F. Harrison, "Ewell at First Manassas," *Southern History Society Papers* (hereinafter *SHSP*), vol. 14 (1886), 356–57; Campbell Brown, "General Ewell at Bull Run," in Johnson and Buel, *Battles and Leaders* 1:259–60; Cutrer, *The Civil War Letters of Thomas J. Goree*, 27–28.

21. *CCW*, 44.
22. Woodbury, *First Rhode Island*, 90–92.
23. *CCW*, 160–61.
24. *CCW*, 30.
25. Lewis H. Metcalfe, "So Eager Were We All," *American Heritage*, vol. 16 (June, 1965), 35.
26. Mrs. J. K. M'Whorter, "Caring for the Soldiers in the Sixties," *Confederate Veteran*, vol. 29 (1921), 410–411; Haynes, *Second New Hampshire*, 23–24.
27. G. Moxley Sorrel, *Recollections of a Confederate Staff Officer* (New York, 1905), 93.
28. E. P. Alexander, "The Battle of Bull Run," *Scribner's Magazine*, vol. 41 (1907), 87–88.
29. J. B. E. Sloan, MS Account, J. B. E. Sloan Papers, Pendleton District Historical and Recreational Commission; Charles L. Dufour, *Gentle Tiger: The Gallant Life of Roberdeau Wheat* (Baton Rouge, 1957), 134; *O.R.* 2:563.
30. *O.R.* 2:559, 560–561, 563; Sloan, MS Account; "Fourth South Carolina Regiment," *Richmond Dispatch*, August 8, 1861.
31. Breazeale, "4th South Carolina," TS Manassas NBP Library, 2; Letter of "R. R.," Wheat's battalion, *Daily True Delta* [New Orleans], August 15, 1861; Letter of "W," *Daily True Delta* [New Orleans], August 8, 1861; *O.R.* 2:561.
32. *O.R.* 2:486–87, 563; Imboden, "Incidents of the First Bull Run," p. 232.
33. Letter of "W," Wheat's battalion, *Daily True Delta* [New Orleans], August 8, 1861; Imboden, "Incidents of the First Bull Run," 232–33; James G. Hudson, MS Diary, July 21, 1861, Alabama Department of Archives and History. The time of arrival of Bee's command and Imboden's battery has long been misunderstood; most historians suggest they arrived after the fight on Matthews Hill commenced. It is clear from the source material cited in the following chapter that at least the 4th Alabama and perhaps Imboden were present prior to the opening of the Rhode Island battery on Matthews Hill, an event that occurred in the earliest phase of the fighting.

CHAPTER 5: Matthews Hill

1. M'Whorter, "Caring for the Soldiers in the Sixties," 29:410–11; J. Albert Monroe, "Reminiscences of the War of the Rebellion of 1861–5," in *Personal Narratives of the Rhode Island Soldiers and Sailors Society, Second Series, No. 11.* (Providence, 1881), 6–7; Charles F. Clarke, *History of Company F, First Regiment Rhode Island Volunteers During the Spring and Summer of 1861* (Newport, 1891), 55.
2. Aldrich, *Battery A*, 18–19.
3. Eckert and Amato, *Ten Years in the Saddle*, 295; *O.R.* 2:383; Augustus T. Francis, *History of the 71st Regiment, N.G.N.Y.* (New York, 1919), 182.
4. *O.R.* 2:331, 395; Robert Hunt Rhodes, ed., *All for the Union: The Diary and Letters of Elisha Hunt Rhodes* (Lincoln, RI, 1986), 36.
5. Woodbury, *Second Rhode Island*, 32; Haynes, *Second New Hampshire*, 24; *O.R.* 2:321, 331.
6. William Greene Roelker, ed., "Civil War Letters of William Ames," *Rhode Island Historical Society Collections*, October, 1940, 12–13; "Correspondence of the Journal" [Letters from the 2nd Rhode Island], *Providence Journal*, July 27, 1861.
7. Aldrich, *Battery A*, 19; Rhodes, *All for the Union*, 26.
8. English letter quoted in Rhodes, *All for the Union*, 33.
9. "Letters from the Second Battery," *Providence Evening Press*, July 31, 1861.
10. Ibid; "The Second Battery," *Providence Journal*, July 31, 1861.
11. Aldrich, *Battery A*, 20; "The Second Battery," *Providence Journal*, July 31, 1861.
12. *O.R.* 2:559, 561.

13. "Letter from the Battlefield," *Worcester Daily Spy*, August 2, 1861; "Correspondence of the Journal," *Providence Journal*, July 27, 1861; Augustus Woodbury, *The Second Rhode Island Regiment: A Narrative of Military Operations* (Providence, 1873), 33.

14. Woodbury, *First Rhode Island*, 93.

15. *O.R.* 2:396; *Providence Evening Press*, July 26, 1861; *Providence Journal*, July 25, 1861. The location of the 1st vis-a-vis the 2nd Rhode Island has been the subject of some debate. The letters published in the newspapers cited above strongly suggest that the 1st Rhode Island entered the fight on the left of the 2nd.

16. *O.R.* 2:384.

17. "Letter from the Field of Battle," July 31, 1861, and "The Tiger Rifles at Manassas," August 1, 1861, *Daily Crescent* [New Orleans]; Letter of "R. R.," *Daily True Delta* [New Orleans], August 15, 1861; *O.R.* 2:384, 559.

18. *Providence Evening Press*, July 31, 1861. The letter of an unidentified member of the 2nd Rhode Island, quoted in Rhodes, *All for the Union*, 33, also gives the distance as 20 yards. *Providence Evening Press*, July 25, 1861; Rhodes, *All for the Union*, 26; Roelker, "Ames Letters," 13. The timing of the 1st Rhode Island's arrival is not entirely clear. A letter cited in Rhodes, *All for the Union*, 37, states that the 1st arrived when the Confederates were within "20 paces" of the battery and is the authority for the narrative given here.

19. *O.R* 2:559; Beauregard, "The First Battle of Bull Run," 207.

20. Zettler, *War Stories*, 62–63; Robert L. Grant to his mother, July 24, 1861, TS, Manassas NBP Library; Thomas L. Wragg to his father, July 23, 1861, Thomas L. Wragg Papers, Library of Congress.

21. R. T. Coles, MS "History of the 4th Alabama Volunteers," Chapter 2, p. 7, Alabama Department of Archives and History, 4th Infantry Regiment Files. Since published as Jeffrey D. Stocker, *From Huntsville to Appomattox: R. T. Coles's History of the 4th Regiment, Alabama Volunteer Infantry* (Knoxville, 1996); Hudson, Diary, July 21, 1861.

22. 4th Alabama report, *Richmond Dispatch*, August 17, 1861; Hudson, Diary, July 21, 1861.

23. 4th Alabama Report, *Richmond Dispatch*, August 17, 1861; Hudson, Diary, July 21, 1861; Coles, "4th Alabama," 7.

24. *Savannah Republican*, August 6, 1861; Zettler, *War Stories*, 64–65. Another source times this little address by Gardner somewhat earlier in the day. Robert Grant to his mother, July 24, 1861, Manassas NBP Library.

25. Joslyn, *Charlotte's Boys*, 44–45; Beauregard, "The First Battle of Bull Run," 207; Coles, "4th Alabama," 7; *O.R.* 2:489–90.

26. Woodbury, *First Rhode Island*, 95; Aldrich, *Battery A*, 20.

27. "Battle of Bull Run—Personal Narrative of a San Franciscan," *San Francisco Bulletin*, August 20, 1861; William B. Styple, ed., *Writing and Fighting the Civil War: Soldier Correspondence of the* New York Mercury (Kearny, NJ, 2000), 34–35; Coles, "Fourth Alabama," 8; *Richmond Dispatch*, August 17, 1861.

28. Zettler, *War Stories*, 66; "Letter from an Oglethorpe," *Savannah Republican*, August 6, 1861; Hudson, Diary, July 21, 1861; Robert Grant to his mother, July 24, 1861, Manassas NBP Library; "The 7th and 8th Georgia Regiments at Manassas," *Augusta [GA] Chronicle*, July 30, 1861; Letter from the 8th Georgia, *Richmond Dispatch*, July 29, 1861.

29. "Letters from the Second Rhode Island Regiment" and "The Rhode Islanders in Battle," *Providence Evening Press*, July 26, 1861; *Providence Journal*, July 26, 1861; Letter of Leonard C. Beeding, *Worcester Daily Spy*, August 2, 1861.

30. Woodbury, *First Rhode Island*, 99.

31. "An Account by an Officer of the Regular Army," *New York Times*, July 27, 1861.

32. Eckert and Amato, *Ten Years in the Saddle*, 297.

33. Carter, *Four Brothers in Blue*, 13; "Reminiscences of Bull Run," *National Tribune*, January 25, 1907; Dangerfield Parker, "Personal Reminiscences: The Battalion of Regular Infantry in the First Battle of Bull Run," in Military Order of the Loyal Legion of the United States, DC, *War Papers 36* (Washington, D.C., 1890), 13–14. Both Carter and Parker state pointedly that the Regulars supported the Rhode Island Battery, and neither claims to have delivered a decisive blow against the Confederate flank. Nor do Burnside or Sykes in their reports, *O.R.* 2:390, 396; "An Account by an Officer in the Regular Army," *New York Times*, July 27, 1861. This officer states explicitly that the Regular battalion went directly to support Reynolds's guns.

34. Patrick O'Rorke to his brother Thomas, July 28, 1861, published digitally at https://bullrunnings.wordpress.com/2008/05/11/838; Howe, *Home Letters of Sherman*, 206. It has often been presumed that the bold Confederate rider was Roberdeau Wheat. This is possible, but it is just as likely the rider belonged to Capt. William Terry's squadron of cavalry, in position near Wheat on the Confederate left.

35. Todd, *Seventy-Ninth Highlanders*, 34; Brooks D. Simpson and Jean V. Berlin, eds., *Sherman's Civil War: Selected Correspondence of William T. Sherman, 1860–1865* (Chapel Hill, 1999), 121–22.

36. *O.R.* 2:369; Simpson and Berlin, *Sherman Letters*, 123; Stedman, *The Battle of Bull Run*, 17. Many modern accounts of the battle attribute the collapse of the Confederate right flank to the arrival on the field of the 1st Minnesota of Heintzelman's division. While there is little doubt the Minnesotans moved to the left of the Union line, none of the source material suggests they came in contact with the Confederate flank. Instead, the head of Sherman's column arrived first and ultimately compelled the Confederate retreat.

37. "Bill Arp's Reminiscences of Manassas," *Aberdeen [SD] Daily News*, January 20, 1887.

38. Sloan, MS Account; *Charleston Mercury*, August 12, 1861; Dufour, *Gentle Tiger*, 137–38.

39. Zettler, *War Stories*, 67; "Letter from an Oglethorpe," *Savannah Republican*, August 6, 1861; James E Bagwell, *James Hamilton Couper, Georgia Rice Planter* (PhD Dissertation, University of Southern Mississippi, 1978), 310.

40. Hudson, Diary, July 21, 1861; Coles, "Fourth Alabama," 8.

41. Carter, *Four Brothers in Blue*, 13.

42. Haynes, *Second New Hampshire*, 25.

43. Tyler in *CCW*, 201; Henry N. Blake, *Three Years in the Army of the Potomac* (Boston, 1865), 16; Todd, *Seventy-Ninth Highlanders*, 34; "The Second Battery," *Providence Journal*, July 31, 1861.

CHAPTER 6: Chasing Victory

1. Letter of "P.W.A.," *Augusta [GA] Chronicle*, July 31, 1861; "Fourth Alabama Regiment at Manassas," *Times-Picayune* [New Orleans], August 3, 1861; "The Eighth Georgia Regiment in the Battle at the Stone Bridge," *Richmond Daily Dispatch*, July 29, 1861.

2. Johnston, "First Bull Run," 247.

3. Beauregard, "First Battle of Bull Run," 209.

4. Johnston, "First Bull Run," 248; Alexander, "Battle of Bull Run," 89.

5. *O.R.* 2:491.

6. Imboden, "Incidents of the First Bull Run," 233.
7. John Coxe, "The Battle of First Manassas," *Confederate Veteran* 23:25; "From a Member of the Washington Light Infantry," *Charleston Mercury*, August 5, 1861; Letter of James Singleton, July 26, 1861, James Singleton Papers, University of Virginia.
8. James Conner to his mother, July 24, 1861, James Conner Papers, Southern Historical Collection, University of North Carolina; "The Manassas Battle," *Charleston Courier*, August 8, 1861.
9. Coxe, "First Manassas," 25; "Extracts of a Private Letter," *Charleston Mercury*, August 5, 1861, August 8, 1861; Wade Hampton, "The Legion at Manassas," *Charleston News and Courier*, July 13, 1885; Rev. Richard Johnson to Lina, October 8, 1861, Museum of the Confederacy, Richmond, VA; C. W. Hutson to his parents, July 22, 1861, Charles W. Hutson Papers, Southern Historical Collection, University of North Carolina.
10. Westervelt, *Lights and Shadows of Army Life* 4; C. B. Fairchild, *History of the 27th Regiment New York Volunteers* (Binghamton, 1888), 12; Hall, "A Volunteer at First Bull Run," 155.
11. Account of Capt. Hugh Miller, published in the *Pontotoc [MS] Examiner*, September 13, 1861. A transcription of Miller's account appears online at www.authentic -campaigner.com/forum/showthread.php?31971-Captain-Hugh-Miller-s-Account-of -First-Manassas&s=d0959c93784aaae0ebb8f472e840c0cb; David Sullivan, ed., "Fowler the Soldier, Fowler the Marine: Letters from an Unusual Confederate," *Civil War Times Illustrated*, February 1988, 30.
12. "The Manassas Battle," *Charleston Courier*, August 8, 1861; "Extracts of a Private Letter," *Charleston Mercury*, August 5, 1861; *O.R.* 2:566.
13. Letter of "Blockhead," *Union [NY] News*, August 8, 1861; Fairchild, *History of the 27th Regiment*, 12; Sullivan, "Fowler the Soldier," 30.
14. Letter of "Blockhead," *Union [NY] News*, August 8, 1861; James Conner to his mother, July 24, 1861, Conner Papers, UNC; "Extracts of a Private Letter," *Charleston Mercury*, August 5, 1861; H. Seymour Hall, "A Volunteer at First Bull Run," MOLLUS, *War Talks in Kansas* 1:165.
15. Imboden, "Incidents of Bull Run," 233–34.
16. Averell in *CCW*, 214–15; Colonel Fowler's Report (14th Brooklyn), *Brooklyn Daily Eagle*, March 17, 1901, 6; Letter of Evert Myers, *Red Hook Journal*, August 1, 1861; Letter of "Richard," 8th NYSM, *New York Herald*, July 25, 1861.
17. Coxe, "First Manassas," 26.
18. Robert Grant to his wife, July 24, 1861, Manassas NBP Library; Coles, "4th Alabama," 9.
19. *O.R.* 2:481.
20. Charles W. Squires, "The 'Boy Officer' of the Washington Artillery—Part I of a Memoir," *Civil War Times Illustrated*, vol. 14 (May 1975), 11–17. The use of the narrow farm road is well documented. Its remnants are still visible on Henry Hill today. John N. Lyle, TS "Sketches Found in a Confederate Veteran's Desk," 202, Rockbridge County Historical Society.
21. D. B. Conrad, "History of the First Battle of Manassas," *SHSP* 19:89; "Newtown Artillery—Beckham's Battery," *Richmond Dispatch*, August 5, 1861; MS Memoir of Charles Wight, Wight Family Papers, Virginia Historical Society; Lyle, "Sketches," 202.
22. Wight, MS Memoir, VHS; Clement D. Fishburne, Rockbridge Artillery, MS Memoir, Alderman Library, University of Virginia.

23. *Charleston Mercury*, July 26, 1861.

24. Imboden, "Incidents of Bull Run," 234–35.

25. Lyle, "Sketches," 202–3; *O.R.* 2:481.

26. William M. Owen, *In Camp and Battle with the Washington Artillery* (Boston, 1885), 36; William Poague to John Warwick Daniel, August 8, 1905, John Warwick Daniel Papers, University of Virginia; Dennis P. Kelly, TS "Plan to Locate Artillery, Manassas National Battlefield Park," 83–89. The number and order of these guns are still very much in question.

27. *O.R.* 2:483.

28. Beauregard, "First Battle of Bull Run," 210.

29. Samuel W. Ferguson, MS Memoirs, Duke University, 7.

30. Beauregard, "First Battle of Bull Run," 210; Johnston, "First Bull Run," 248; Coles, "4th Alabama," 9–10; Kenneth Jones, "The Fourth Alabama Infantry: First Blood," *Alabama Historical Quarterly*, 36:45–46; Owen, *Washington Artillery*, 38; James Singleton to his mother, July 26, 1861, Singleton Papers, UVA.

31. Zettler, *War Stories*, 69–70.

32. *O.R.* 2:492.

33. Fry, "McDowell's Advance to Bull Run," 187.

34. *CCW*, 214.

35. Lyle, "Sketches," 204–5.

36. John G. Merritt, "A Minnesota Boy's First Battle," in Theodore F. Rodenbaugh, ed., *Sabre and Bayonet* (New York, 1897), 39.

CHAPTER 7: To Henry Hill

1. Tyler testimony, *CCW*, 201; Fry confirmed he expressed claims of victory. See Fry, *Campaign of Bull Run*, 56.

2. *O.R.* 2:349–350, 352. Fry, *Campaign of Bull Run*, 56; J. R. H., "Notes on the Battle of Bull Run," *Hartford Evening Press*, August 8, 1861 (this is Part 4 of an excellent account of the battle written within days of its conclusion); Letter of "C. E. P.," *Winsted [CT] Herald*, July 26, 1861.

3. *O.R.* 2:349, 353.

4. Coxe, "First Manassas," 26.

5. Coxe, "First Manassas," 26; Hutson to his parents, July 22, 1861, Charles W. Hutson Papers, UNC; James Conner to his mother, July 24, 1861, Conner Papers, UNC; *O.R.* 2:566; James Simpson to his sister, July 26, 1861, James Simpson Papers, Duke University; "The Manassas Battle," *Charleston Courier*, August 8, 1861.

6. Coxe, "First Manassas," 26; *O.R.* 2:353.

7. Styple, *Writing and Fighting the Civil War*, 39–40; "The Fifth Virginia Regiment in the Battle of Manassas," *Richmond Dispatch*, August 16, 1861; "Position of the Second," *Bangor Daily Whig and Courier*, August 3, 1861; Letter of James Kelly, *Bangor Daily Whig and Courier*, August 6, 1861; Letter of Hugh Miller, *Pontotoc [MS] Examiner*, September 13, 1861, www.authentic-campaigner.com/forum/showthread .php?31971-Captain-Hugh-Miller-s-Account-of-First-Manassas&s=d0959c93784aaa e0ebb8f472e840c0cb.

8. *O.R.* 2:566–67; "The 5th Virginia Regiment," *Richmond Dispatch*, August 16, 1861; Letter of James Kelly, *Bangor Daily Whig and Courier*, August 6, 1861; William H. Shaw, Diary, July 21, 1861, Manassas NBP Library; *O.R.* 2:353; Wight MS Memoir, VHS.

9. Fry, "McDowell's Advance to Bull Run," 188.

10. "An Account by an Officer of the Regular Army," *New York Times*, July 27, 1861; C. D. Fishburne, "Sketch of the Rockbridge Artillery," *SHSP* 23:112; *CCW*, 168.

11. McDowell's commands and the protests against them are revealed in various officers' testimony to the Joint Committee on the Conduct of the War. See *CCW*, 149, 168, 169, 172, 219, 243; *O.R.* 2:347.

12. *O.R.* 2:347, 385, 392, 402; *O.R.* 51:21; *CCW*, 216; Charles E. Davis to his wife, July 24, 1861, Charles E. Davis Papers, Minnesota Historical Society; H. H. Comings, *Personal Reminiscences of Company E, New York Fire Zouaves* (Malden, MA, 1886), 9; Lewis Metcalfe, "So Eager Were We All," *American Heritage*, June 1965, 37. For a complete discussion of the evidence relating to the sequence of events during the early part of the Henry Hill fight, see John Hennessy, TS "The First Hour's Fight on Henry Hill," 1985, Manassas NBP Library.

13. *CCW*, 168–69.

14. *CCW*, 145. One of Griffin's guns had a shell lodged in its bore and did not join the movement to Henry Hill.

15. James A. Wright, *No More Gallant a Deed: A Civil War Memoir of the First Minnesota Volunteers*, ed. Steven J. Keillor (Minneapolis, 2001), 54; *CCW*, 169, 219, 243.

16. *CCW*, 243; Joseph Mills Hanson, *Bull Run Remembers* (Manassas, 1953), 88–89. The slave was also wounded in the barrage.

17. *CCW*, 219, 243; George B. Haskins, *The History of the First Regiment of Artillery* (Portland, 1879), 505; *O.R.* 2:394.

18. *CCW*, 143, 216; *Brooklyn Daily Eagle*, July 31, 1861; C. V. Tevis, *History of the Fighting Fourteenth* (New York, 1911), 25; *CCW*, 216; *O.R.*, 51:21; Wright, *No More Gallant a Deed*, 54. For a discussion and documentation of the sequence of events on Henry Hill, see Hennessy, "First Hour's Fight," 8–9.

19. That the 38th New York ascended Henry Hill with the initial Union surge is clear from Averell's testimony to the *CCW*, p. 215, and the testimony of participants, notably Capt. William Baird, *Geneva [NY] Gazette*, August 2, 1861, and Capt. Calvin S. DeWitt, *Elmira Weekly Advertiser*, August 10, 1861. See also Farnsworth's report, *O.R.* 2:113–14.

20. Fishburne, MS Memoir, University of Virginia; W. Morton Brown to Dr. Lee Hold, August 19, 1861, Bowman-Howard-Domingos Collections, Middle Georgia Archives, Washington Library, Macon, GA; "Extract of a Letter from Lieut. John Pelham to his Father," *Jacksonville Republican*, August 8, 1861.

21. John H. B. Jones, "Reminiscences of a Famous Company," *Richmond Times-Dispatch*, February 2, 1911. This cannonball also killed Cpl. William Paxton, another Washington College student. See Alexander Tedford Barclay to his mother, July 27, 1861, Barclay Papers, Washington and Lee University, and letter of Robert Glasgow, *Lexington [VA] Gazette*, August 1, 1861.

22. Fishburne, MS Memoir, University of Virginia. This memoir was the basis for Fishburne's published account in *SHSP*, cited elsewhere; Lyle, "Sketches," 205–6; Wight, MS Memoir, VHS; Jackson to J. M. Bennett, July 28, 1861, in John Esten Cooke, *Stonewall Jackson: A Military Biography* (New York, 1866), 508. Cummings's letter appears in John O. Casler, *Four Years in the Stonewall Brigade* (repr. Dayton, 1971), 36.

23. Wright, *No More Gallant a Deed*, 55.

24. W. Morton Brown to Dr. Lee Hold, August 19, 1861, Bowman-Howard-Domingos Collection.

25. Casler, *Four Years in the Stonewall Brigade*, 42.
26. Wright, *No More Gallant a Deed*, 55; Alexander Wilkin to his father, July 23, 1861, Wilkin Papers, Minnesota Historical Society.
27. Merritt, "First Battle," 39; Letter of Edward Foster, *St. Paul Press*, August 1, 1861; Richard Moe, *The Last Full Measure: The Life and Death of the First Minnesota Volunteers* (New York, 1993), 49; Casler, *Four Years in the Stonewall Brigade*, 26; *CCW*, 30–31, 216; *O.R.* 51:21; George W. Baylor, *Bull Run to Bull Run or Four Years in the Army of Northern Virginia* (Richmond, 1900), 20.
28. Letter of "Typo," *St. Paul Press*, August 4, 1861; Charles E. Davis to his wife, July 24, 1861, Davis Papers, MHS; Metcalfe, "So Eager Were We All," 37; "Services and Sufferings of the 33rd Virginia Regiment," *Richmond Daily Enquirer*, August 5, 1861.
29. *CCW* 216; *O.R.* 2:385.
30. Both Captains DeWitt and Baird of the 38th stated that the 38th advanced with the Fire Zouaves on their right, Dewitt in the *Elmira Weekly Advertiser*, August 10, 1861, and Baird in the *Geneva Gazette*, August 2, 1861. See also Averell's testimony, *CCW*, 217. Averell said the 38th "led the column on the left."
31. *CCW*, 216; Metcalfe, "So Eager Were We All," 37; Haskins, *First Artillery*, 505.
32. *O.R.* 2:483.
33. Letter of Lieutenant Knox, *Chicago Tribune*, July 30, 1861; Letter of John Johnson, *New York Leader*, August 3, 1861; *Richmond Dispatch*, August 13, 1861.
34. William W. Blackford, *War Years with Jeb Stuart*, (New York, 1945), 30.
35. Letter of Edward Foster, *St. Paul Press*, August 1, 1861; *O.R.* 2:393, 405. A small detachment of Union cavalry gave chase to Stuart's horsemen, but the junket accomplished little beyond the capture of Lt. Col. (and future general) George H. Steuart.
36. Alexander, "The Battle of Bull Run," 92–93.
37. *O.R.* 51:29; 2:475.
38. *O.R.* 2:475, 522, 561; John W. Bell, *Memoirs of Governor William Smith of Virginia: His Political, Military and Personal History* (New York, 1891), 30.
39. This account of Jackson's naming is based on the only four known eyewitness accounts of the incident. See the 4th Alabama report, *Richmond Dispatch*, August 17, 1861; Coles, "4th Alabama," 11; clipping of an account by an unidentified officer of the 4th Alabama in the Jedediah Hotchkiss Papers, container #70, Library of Congress; and William M. Robins, "The Sobriquet Stonewall," *SHSP* 19:166. While the four accounts vary as to some details, they clearly provide a context for Bee's legendary utterings, placing the occurrence much later in the day than has been commonly supposed. These accounts also show with certainty that, contrary to popular perception, Bee was not rallying anyone at the time of the event—hence the phrase "Rally around the Virginians!" commonly attributed to Bee is illogical. The accepted location of Bee at the time of the episode—in the fields directly south of the Robinson house—is also exploded as a possibility. For a complete discussion of the Bee–Jackson incident, see John Hennessy, "Jackson's Stone Wall: Fact or Fiction?" in *Civil War: The Magazine of the Civil War Society*, March–April 1990.
40. Robert Garth Scott, ed., *Forgotten Valor: The Memoirs, Journals, & Civil War Letters of Orlando B. Willcox* (Kent, OH, 1999), 293.
41. Tevis, *Fighting Fourteenth*, 25; *O.R.* 2:414; Hennessy, "First Hour's Fight," 17–18.
42. *CCW*, 219, 220, 243; Haskins, *First Artillery*, 505–6; *O.R.* 2:394. Griffin references the presence of the rallied detachment of Zouaves behind his guns, and their presence is suggested by "The New York Fire Zouaves in Battle, Taken from Notes Furnished by John Johnson . . . Marion of Engine 9 . . . Captain Edward Burns," an undated

clipping from the *New York Leader*, in the files of the 11th New York Regiment, New York State Division of Military and Naval Affairs (DMNA), accessed online at https://dmna.ny.gov/historic/reghist/civil/infantry/11thInf/11thInfCWN.htm.
43. Letter of Arthur C. Cummings in Casler, *Four Years*, 36.
44. Letter of Randolph Barton, January 15, 1897, in Casler, *Four Years*, 41; see also Hennessy, "First Hour's Fight," 30–31.
45. Bell, *Memoirs of William Smith*, 146–47; Scott Mingus, *Confederate General William "Extra Billy" Smith* (El Dorado Hills, 2013), 162–63.
46. The details of this pivotal moment of the battle are embodied mostly in the reports and testimony of Barry and Griffin. *CCW*, 143–45, 169; *O.R.* 2:552. In his memoir, Smith misidentified the battery at Ricketts's (a common error that day) and declared "it never fired on us more than once, if that."
47. Casler, *Four Years*, 26, 42; *Richmond Daily Enquirer*, August 5, 1861. For a complete discussion of the evidence regarding the capture of Griffin's guns see Hennessy, "First Hour's Fight," 25–36.

CHAPTER 8: Maelstrom
1. "Services and Sufferings of the 33rd Virginia Regiment," *Richmond Daily Enquirer*, August 5, 1861; Casler, *Four Years*, 29; "The Thirty-Third Virginia at First Manassas," *Richmond Times-Dispatch*, June 4, 1905; *CCW*, 147.
2. The report of Colonel Allen appears in "Thirty-Third Virginia at First Manassas," *Richmond Times-Dispatch*, June 4, 1905, and also in *SHSP* 19:365–66.
3. J. H. B. Jones, "The Liberty Hall Volunteers at First Manassas," *Rockbridge County News*, February 2, 1911; Lyle, "Sketches," 209.
4. Unidentified letter from Camp Porter, *Brooklyn Daily Eagle*, July 29, 1861; Letter of John P. Victory, (ibid., July 31, 1861); Letter of G. H. Prick, (ibid., July 26, 1861); Letter of Joseph Sands, (ibid.); Letter of Albert Pendell, (ibid., July 25, 1861); Caleb Beal to his parents, July 23, 1861, private collection of Anthony Dellarocca. Text accessed at Bull Runnings, https://bullrunnings.wordpress.com/?s=Dellarocca. The proximity of the Federal infantry is attested to by Jackson in Cooke, *Stonewall Jackson*, 508, and Pendleton's report in *O.R.* 51:36. See also Hennessy, "First Hour's Fight," 15–16.
5. *O.R.* 51:35.; C. D. Fishburne, "Sketch of the Rockbridge Artillery," *SHSP* 23:114. The timing of the artillery's withdrawal is further confirmed by members of the 4th Alabama who at that moment—after Bee's immortal utterance—were following Bee to the field. Three members confirm that as they advanced, Jackson's artillery retreated, splitting the regiment's column. See Hennessy, "Jackson's Nickname: Fact or Fable," in *Civil War: The Magazine of the Civil War Society*, March–April 1990.
6. John Warwick Daniel, "A Charge at First Manassas," *SHSP* 39:345; Watkins Kearns, Diary, Virginia Historical Society. Several Confederates later claimed this was the first use of the soon-to-be-feared rebel yell.
7. Haskins, *First Artillery*, 505–6.
8. C. A. Fonerden, *A Brief History of the Military Career of Carpenter's Battery* (New Market, 1911), 10–11.
9. Robert R. Murray, "On the Battle of Manassas," *Marietta [GA] Journal*, April 19, 1888; "The Eighth Georgia in the Battle at Stone Bridge," *Richmond Dispatch*, July 27, 1861.
10. "The Sixth North Carolina Regiment," *Richmond Dispatch*, August 5, 1861; Letter of B. Rush Smith, *North Carolina Whig* [Charlotte], August 6, 1861. Before the construction of the modern National Park Service visitor center on Henry Hill, the location of

Fisher's death was marked. The marker stood approximately where the flagpole in front of the visitor center stands today. Walter Clark, ed., *Histories of the Several Regiments and Battalions from North Carolina* 5:344–45, 583–84.

11. *O.R.* 2:409, 412; William H. Randall, MS Reminiscences, Bentley Historical Library, University of Michigan. In his report, Willcox claimed to have "expelled" the Virginians from the guns, but other sources make it clear this did not happen.

12. Fonerden, *Carpenter's Battery*, 12–13.

13. Charles M. Smith to his mother, July 31, 1861, Drew Archival Library, Duxbury Rural and Historical Society.

14. Ibid.; "The Massachusetts Fifth in the Fight," *Boston Daily Advertiser*, July 30, 1861; Letter of "R," *Boston Evening Journal*, July 30, 1861; Alfred S. Roe, *The Fifth Regiment Massachusetts Volunteer Infantry in its Three Years of Duty* (Boston, 1911), 81; John Robertson to his parents, July 27, 1861, Tufts-Robertson Family Papers, Massachusetts Historical Society; *O.R.* 2:406.

15. Roe, *Fifth Massachusetts*, 81; Blake, *Three Years*, 21.

16. Beauregard's report, *O.R.* 2:494.

17. Letter of James Singleton, July 26, 1861, Singleton Papers, UVA; Captain Conner of the Hampton Legion mentions being attached at this time to a Virginia regiment. James Conner to his mother, July 24, 1861, James Conner Papers, UNC. "The Battle of Manassas," *Charleston News and Courier*, July 13, 1885, also makes reference to the Legion fighting with some of Jackson's Virginians. Unknown Letter, *Richmond Dispatch*, August 16, 1861; Samuel S. Seig to his parents, July 25, 1861, Samuel S. Seig Papers, Duke University; Wight, MS Memoir, VHS.

18. Hudson, Diary, July 21, 1861; Letter of Capt. Hugh Miller, 2nd Mississippi, in the *Pontotoc [MS] Examiner*, September 13, 1861.

19. Letter from unidentified soldier, *Richmond Dispatch*, August 16, 1861; Wight, MS Memoir, VHS; Hudson, Diary, July 21, 1861; John Newton Opie, *A Rebel Cavalryman with Lee, Stuart and Jackson* (Chicago, 1899), 32; James Conner to his mother, July 24, 1861, Conner Papers, UNC.

20. *O.R.* 2:418; Howard, *Autobiography*, 11:158–59. It's possible that Arnold's battery was in position on Chinn Ridge. Howard later misstated his destination as Ricketts's battery.

21. *O.R.* 2:369; Letter of Nathaniel Rollins, July 25, 1861 in E. B. Quiner, "Correspondence of Wisconsin Volunteers," 1:115, State Historical Society of Wisconsin.

22. "Civil War Letters of Samuel S. Partridge of the 'Rochester Regiment'," *Rochester Historical Society Publications*, 1944, 80; Letter of Capt. H. B. Williams, *Rochester Union and Advertiser*, July 29, 1861; Ibid., July 27, 30, 1861; Letter of Lt. Eugene P. Fuller, *Brockport [NY] Republic*, August 1, 1861.

23. Letter of Nathaniel Rollins, July 25, 1861, in Quiner, "Correspondence," 1:102–3. As of 2015, all of the Quiner correspondence related to the 2nd Wisconsin is transcribed and available online at www.secondwi.com/fromthefront/fromthe.htm. For access to the originals (in the State Historical Society of Wisconsin), see http://content.wisconsin history.org/cdm/compoundobject/collection/quiner/id/13015/show/12868/rec/1.

24. Quiner, "Correspondence," 1:102; Otis, *Second Wisconsin Infantry*, 35; Letter of Nathaniel Rollins, July 25, 1861, in Quiner, "Correspondence" 1:102; "The Battle at Bull Run," *New York Herald*, July 29, 1861. This letter from the 79th New York references a Confederate fort on Henry Hill. Thomas S. Allen, "The Second Wisconsin at the First Battle Of Bull Run," in *War Papers Read Before the Commandery of the State of Wisconsin, Military Order of the Loyal Legion of the United States* 1:390; *O.R* 2:370.

25. Letter of James H. Langhorne, July 21, 1861, Langhorne Family Papers, VHS; Wight, MS Memoir, VHS; Opie, *Rebel Cavalryman*, 36.

26. William T. Lusk, *The War Letters of William Thompson Lusk* (New York, 1911), 58–59; Todd, *Seventy-Ninth Highlanders*, 37–38.

27. Letter of James Singleton, July 25, 1861, Singleton Papers, UVA; *O.R.* 2:566.

28. *O.R.* 2:414, 547; Letter of George W. Cooney, *New York Times*, July 29, 1861; "Statement of a Returned Soldier of the Sixty-Ninth," *New York Times*, July 26, 1861.

29. "Lieutenant Simpson's Account of the Battle of Bull's Run," *New York Herald*, July 25, 1861.

30. J. Albert Monroe, "The Rhode Island Artillery at the First Battle of Bull Run," *Personal Narratives of Rhode Island Soldiers and Sailors Historical Society* 2:21; Letter of Jonathan Coward, *New York Herald*, July 29, 1861; James Conner to his mother, July 24, 1861, Conner Papers, UNC.

31. Simpson and Berlin, *Selected Correspondence of William T. Sherman*, 124.

32. *O.R.* 2:414.

33. "Statement of a Returned Soldier of the Sixty-Ninth," *New York Times*, July 26, 1861; "News from the Sixty-Ninth," *New York Herald*, July 25, 1861.

34. *O.R.* 2:545, 547; James Conner to his mother, July 24, 1861, Conner Papers, UNC; Robert Enoch Withers, *Autobiography of an Octogenarian* (Roanoke, 1907), 149.

35. *O.R.* 2:414; "Statement of a Returned Soldier of the Sixty-Ninth," *New York Times*, July 26, 1861; Letter of Alexander Carolin, *New York Herald*, July 25, 1861; Letter of John Stacom, *Irish American Weekly*, August 3, 1861; Christopher-Michael Garcia, "The 'Fighting' Sixty-Ninth New York State Militia at Bull Run," in Pia Seija Seagrave, ed., *The History of the Irish Brigade* (Fredericksburg, 1997), 50.

36. "Partridge Letters," 80–81.

37. *O.R.* 2:547–48; Henry T. Owen to Richard Irby, November 9, 1878, H. T. Owen Papers, Virginia State Library; Withers, *Autobiography*, 149.

CHAPTER 9: Denouement

1. *O.R.* 2:332, 747; Fry, "McDowell's Advance to Bull Run," 190; George E. French, 5th Maine Infantry, Letter of July 23, 1861, retrieved from www.mqamerica.com /Bull_Run_Battle_Letters.htm; transcript in the author's files.

2. Letter from Lt. J. P. Drouillard, *Gallipolis [OH] Journal*, August 8, 1861.

3. Howard, his division commander Heintzelman, army commander McDowell, and McDowell's staff officers make no claim of a plan to use Howard's brigade to mount a flanking movement via Chinn Ridge.

4. "A Personal Account of Bull Run," Frank L. Lemont of the 5th Maine to his father, *Lewiston Daily Evening Journal*, August 12, 1861; Letter from the 2nd Vermont, *Rutland [VT] Herald*, August 8, 1861.

5. Lemont, "A Personal Account of Bull Run," *Lewiston Daily Evening Journal*, August 12, 1861; Howard, *Autobiography* 1:158; "Second Vermont at Bull Run," *St. Albans Messenger*, August 15, 1861.

6. "From the Archives: The First Battle of Manassas" (letter from an unknown member of the 2nd South Carolina), South Carolina Historical Society, accessed on www.southcarolinahistoricalsociety.org/wp-content/uploads/2015/01/Summer2011.pdf; "Battle Field of Bull Run," *Charleston Mercury*, July 29, 1861 (letter from the 2nd South Carolina); "Private Letter," *Charleston Mercury*, August 2, 1861.

7. *O.R.* 2:522–23, 530–31; "From the Archives: The First Battle of Manassas," www.south carolinahistoricalsociety.org/wp-content/uploads/2015/01/Summer2011.pdf.
8. *O.R.* 2:476, 523; "Battlefield of Bull Run," *Charleston Mercury*, August 1, 1861; "Private Letter," *Charleston Mercury*, August 2, 1861; Arnold Elzey MS, July 25, 1861, Bradley T. Johnson Papers, Duke University; "Letter from Dr. J. C. Nott, of South Carolina," *New York Times*, August 6, 1861.
9. Washington Hands (1st Maryland), MS Memoir, University of Virginia, 37; T. O. Chesney, "Blucher of the Day at Manassas," *Confederate Veteran*, 7:310; "Letter from an Officer in the Maryland Brigade to his Wife," *Richmond Examiner*, August 17, 1861.
10. Elzey MS, Johnson Papers, Duke; "Letter from an Officer," *Richmond Examiner*, August 17, 1861.
11. Early, *Autobiographical Sketch*, 21.
12. *O.R.* 2:523; "Second Vermont at Bull Run," *St. Albans Messenger*, August 1, 1861.
13. McHenry Howard, *Recollections of Maryland Confederate Staff Officer* (repr. Dayton, 1975), 38. Bradley Johnson offered a version of this period only slightly different from Howard's. B. T. Johnson, "Memoir of the First Maryland Regiment," *SHSP* 9:483; "Letter from an Officer," *Richmond Examiner*, August 17, 1861.
14. Howard, *Autobiography*, 1:159; "The Late Battle," *The Caledonian* [St. Johnsbury, VT], August 9, 1861; "Letter from the Second Regiment," *Vermont Phoenix*, August 15, 1861.
15. George W. Bicknell, *History of the Fifth Regiment Maine Volunteers* (Portland, 1871), 30; Howard, *Autobiography*, 1:159.
16. "Army Correspondence," *Portland Daily Advertiser*, August 2, 1861; Bicknell, *Fifth Regiment Maine Volunteers*, 30–31.
17. Gerald S. Henig, ed., "'Give My Love to All': The Civil War Letters of George S. Rollins," *Civil War Times Illustrated*, November 1972, 24; Howard, *Autobiography*, 1:159–60.
18. "First Maryland Battalion," *Richmond Examiner*, August 17, 1861.
19. McHenry Howard, *Recollections*, 38–39.
20. "First Maryland Battalion," *Richmond Examiner*, August 17, 1861.
21. Henig, "Rollins Letters," 24; Bicknell, *Fifth Maine*, 31.
22. Carter, *Four Brothers in Blue*, 15; Dangerfield Parker, "Personal Reminiscences," MOLLUS, DC, *War Papers*, 17–18; *O.R.* 2:390.
23. Fry, "McDowell's Advance to Bull Run," 191; "Correspondence of the Journal," *Providence Journal*, July 27, 1861.
24. "A Volunteer's Narrative," *Providence Evening Press*, July 26, 1861.
25. Fry, "McDowell's Advance to Bull Run," 191; Thomas Scharf, *History of Maryland* (Hatboro, PA, 1967), 3:449–50.
26. Todd, *Seventy-Ninth Highlanders*, 42; Howard, *Autobiography*, 162; *O.R.* 2:390, 416. The eight captured guns were those of Ricketts's and Griffin's batteries. Griffin did manage to get four pieces off the field, only to lose them later at Cub Run.
27. George J. Hundley, "Reminiscences of the First and Last Days of the War," *SHSP* 23:304; *O.R.* 2:524, 547–48; Henry T. Owen to Richard Irby, November 9, 1878, Owen Papers, VSL.
28. Letter of Benjamin Irby Scott to his mother, July 25, 1861, Scott Family Papers, Virginia Historical Society; Johnson, "First Maryland," 488; Hands, MS Memoirs, UVA, 38.

CHAPTER 10: The War Watchers' Surprise

1. John C. Tidball, MS Memoir, Tidball Papers, United States Military Academy, 265.
2. William Howard Russell, *My Diary North and South* (Boston, 1863), 448–49; Charles Lanman, ed., *The Journal of Alfred Ely, A Prisoner of War in Richmond* (New York, 1862), 11.
3. Russell, *My Diary*, 449.
4. Ibid., 450.
5. Tidball, MS Memoir, USMA, 265–66, 269–70.
6. Daniel McCook to "My Dear Son," July 26, 1861, McCook Family Papers, Library of Congress; Hunt, *Washburn: An American Biography*, 200–01.
7. Ibid., 201.
8. Henry Villard, *Memoirs of Henry Villard* (Boston & New York, 1904), 192–93.
9. Lanman, ed., *Journal of Alfred Ely*, 14.
10. "Letter from one of McDowell's Aids," *New York Herald*, July 30, 1861; Parker, "The Battalion of Regular Infantry," 18.
11. *O.R.* 2:551.
12. Early, *Autobiographical Sketch*, 26. The troops Early pursued and lost were probably those of Sherman's brigade, which recrossed Bull Run at Farm Ford, just east of Pittsylvania.
13. Lemont, "A Personal Account of Bull Run," *Lewiston Daily Evening Journal*, August 12, 1861.
14. *O.R.* 2:483; "Stuart's Regiment at Manassas," *Richmond Dispatch*, July 29, 1861; Edmund Berkeley (8th Virginia), "Some Things I saw at 1st Manassas," in the First Bull Run folder, John Warwick Daniel Papers, Box 22, University of Virginia.
15. M'Whorter, "Caring for the Soldiers in the Sixties," 29:411–12.
16. Letter from a member of the 5th Massachusetts, *Charlestown Advertiser*, July 31, 1861.
17. Withers, *Autobiography*, 149–50; *O.R.* 2:524.
18. "The Pursuit at Manassas," letter from a member of the Albemarle Light Horse, *Richmond Dispatch*, July 29, 1861.
19. *O.R.* 2:532–33, 534; "Col. T. T. Munford and His Cavalry," *Richmond Examiner*, August 10, 1861.
20. Daniel McCook to his son, July 26, 1861, McCook Family Papers, LOC; Taylor, *The Story of a Battle*, 10–11. See also a letter from Charles's cousin, "Death of Captain McCook," *Cleveland Plain Dealer*, July 25, 1861.
21. Hains, "First Gun at Bull Run," 396; "Bull's Run Panic," memoir of A. G. Riddle, *Trenton Evening Times*, February 5, 1887.
22. "Col. T. T. Munford and his Cavalry," *Richmond Daily Enquirer*, August 10, 1861; "The Pursuit at Manassas," *Richmond Dispatch*, July 29, 1861; *O.R.* 2:534; "Bull's Run Panic," memoir of A. G. Riddle, *Trenton Evening Times*, February 5, 1887.
23. Lanman, ed., *Journal of Alfred Ely*, 16; Gallagher, *Fighting for the Confederacy*, 55. These two accounts of Ely's capture are largely consistent.
24. Charles M. Blackford, *Letters from Lee's Army*, 32–33; Otho Scott Lee, MS "Reminiscences of Four Years Service in the Confederate Army" (1st Virginia Cavalry), Manassas NBP Library; *Charleston Mercury*, August 5, 1861.
25. *O.R.* 2:525, 536; William Kauffman Scarborough, ed., *The Diary of Edmund Ruffin: Vol. 2, The Years of Hope* (Baton Rouge, 1976), 89.
26. Aldrich, *Battery A*, 23–24.

27. Roelker, "Ames Letters," 16; "The Reverse" (1st Rhode Island), *Providence Journal*, July 27, 1861; Ai Baker Thompson to his father, July 27, 1861, Thompson Letters, Manassas NBP Library.
28. Rhodes, *All for the Union*, 39.
29. Russell, *My Diary North and South*, 453.
30. "A Volunteer's Narrative" (1st Rhode Island), *Providence Evening Press*, July 26, 1861.
31. "Bull Run's Panic," memoir of A. G. Riddle, *Trenton Evening Times*, February 5, 1887.
32. Hunt, *An American Biography*, 201–2; Stedman, *Battle of Bull Run*, 35; "Bull Run's Panic," memoir of A. G. Riddle, *Trenton Evening Times*, February 5, 1887. A contemporary letter of Riddle's, also quoted here, appears in the *New York Times*, August 13, 1861.
33. Taylor, *The Story of a Battle*, 13.
34. Hains, "The First Gun at Bull Run," 398.
35. *CCW*, 24–28; *O.R.* 2:375–76, 424–25, 427, 430–31, 438–39; Jack C. Mason, *Until Antietam: The Life and Letters of Major General Israel B. Richardson* (Carbondale, IL, 2009), 100.
36. Gallagher, *Fighting for the Confederacy*, 56; Beauregard, "First Battle of Bull Run," 215.
37. "Battlefield of Bull Run" (2nd South Carolina), *Charleston Mercury*, July 29, 1861.
38. Tidball, MS Memoir, 277–80.
39. "Letter from the Adjutant of the 18th Regiment," *Albany Evening Journal*, July 29, 1861. Other sources make reference to regiments stopping in Centreville that evening and squeezing in an hour or two of sleep. "Letter from One of the Hillsboro Band" (2nd Ohio), *Highland [OH] Weekly News*, August 8, 1861; Keillor, *No More Gallant a Deed*, 60–61.
40. "The Reverse," *Providence Journal*, July 27, 1861; Letter from a member of the 1st Rhode Island, *Providence Journal*, July 26, 1861.

CHAPTER 11: Wreckage
1. "The Pursuit at Manassas," *Richmond Dispatch*, July 29, 1861.
2. Beauregard, "First Battle of Bull Run," 215; Johnston, "First Bull Run," 252.
3. Hunter McGuire, "General Thomas J. Jackson: Reminiscences of the Famous Leader," *SHSP* 19:303.
4. Morgan, *Personal Reminiscences*, 75; Hunter, MS "Four Years in the Ranks," 47.
5. Breazeale, "4th South Carolina," TS Manassas NBP Library, 10.
6. Beauregard, "First Battle of Bull Run," 219; Joseph E. Johnston, *Narrative of Military Operations, Directed, During the Late War Between the States* (New York, 1874), 60.
7. "A Search for the Dead by Moonlight," *North Carolina Whig*, September 3, 1861; "The Battle-Field Near Manassas—The Graves of the Slain," from the *Richmond Daily Enquirer*, reprinted in the *Columbian Register* [New Haven], August 17, 1861.
8. "The Battle-Field Near Manassas—The Graves of the Slain," from the *Richmond Daily Enquirer*, reprinted in the *Columbian Register* [New Haven], August 17, 1861.
9. Wiley C. Tunstall to his mother, August 6, 1861. Copy and transcription retrieved from Bull Runnings, https://bullrunnings.wordpress.com/2009/11/07/w-c-tunstall -co-d-5th-al-on-the-aftermath-of-the-battle. Tunstall stated his visit to the field was on Sunday, but given the advanced state of burial operations, it must have been Monday.

10. A good example of the penchant for setting up aid stations too close to the front appears in John Herbert Roper, ed., *Repairing the March of Mars: The Civil War Diaries of John Samuel Apperson* (Macon, GA, 2001), 114.

11. "Letter from an Eye-Witness," *The National Republican*, July 26, 1861; see also *CCW*, 469. Local resident Marianne Compton confirmed the use of Pittsylvania as a field hospital: "A large part of the house was disused and out of repair. Here, in great old rooms, with paper brought from England hanging in strips from the walls; and floors covered with fallen plaster, we saw the wounded; some lying in tall old four-posted bedsteads, some on pallets." "Woman's Recollections of Two Famous Battles," *Manassas Journal*, July 4, 1913.

12. Horace H. Cunningham, *Field Medical Services at the Battles of Manassas* (Athens, GA, 1968), 31.

13. Roper, *Diaries of John Samuel Apperson*, 115, testifies to the need to constantly relocate aid stations farther from the firing line.

14. William S. King's report, *Medical and Surgical History*, Appendix to Part 1, 2–3; William Williams Keen, *Addresses and Other Papers* (Philadelphia, 1905), 421; Letter of Surgeon Frank Hamilton of the 31st New York (Miles Brigade), *American Medical Times*, August 3, 1861, 77–78; George Miller Sternberg, surgeon with Sykes's battalion, in *Proceedings of the Fifth Annual Meeting of the Association of Military Surgeons* (Cincinnati, 1896), 13.

15. A list of surgeons and assistant surgeons on the field at Manassas appears in the *American Medical Times*, July 27, 1861, 63. King's and Magruder's reports appear in *Medical and Surgical History*, Appendix to Part 1, 2–5. Magruder refers to an "old stone church," and many subsequent historians have therefore connected his service with a stone church in Centreville. It is clear, however, from virtually all other accounts that Magruder in fact referred to Sudley Church, which was brick. Magruder misremembered the construction material, not the location.

16. Magruder in *Medical and Surgical History*, Appendix to Part 1, 4–5; Keen, *Addresses*, 421.

17. Edward Neill, "Extracts from a Chaplain's Journal," in Edward D. Neill, *History of Minnesota* (Minneapolis, 1878), 678.

18. William Croffut, *American Procession, 1855–1914: A Personal Chronicle of Famous Men* (Boston, 1931), 51–52; Keen, *Addresses*, 422.

19. Roper, *Diaries of John Samuel Apperson*, 114; Gallagher, *Fighting for the Confederacy*, 54.

20. W. W. Blackford, *War Years with Jeb Stuart*, 27–28.

21. Keen, *Addresses*, 423.

22. George Edward Ellis, *Memoir of Luther V. Bell* (Boston, 1863), 60.

23. Charles Carroll Gray Diary, July 21, 1861, Southern Historical Collection, UNC.

24. Charles Coffin, *Stories of Our Soldiers* (Boston, 1893), 109.

25. Charles J. Murphy, *Reminiscences of the Mexican and Civil War* (New York, 1882), 61; "Report of a Surgeon of the Eighth," *New York Times*, August 16, 1861.

26. Scott, *Willcox Memoirs*, 300–301; Fanny Ricketts, MS Diary, July 26, 1861, Manassas NBP Library. Hospitals used for an extended time included Portici, Sudley, the Old Stone Church in Centreville, the John Dogan house, and the Stone House in the middle of the battlefield.

27. For commentary on the Stone House hospital, see "The Field of the Second Battle," *Macon Telegraph*, July 30, 1861.

28. For the hospitals on the rail lines south, see *Charleston Mercury*, July 29 and 31, and August 9, 1861; and the *Richmond Examiner*, July 26, 1861; Daniel E. Sutherland,

Seasons of War: The Ordeal of a Confederate Community (New York, 1995), 63–64. A good description of the hospitals in Charlottesville appears in the *Richmond Dispatch*, August 1, 1861.

CHAPTER 12: Tallying Failure and Virtue
1. The quote from the Congressional chaplain appears in "The War on Sunday," *Jamestown [NY] Journal*, August 23, 1861, and was echoed by Reverend Lamson in Brookline, MA: "Rev. Dr. Lamson on the War," *Portsmouth Journal of Literature and Politics*, August 24, 1861.
2. *Syracuse Journal* quoted in "About the Civilians at the Battle," *Rochester Democrat and American*, July 27, 1861. See also *Rockland County Messenger*, August 1, 1861.
3. The best summary of Union commentary appears in the *New York Herald*, July 23, 1861. Other views cited here come from "Several Lessons from Bull Run," *Springfield Republican*, August 3, 1861; "Editorial Correspondence of the *Albany Evening Journal*," *Albany Evening Journal*, July 29, 1861.
4. Beauregard, "First Battle of Bull Run," 218–19.
5. Samuel S. Seig to his cousin, Carrie Davis, July 25, 1861, Samuel S. Seig Papers, Duke.
6. The first known reference to Jackson as Stonewall appeared in the *Charleston Mercury*, July 25, 1861.

CHAPTER 13: Awakening
1. "Woman's Recollections," *Manassas Journal*, July 4, 1913; Rev. Alexander Compton to Mrs. Davis, July 30, 1861, Schoff Collection, UM.
2. Fletcher, "A few memories of the 'War Between the States' by an eye witness," TS, Manassas NBP Library.
3. George Mason Bohannon to Bettie Bohannon Clare, July 30, 1861, Graves-Bohannon Family Papers, University of Virginia; Hugh Henry to his sister, Ellen, May 30, 1861, Henry Family Papers, Manassas NBP Library; "Woman's Recollections," *Manassas Journal*, July 4, 1913; Rev. Alexander Compton to Mrs. Davis, July 30, 1861, Schoff Collection, UM. A good testament to Mrs. Henry's status as a martyr is in "The Graves of the Slain," *Columbian Register* [New Haven], August 17, 1861, reprinted from the *Richmond Daily Enquirer*.
4. "Those Handcuffs," *Macon Telegraph*, August 13, 1861.
5. "The Handcuffs," *Macon Telegraph*, August 13, 1861; "Those Hand-Cuffs," *Richmond Whig*, July 30, 1861; "Extracts from a Private Letter" [Hampton's Legion], *Charleston Mercury*, August 7, 1861. Even Richard Ewell trumpeted the story of the handcuffs. See Ewell to Mary Custis Lee, July 31, 1861, Mary Lee Papers, Virginia Historical Society.
6. "The Mystery of the Hand Cuffs," *Cleveland Plain Dealer*, August 20, 1861; "The 'Manacle' Story," *San Francisco Bulletin*, October 9, 1861.
7. Styple, *Writing and Fighting the Civil War*, 33–34, 35; "A Soldier's Letter" (2nd NYSM), *New York Evening Post*, July 29, 1861. The committee's final report on "rebel barbarities" appears in *CCW* 3:449–57.
8. "Serious Thoughts Since the Bull Run Battle," *Albany Argus*, August 14, 1861.
9. "A Letter from the 27th Regiment," *Lockport [NY] Daily Journal Courier*, August 2, 1861; "Letter from the Adjutant of the 18th Regiment," *Albany Evening Journal*, July 29, 1861.
10. "The Fourteenth Regiment," *Oneida Weekly Herald*, August 6, 1861; *Boston Medical and Surgical Journal*, August 15, 1861; "Rev. Dr. Lamson on the War," *Portsmouth*

Journal of Literature and Politics, August 24, 1861; "What We Learn from Defeat," *New York Times*, July 23, 1861; "Latest from the Seat of War," *Washington Star*, July 23, 1861.

11. Editorial of the *New York Daily News*, quoted in the *New York Tribune*, July 23, 1861; Roy P. Basler, ed., *Collected Works of Abraham Lincoln* (New Brunswick, NJ, 1953), 4:457;

12. "The Manassas Victory," *Charleston Courier*, July 25, 1861; Kerri S. Barile and Barbara P. Willis, eds., *A Woman in a War-Torn Town: The Journal of Jane Howison Beale, Fredericksburg, Virginia 1850–1862* (Virginia Beach, 2011), 65; Isabella D. Martin and Myrta Lockett Avary, eds., *Mary Chesnut's Diary from Dixie* (Gretna, LA, 2011), 113–14.

13. "Last Honors to the Heros [*sic*] of Manassas," *Charleston Mercury*, July 27, 1861.

14. Virginia Bedinger to "Ma," July 27, 1861, Bedinger-Dandridge Family Papers, Duke University.

15. "A Suggestion," *Richmond Whig*, July 26, 1861.

16. T. Conn Bryan, ed., "Letters of Two Confederate Officers: William Thomas Conn and Charles Augustus Conn" (9th Georgia), *Georgia Historical Quarterly* 46 (1962): 170–71; Virginia Soutter Knox to her son, Robert, July 30 and October 18, 1861, Knox Family Papers, Central Rappahannock Heritage Center; John Gallatin Paxton, comp., *Memoir and Memorials: Elisha Franklin Paxton, Brigadier-General, C.S.A.* (n.p., 1905), 12.

17. Asher W. Harman to "My dear wife," July 25, 1861, TS from an original posted on an online auction site; copy in the author's files. For similar sentiments, see the untitled editorial in the *Richmond Daily Examiner*, July 25, 1861.

18. *Boston Medical and Surgical Journal*, August 15, 1861.

19. Sumner quoted in Gary W. Gallagher, *The Union War* (Cambridge, MA, 2011), 90. For an excellent editorial that highlights the emergence of these issues, see the *Rockland County [NY] Messenger*, August 22, 1861. For the need for harsher treatment of Confederates, see "Several Lessons from Bull Run," *Springfield Republican*, August 3, 1861.

20. Robert L. Dabney to his wife, July 30, 1861, Robert Lewis Dabney Papers, Virginia Historical Society; "Notes of the Rebellion," *New York Times*, July 24, 1861; Samuel Wickliffe Melton to his wife, July 25, 1861, Melton Papers, USC.

Bibliography

UNPUBLISHED MATERIALS

Aiken, David W. Papers. University of South Carolina.

Alexander, Edward Porter. Papers. Southern Historical Collection, University of North Carolina.

Andrew, John A. Papers. Massachusetts Historical Society.

Avery, Alphonso Calhoun. Papers. Southern Historical Collection, University of North Carolina.

Bagwell, James E. "James Hamilton Couper, Georgia Rice Planter." PhD Dissertation, University of Southern Mississippi, 1978.

Ballou, Sullivan. Letter, July 14, 1861. Civil War Letters Collection, Chicago Historical Society.

Barclay, Alexander T. Letters. Washington and Lee University.

Bean, Paul W. Collection of Civil War Papers. University of Maine.

Bowman-Howard-Domingos Collections, Middle Georgia Archives, Washington Library, Macon, Georgia.

Branch, Margaret Sexton. Papers. University of Georgia.

Breazeale, B. B. "Co. J, 4th South Carolina Infantry at the First Battle of Manassas." Manassas National Battlefield Park Library.

Cocke, Philip St. George. Papers. University of Virginia.

Coles, R. T. "History of the 4th Alabama Volunteers." Alabama Department of Archives and History.

Compton, Alexander. Letter, July 30, 1861. James S. Schoff Collection, William Clements Library, University of Michigan.

Conner, Henry Calvin. Papers. University of South Carolina.

Conner, James. Papers. Southern Historical Collection, University of North Carolina.

Dabney, Robert Lewis. Papers. Virginia Historical Society.

Daniel, John Warwick. Papers. University of Virginia.

Davis, Charles E. Papers. Minnesota Historical Society.

Ferguson, Samuel Wragg. Memoirs. Duke University.

Fletcher, Laura Thornberry. "A Few Memories of the 'War Between the States' by an Eyewitness, for My Grandson, Westwood Hugh Fletcher." Unpublished TS, copy on file at Manassas National Battlefield Park.

Grant, Robert L. Letter, July 24, 1861. Manassas National Battlefield Park Library.

Hands, Washington. Memoir. University of Virginia.

Hall, N. D. Papers. Manassas National Battlefield Park Library.

Heffelfinger, Christopher. Papers. Minnesota Historical Society.

Heintzelman, Samuel P. Diary. Library of Congress.

Hennessy, John J. "The First Hour's Fight on Henry Hill." Manassas National Battlefield Park Library.
Hennessy, John J. "Jackson's Stone Wall: Fact or Fable?" Manassas National Battlefield Park Library.
Henry Family Papers. Manassas National Battlefield Park.
Hotchkiss, Jedediah. Papers. Library of Congress.
Hough, Franklin B. Papers. New York State Library.
Hudson, James G. Diary. Alabama Department of Archives and History.
Hunter, Alexander. "Four Years in the Ranks." Virginia Historical Society.
Hutson, Charles W. Papers Southern Historical Collection, University of North Carolina.
Johnson, Bradley T. Papers. Duke University.
Johnson, Rev. Richard. Letter, October 8, 1861. Museum of the Confederacy.
Kearns, Watkins. Diary. Virginia Historical Society.
Kelly, Dennis P. "Plan to Locate Artillery, Manassas National Battlefield Park." Manassas National Battlefield Park Library.
Kemper, James L. Papers. Alderman Library, University of Virginia.
King Family Papers, Alderman Library, University of Virginia.
Lyle, John N. "Sketches Found in a Confederate Veteran's Desk." Rockbridge County Historical Society.
McLintock, Andrew. Papers. Copies at Manassas National Battlefield Park Library.
Melton, Samuel W. Papers. University of South Carolina.
Owen, Henry T. Papers. Virginia State Library.
Potts, Frank. Diary. Virginia Historical Society.
Quiner, E. B. "Correspondence of Wisconsin Volunteers." State Historical Society of Wisconsin (available online at www.wisconsinhistory.org).
Randall, William H. Reminiscences. Bentley Historical Library, University of Michigan.
Rollins, Nathaniel. Diary. State Historical Society of Wisconsin.
Ropes, John C. Papers. Boston University.
Scott Family. Papers. Virginia Historical Society.
Seig, Samuel S. Papers. Duke University.
Shanklin, Henry S. Letters. Virginia State Library.
Shaw, William H. Diary. Manassas National Battlefield Park Library.
Simpson, James. Papers. Duke University.
Singleton, James. Papers. University of Virginia.
Sloan, J. B. E. Papers. Pendleton District Historical and Recreational Commission, Pendleton, South Carolina.
Smith, Charles. Letter. The Drew Archival Library of Duxbury Rural and Historical Society.
Thompson, Ai Baker. Letters. Manassas National Battlefield Park Library.
Tidball, John C. Memoir. United States Military Academy.
Tufts-Robertson Family. Papers. Massachusetts Historical Society.
Wells, William R. Papers. Southern Historical Collection, University of North Carolina.
White, Benjamin F. Papers. North Carolina Department of Archives and History.
Wilkin, Alexander and Family. Papers. Minnesota Historical Society.
Wight, Charles C. Reminiscences. Virginia Historical Society.
Wragg, Thomas L. Papers. Library of Congress.

DIGITAL SOURCES
New York State Division of Military and Naval Affairs (DMNA). For this book, the files of the 11th New York and 38th New York were accessed at https://dmna.ny.gov/historic/reghist/civil/infantry/11thInf/11thInfCWN.htm.

Smeltzer, Harry. Bull Runnings: A Journal of the Digitization of a Civil War Battle, https://bullrunnings.wordpress.com.

NEWSPAPERS
Albany Evening Journal
Augusta [GA] *Chronicle*
Bangor Daily Whig and Courier
[Batavia, NY] *The Daily Republican Advocate*
Boston Daily Advertiser
Boston Evening Journal
[Brattleboro] *Vermont Phoenix*
The British Colonist
Brockport [NY] *Republic*
Brooklyn Daily Eagle
Charleston Courier
Charleston Mercury
Charleston News and Courier
Charlestown [MA] *Advertiser*
[Charlotte] *North Carolina Whig*
Chelsea Telegraph and Pioneer
Chicago Tribune
Cleveland Plain Dealer
Detroit Free Press
Elmira Weekly Advertiser
Gallipolis [OH] *Journal*
Geneva Gazette
Hartford Evening Press
Highland [OH] *Weekly News*
Jacksonville Republican
Lewiston [ME] *Daily Evening Journal*
Lexington [VA] *Gazette*
Marietta [GA] *Journal*
New Haven Daily Morning and Courier
[New Orleans] *Daily Crescent*
[New Orleans] *Daily True Delta*
New York Herald
New York Leader
New York Times
Pontotoc [MS] *Examiner*
Portland Daily Advertiser
[Portsmouth, NH] *Journal of Literature and Politics*
Providence Evening Journal
Providence Evening Press
[Providence] *Manufacturers and Farmers Journal*
Red Hook [NY] *Journal*
Richmond Daily Enquirer
Richmond Dispatch
Richmond Examiner
Richmond Times-Dispatch
Rochester Union and Advertiser

Rutland [VT] *Herald*
St. Albans [VT] *Messenger*
[St. Johnsbury, VT] *The Caledonian*
St. Paul Press
San Francisco Bulletin
Savannah Republican
Syracuse Daily Courier and Union
Trenton Evening Times
Union [NY] *News*
Washington Star
Winsted [CT] *Herald*
Worcester Daily Spy

ARTICLES
Alexander, Edward Porter. "The Battle of Bull Run." *Scribners Magazine*, Vol. XLI (1907), pp. 80–94.

Allen, Thomas S. "The Second Wisconsin at the First Battle of Bull Run." *War Papers Read Before the Commandery of the State of Wisconsin, Military Order of the Loyal Legion of the United States*, Vol. I.

Anon. "Reminiscences of Bull Run." *National Tribune*, January 25, 1907.

Beauregard, Pierre Gustave Toutant. "The First Battle of Bull Run." *Battles and Leaders of the Civil War*, Vol. I, pp. 196–227.

Brown, Campbell. "General Ewell at Bull Run." *Battles and Leaders of the Civil War*, Vol. I, pp. 259–60.

Bryan, T. Conn, ed., "Letters of Two Confederate Officers: William Thomas Conn and Charles Augustus Conn." *The Georgia Historical Quarterly*, Vol. 46 (1962).

Chesney, T. O. "Blucher of the Day at Manassas." *Confederate Veteran*, Vol. 7, p. 310.

Conrad, D. B. "History of the First Battle of Manassas and the Formation of the Stonewall Brigade." *Southern Historical Society Papers*, Vol. 19, pp. 88–94.

Coxe, John. "The Battle of First Manassas." *Confederate Veteran*, Vol. 23, pp. 24–26.

Daniel, John Warwick. "A Charge at First Manassas." *Southern Historical Society Papers*, Vol. 29, pp. 345–46.

Fishburne, Clement D. "Sketch of the Rockbridge Artillery." *Southern Historical Society Papers*, Vol. 23, pp. 22–25.

Fry, James B. "McDowell's Advance to Bull Run." *Battles and Leaders of the Civil War*, Vol. I, pp. 167–93.

Hains, Peter C. "The First Gun at Bull Run." *Cosmopolitan* magazine, Vol. 51 (1911), pp. 388–400.

Hall, Seymour. "A Volunteer at First Bull Run." MOLLUS *War Talks in Kansas*, Vol. I.

Hampton, Wade. "The Legion at Manassas." *Charleston News and Courier*, July 13, 1885.

Harrison, George F. "Ewell at First Manassas." *Southern Historical Society Papers*, Vol. 14 (1886), pp. 355–57.

Henig, Gerald S., ed. "'Give My Love to All': The Civil War Letters of George S. Rollins." *Civil War Times Illustrated*, November 1972.

Hennessy, John J. "Jackson's Stone Wall: Fact or Fiction?" in Vol. VIII, No. 2, of *Civil War: The Magazine of the Civil War Society*, March–April 1990.

Hundley, George J. "Reminiscences of the First and Last Days of the War." *Southern Historical Society Papers*, Vol. 23 (1895), pp. 294–313.

Imboden, John D. "Incidents of the First Bull Run." *Battles and Leaders of the Civil War*, Vol. I, pp. 229–239.

Johnson, Bradley T. "Memoir of the First Maryland Regiment." *Southern Historical Society Papers*, Vol. 9 (1881), pp. 344–353.

Johnston, Joseph E. "Responsibilities of the First Bull Run." *Battles and Leaders of the Civil War*, Vol. I, pp. 240–260.

Jones, J. H. B. "The Liberty Hall Volunteers at First Manassas." *Rockbridge County News*, February 2, 1911.

Jones, Kenneth. "The Fourth Alabama Infantry: First Blood." *Alabama Historical Society Quarterly*, Vol. 36.

Metcalfe, Lewis H. "So Eager Were We All." *American Heritage*, Vol. 16 (1965), pp. 32–41.

M'Whorter, Mrs. J. K. "Caring for the Soldiers of the Sixties," *Confederate Veteran*, Volume 29 (1921), pp. 410–411.

Monroe, J. Albert. "The Rhode Island Artillery at the First Battle of Bull Run." *Personal Narratives of Rhode Island Soldiers and Sailors Historical Society. No. 2*. Providence: 1878.

Parker, Dangerfield. "Personal Reminiscences: The Battalion of Regular Infantry at the First Battle of Bull Run." MOLLUS, District of Columbia. *War Papers*. Washington: 1900.

Partridge, Samuel S. "Civil War Letters of Samuel S. Partridge of the 'Rochester Regiment.'" *Rochester Historical Society Publications*, 1944.

Roelker, William Greene, ed. "Civil War Letters of William Ames." *Rhode Island Historical Society Collections*, October 1940, pp. 10–23.

Smith, William. "Reminiscences of the First Battle of Manassas." *Southern Historical Society Papers*, Vol. 10, pp. 433–44.

Squires, Charles W. "The 'Boy Officer' of the Washington Artillery—Part I of a Memoir," *Civil War Times Illustrated*, Vol. 14 (May 1975), pp. 11–17.

Sullivan, David, ed., "Fowler the Soldier, Fowler the Marine: Letters from an Unusual Confederate," *Civil War Times Illustrated*, February 1988, p. 28–35, 44.

BOOKS
Aldrich, Thomas M. *The History of Battery A, First Regiment Rhode Island Light Artillery*. Providence: 1904.

Anon. *Battlefields of the South*. London: 1863.

Bagwell, James E. "James Hamilton Couper, Georgia Rice Planter." PhD Dissertation, University of Mississippi: 1978.

Barile, Kerri S., and Barbara P. Willis, eds. *A Woman in a War-Torn Town: The Journal of Jane Howison Beale, Fredericksburg, Virginia 1850–1862*. Virginia Beach: 2011.

Barnard, John G. *The C.S.A. and the Battle of Bull Run*. New York: 1862.

Baylor, George W. *Bull Run to Bull Run; or Four Years in the Army of Northern Virginia*. Richmond: 1900.

Bearss, Edwin C. *Troop Movement Maps: Battle of First Manassas and Blackburn's Ford*. Washington: 1981.

Bell, John W. *Memoirs of Governor William Smith of Virginia: His Political, Military and Personal History*. New York: 1891.

Bicknell, George W. *History of the Fifth Regiment Maine Volunteers*. Portland: 1871.

Blackford, Charles Minor. *Annals of the Lynchburg Home Guard*. Lynchburg: 1891.

Blackford, William W. *War Years with Jeb Stuart*. New York: 1945.

Blake, Henry N. *Three Years in the Army of the Potomac.* Boston: 1865.

Bosang, James N. *Memoirs of a Pulaski Veteran.* Pulaski, Virginia: 1912.

Carroll, Nannie Neville Leachman. *Folly Castle Folks.* Newport News: 1976.

Carter, Robert G. *Four Brothers in Blue.* Washington: 1913.

Casler, John. *Four Years in the Stonewall Brigade.* Girard, Kansas: 1906.

Clark, Walter, ed. *Histories of the Several Regiments and Battalions from North Carolina.* 5 vols. Goldsboro: 1901.

Comings, H. H. *Personal Reminiscences of Company E, New York Fire Zouaves.* Malden, MA: 1886.

Cooke, John E. *Stonewall Jackson: A Military Biography.* New York: 1866.

Crawford, Martin, ed. *William Howard Russell's Civil War: Private Diary and Letters, 1861–1862.* Athens, GA: 1992.

Crotty, Daniel G. *Four Years Campaigning in the Army of the Potomac.* Grand Rapids: 1874.

Cutrer, Thomas W., ed. *Longsreet's Aide: The Civil War Letters of Major Thomas J. Goree.* Charlottesville: 1995.

Cudworth, Warren H. *History of the First Regiment [Massachusetts] Infantry.* Boston: 1866.

Dufour, Charles L. *Gentle Tiger: The Gallant Life of Roberdeau Wheat.* Baton Rouge: 1957.

Dickert, Augustus D. *History of Kershaw's Brigade.* Newberry, SC: 1899.

Early, Jubal A. *Autobiographical Sketch and Narrative of the War Between the States.* Philadelphia: 1912.

Eckert, Edward K., and Nicholas J. Amato, eds. *Ten Years in the Saddle: The Memoir of William Woods Averell.* San Rafael: 1983.

Ely, Alfred. *The Journal of Alfred Ely.* New York: 1862.

Fairchild, C. B. *History of the 27th Regiment New York Volunteers.* Binghamton: 1888.

Fonerden, C. A. *Military History of Carpenter's Battery.* New Market: 1911.

Francis, Augustus T. *History of the 71st Regiment N.G.N.Y.* New York: 1919.

Fry, James B. *McDowell and Tyler in the Campaign of Bull Run.* New York: 1884.

Gaff, Alan D. *If This is War.* Dayton: 1991.

Gallagher, Gary W., ed. *Fighting for the Confederacy.* Chapel Hill: 1989

Goldsborough, W. W. *The Maryland Line in the Confederate Army.* Baltimore: 1900.

Grabill, John H. *Diary of a Soldier of the Stonewall Brigade.* N.p.: n.d.

Hanson, Joseph Mills. *Bull Run Remembers.* Manassas: 1953.

Haskins, George B. *The History of the First Regiment of Artillery.* Portland: 1879.

Haynes, Martin D. *History of the Second Regiment New Hampshire Volunteers in the War of the Rebellion.* Lakeport: 1896.

Howard, James McHenry. *Recollections of a Maryland Confederate Soldier and Staff Officer.* Repr., Dayton: 1975.

Howard, Oliver O. *Autobiography of Oliver Otis Howard.* 2 Volumes. New York: 1908.

Howe, M. A. DeWolfe, ed. *Home Letters of General Sherman.* New York: 1909.

Hunt, Gaillard. *Israel, Elihu, and Cadwallader Washburn: An American Biography.* New York: 1925.

Hutchinson, Gustavas B. *A Narrative of the Formation and Services of the Eleventh Massachusetts Volunteers.* Boston: 1893.

Johnson, E. A., ed. *The Hero of Medfield: Containing the Journals and Letters of Amos Alonzo Kingsbury.* Boston: 1862.

Johnson, John Lipscomb. *Autobiographical Notes.* n.p.: 1958.

Johnson, Robert U., and Clarence C. Buel, eds. *Battles and Leaders of the Civil War*. 4 Vols. New York: 1956.

Johnston, Joseph E. *Narrative of Military Operations, Directed, During the Late War Between the States*. New York: 1874.

Joslyn, Muriel Phillips. *Charlotte's Boys: The Civil War Letters of the Branch Family of Savannah*. Berryville, VA: 1996.

Keyes, Erasmus D. *Fifty Years Observations of Men and Events*. New York: 1884.

Lee, Susan Pendleton, ed. *Memoir of William Nelson Pendleton, D. D*. Philadelphia: 1893.

Loehr, Charles T. *War History of the Old First Virginia*. Repr. Dayton: 1970.

Longstreet, James. *From Manassas to Appomattox*. Philadelphia, 1896.

Lusk, William T. *The War Letters of William Thompson Lusk*. New York: 1911.

Mason, Jack C. *Until Antietam: The Life and Letters of Major General Israel B. Richardson*. Carbondale, IL: 2009.

Meagher, T. F. *The Last Days of the 69th in Virginia*. New York: 1861.

Mingus, Scott. *Confederate General William "Extra Billy" Smith*. El Dorado Hills: 2013.

Moore, Frank E., ed. *Rebellion Record: A Diary of American Events*. 2 Vols. New York: 1892.

Morgan, W. H. *Personal Reminiscences of the War of 1861–65*. Lynchburg: 1911.

Opie, John N. *A Rebel Cavalryman with Lee, Stuart and Jackson*. Chicago: 1899.

Otis, George. *The Second Wisconsin Infantry*. Alan D. Gaff, ed. Dayton: 1984.

Owen, William M. *In Camp and Battle With the Washington Artillery*. Boston: 1885.

Paxton, John G., ed. *Memoir and Memorials: Elisha Franklin Paxton, Brigadier General, C.S.A*. N.p.: 1905.

Poague, William T. *Gunner with Stonewall*. Jackson, Tennessee: 1957.

Reid, J. W. *History of the Fourth Regiment of South Carolina Volunteers*. Rpt. Dayton: 1975.

Rhodes, Robert Hunt, ed. *All for the Union: A History of the 2nd Rhode Island Infantry in the War of the Great Rebellion*. Lincoln, RI: 1986.

Robinson, Frank T. *History of the Fifth Regiment, M.V.M*. Boston: 1879.

Rodenbaugh, Theodore F., ed. *Sabre and Bayonet*. New York: 1897.

Roe, Alfred S. *The Fifth Regiment Massachusetts Volunteer Infantry in its Three Years of Duty*. Boston: 1911.

Russell, William Howard. *My Diary North and South*. Boston: 1863.

Scharf, Thomas. *History of Maryland*. Rpt. Hatboro, PA: 1967.

Scott, Robert Garth, ed. *Forgotten Valor: The Memoirs, Journals, & Civil War Letters of Orlando B. Willcox*. Kent, OH: 1999.

Sherman, William T. *Memoirs of William T. Sherman*. 2 Vols. New York: 1886.

Simpson, Brooks D., and Berlin, Jean V. *Sherman's Civil War: Selected Correspondence of William T. Sherman, 1860–1865*. Chapel Hill, 1999.

Smith, James E. *A Famous Battery and its Campaigns, 1861–64*. Washington: 1892.

Snow, W. P. *Southern Generals*. N.p.: 1865.

Sorrell, G. Moxley. *Recollections of a Confederate Staff Officer*. New York: 1905.

Stedman, Edmund D. *The Battle of Bull Run*. New York: 1861.

Stocker, Jeffrey D. *From Huntsville to Appomattox: R.T. Coles' History of the 4th Regiment, Alabama Volunteer Infantry*. Knoxville: 1996.

Styple, William B., ed. *Writing and Fighting the Civil War: Soldier Correspondence of the* New York Mercury. Kearny, NJ: 2000.

Taylor, John. *The Story of a Battle: Recited Before the Young Men's Catholic Club, at Trenton, Monday Evening, Dec. 11, 1893*. Trenton: n.d.

Tevis, C. *History of the Fighting Fourteenth.* New York: 1911.

Todd, William. *The Seventy-Ninth Highlanders New York Volunteers in the War of the Rebellion.* Albany: 1886.

Tyler, Daniel. *A Memorial Volume Containing his Autobiography and War Record.* New Haven: 1883.

United States Congress. *Report of the Joint Committee on the Conduct of the War, In Three Parts.* Washington: 1863.

United States War Department. *War of the Rebellion. A Compilation of the Official Records of the Union and Confederate Armies.* 128 Vols. Washington: 1881–1902.

Villard, Henry. *Memoirs of Henry Villard.* Boston & New York: 1904.

Westervelt, William B. *Lights and Shadows of Army Life as Seen By a Private Soldier.* Marlboro, NY: 1886.

Withers, Robert Enoch. *Autobiography of an Octogenarian.* Roanoke: 1907.

Woodbury, Augustus. *A Narrative of the Campaign of the First Rhode Island Regiment in the Spring and Summer of 1861.* Providence: 1862.

———. *The Second Rhode Island Regiment: A Narrative of Military Operations.* Providence: 1875.

Wright, James A. *No More Gallant a Deed: A Civil War Memoir of the First Minnesota Volunteers,* Steven J. Keillor, ed. Minneapolis: 2001.

Zettler, Berrien M. *War Stories and School-Day Incidents for the Children.* New York: 1912.

Acknowledgments

Foremost I owe a debt of gratitude to that small legion of dedicated National Park Service history professionals working in Virginia. These historians often labor in misunderstood obscurity, but are bastions of scholarship, dedication, and good humor. Foremost in assisting with the original research for this book was Michael Andrus, formerly my colleague at Manassas National Battlefield. He and I spent hours hashing around the interpretations of the battle presented in this work. Ed Raus, the former chief historian at Manassas, passed along great amounts of primary material and was always cheerful in making the battlefield's considerable resources available to me. Jim Burgess—who, as of 2015, has worked at Manassas Battlefield longer than anyone ever has or likely ever will—also provided important material for this work, and cast his ever-skeptical eye on some of my more controversial conclusions, always to good purpose.

Other individuals who assisted in the original endeavor were: Bob Krick, the former chief historian at Fredericksburg & Spotsylvania NMP; Keith Bohannon, University of Western Georgia; Frederick W. Chesson of Waterbury, Connecticut; Dalton Rector of Manassas; and the staffs of the numerous libraries and repositories cited in the bibliography.

In preparing this updated edition of the book, I am indebted to Harry Smeltzer, whose blog Bull Runnings is an ever-expanding online repository of source material and thought related to the First Battle of Manassas. Harry has not only blazed a new path in making source material related to an individual battle available to the public, but also challenged me and others to consider anew certain aspects of the battle.

In completing the original work on this book in 1989, I deposited virtually all the source material I discovered in the files at Manassas National Battlefield Park. In finishing the updated volume, I have shared most new source material (and certainly anything of note) with both the park and Harry's Smeltzer's Bull Runnings. Due to Harry's efforts, much of it has been posted online.

Index

Page numbers in italics indicates illustrations.

defense of Manassas Junction, 3–5
Matthews Hill defeat, 71–72
Order of Battle, 170–72
pursuit, 135
reasons for victory of, 157–58
victory affirming the Confederacy, 163
Confederate battle flag, birth of, 113
Conner, James, 77, 89, 114
Coward, Jonathan, 115
Coxe, John, 78
Croffut, William, 148, 149–50
Cub Run, 139–42
advance on, *43*
bridge over, 41, 145
panic at bridge over, 141
Cummings, Arthur C., 81, 93, 100–2
Cushing, Christopher, 1

Daniel, Charles, 83
Davidson, George S., 44
Davies, Thomas, 142
Davis, Jefferson, battlefield visit, 146
Davis, Varina, 163
DeWitt, Calvin, 97
Dogan Ridge, 60, 78, 84, 92

Early, Jubal, 15–17, 25, 73, 121–28
Poplar Ford advance, 133–34
8th Georgia, 53, 62–64, 68, 72, 148
8th New York Militia, 78
8th South Carolina, 116, 121–28, 133, 138
8th Virginia, 11, 116–18, 121–28, 133
11th Massachusetts, 99–102, 108–10
11th Mississippi, 53
11th New York, 49, 91–102, 108–10, 115
18th Virginia, 116–18, 121–28, 133, 136
Ellis, John, 63
Ely, Alfred, 130, 132
taken prisoner, 138
Elzey, Arnold, 121–28, 158
English, Sam, 57
Evans, Nathan "Shanks," 36, 44
at Stone Bridge, 49–52
Ewell, Richard, 11, 47–48
at Union Mills Ford, 15

Farnsworth, Addison, 115
Federals, *see* Union army
Ferguson, Samuel, 142, 145

field hospitals, 148–52
5th Maine, 125–28
5th Massachusetts, 99–102, 108–10
5th U.S. Artillery, Battery D, 42, 90
5th Virginia, 79–83, 89, 109–10, 113, 115
Fire Zouaves, *see* 11th New York
First Battle of Manassas
aftermath, 159–65
caring for wounded of, 148–52
casualties, 147–48
on eve of, 38–39
naive illusions about, v–vi
spectators, 129–43
see also specific areas of battle
1st Connecticut, 86
1st Massachusetts, 20–26, 46
1st Michigan, 99–102, 107, 108–10
1st Minnesota, 91–102, 108–10
1st Rhode Island, 42, 60, 127
1st U.S. Artillery, Battery I, 90
1st Virginia, 15–26
Fisher, Charles, 99, 106
Fonerden, C. A., 106
4th Alabama, 53, 62–64, 68, 72, 76, 110
4th Maine, 123–28
4th Pennsylvania, 32
4th South Carolina, 44, 58
4th Virginia, 81, 109–10
14th Brooklyn, 42, 78, 91–102, 103, 107–10, 114–18
49th Virginia, 103
Franklin, William B., 108
Fry, James B., 18, 86

Gardner, W. M., 63
Gray, Charles, 151
Greenhow, Rose, 10
Griffin, Charles, 42, 90–102

Haggerty, James, 67
Hains, Peter, 7, 137, 141
opening battle with 30-pound Parrott, 44–45
Hampton Legion, 11, 35, 73–79, 89, 109–16, 158
Hampton, Wade, III, 11, 35, 74–76, 77, 88, 158
Harding, Thomas, 24
Harper, Kenton, 81, 88
Hawley, Joseph, 86